JOURNEYS TOWARD GOD

This volume is also Volume 5
of the
Occasional Studies Series
sponsored by the
Medieval and Renaissance Studies Program
of the
University of Pittsburgh

JOURNEYS
TOWARD
GOD

Pilgrimage and Crusade

edited by
Barbara N. Sargent-Baur

SMC XXX
Medieval Institute Publications

WESTERN MICHIGAN UNIVERSITY

Kalamazoo, Michigan
1992

Library of Congress Cataloging-in-Publication Data

Journeys toward God : pilgrimage and crusade / edited by Barbara N.
Sargent-Baur.
      p.   cm. -- (SMC ; 30) (Occasional studies series / Medieval
and Renaissance studies Program of the University of Pittsburgh ; v.
5)
   Papers presented at a conference at the University of Pittsburgh.
Oct. 27-28, 1988.
   Includes index.
   ISBN 1-879288-03-6. -- ISBN 1-879288-04-4 (pbk.)
   1. Christian pilgrims and pilgrimages in literature--Congresses.
2. Crusades in literature--Congresses. 3. Literature, Medieval-
-Themes, motives--Congresses. 4. Christian pilgrims and
pilgrimages--Europe--History--Congresses. 5. Crusades--History-
-Congresses. I. Sargent-Baur, Barbara Nelson. II. Series: Studies
in medieval culture ; 30. III. Series: Occasional studies series
(University of Pittsburgh. Medieval and Renaissance Studies Program)
; v. 5.
PN682.P5J6 1992   92-4356
809'.93355--dc20   CIP

Cover design by Linda K. Judy
Printed in the United States of America

CONTENTS

Preface

  Barbara N. Sargent-Baur   vii

Pilgrimage and Crusade Literature

  †*J. G. Davies*   1

Pilgrimage and Sacral Power

  Robert Worth Frank, Jr.   31

Journeys to the Center of the Earth:
Medieval and Renaissance Pilgrimages
to Mount Calvary

  Dorothea R. French   45

Stephen of Cloyes, Philip Augustus, and the
Children's Crusade of 1212

  Gary Dickson   83

Militia Dei: A Central Concept for the Religious
Ideas of the Early Crusades and the German
Rolandslied

      Horst Richter   107

Christians and Moors in *¡Ay Jherusalem!*

      Donna M. Rogers   127

The Letter of Jean Sarrasin, Crusader

      Jeanette M. A. Beer   135

Crusade Propaganda in the Epic Cycles
of the Crusade

      Robert Francis Cook   157

The Siege of Jerusalem As a Crusading Poem

      Mary Hamel   177

Structural Convergence of Pilgrimage and
Dream-Vision in Christine de Pizan

      Susan Stakel   195

Isabel of Portugal and the Fifteenth-Century
Burgundian Crusade

      Charity Cannon Willard   205

Notes on Contributors   215

Index   219

PREFACE

Of all the enterprises that absorbed the time, the treasure, and the very lives of Western Europeans from the early Christian centuries until the early Renaissance, perhaps the most pervasive were pilgrimage and its younger but close relation, crusade. There is no risk in asserting that for over a millennium there were few—and increasingly fewer—who escaped knowledge of these activities; a great many actively engaged in them.

Pilgrimage was a last or first resort for any number of problems. As assigned penance, as self-imposed expiation, as avenue for petition or for thanksgiving it was open to all, particularly if it involved a short trip to a nearby shrine. For those whose spiritual or physical peril was extreme and who could somehow manage the journey there awaited the great pilgrimages: to Compostela, to Rome, and to the Holy Land. This last was the supreme goal of penitents and was sought by them in increasing crowds from the third century onward. In spite of the Arab conquests, the long journey to Jerusalem was by the eleventh century being made by the faithful in their hundreds and thousands. Those who would not or could not engage in so ambitious a venture supported those who did, through prayers, preaching, hospitality, and various forms of material subvention. The nearly universal adoption of Christianity in Europe brought with it the generally-held cult of the saints and their relics, the familiarity with certain holy places, and the notion of travel to these places as being conducive to salvation.

In addition to possessing a contritionist side, medieval Christianity had a militant aspect. Non-Christians were, ipso facto, enemies of God; to oppose them could not be other than meritorious. This opposition was effected by a whole spectrum of means: persuasion, intimidation, coercion, inquisitions, and force of arms. The struggle was joined with pagan Saxons, Magyars, and Northmen, as well as with Moslems and Jews. When Pope Urban II summoned the French chivalry in 1095 to cease fighting among themselves and direct their energies against the Turkish conquerors of the Holy Land, he founded his appeal on a multiplicity of long-maturing phenomena. Among these were the establishment, by the late eleventh century, of the authority of the Catholic Church as centered in the papacy; the veneration of holy places and especially the Holy Land; the conviction that sin could be expunged and salvation achieved through "works"; the tradition of long-distance pilgrimages in large groups; the existence of a professional fighting caste whose *raison d'être* was, precisely, fighting; the protracted struggle against the Moors in Spain; and the formation of various peace movements intended to limit warfare within Christendom (with the consequent appeal of carrying combat beyond its borders). Specific events combined to channel these developments. The Turkish encroachments in the Christian East, the appeal of the Byzantine Emperor for help against the infidel, the perceived threat to the pilgrimage routes in Palestine, and, not least, the inducements of adventure and enrichment—all of these constituted powerful incentives to the Church-sanctioned military expeditions to the Holy Land. These Crusades, prolonged as they were over nearly two centuries, influenced the lives of practically every inhabitant of Europe and of many dwellers in the Near East. The crusaders themselves were of course the most directly involved. But their enterprise affected others as well: the dependents who travelled with them, the families who remained behind to cope as best they could, the non-combatants who contributed in cash or in kind to the expeditions, the landowners and peasants whose foodstuffs were seized by foraging armies on the march, the ship-owners and bankers to whom the crusaders turned for transport, the clergy who accompanied them (and those who did not, but preached and prayed on their behalf), the Greek Christians who invited them and were conquered by them, and the Moslem natives of Palestine (first defeated enemies, then increasingly successful opponents). Even the inhabitants of Jewish communities in Europe and particularly in the Rhineland were not immune, for they felt the violence of Christian mobs stirred up by crusading fervor.

Although for all practical purposes the Crusades ended with the second expedition of Louis IX in 1270 and still more definitively with the fall of Acre in 1291, the crusade as an ideal had an afterlife of another two centuries or so. Throughout the 1400s the idea of a crusade, specifically against the Turks, retained its potency in the European imagination. Rulers and nobles ostentatiously swore to go on crusade; writers and clergy encouraged others to do so. The fall of Constantinople to the Turks in 1453 breathed new life into the crusading spirit, and indeed some efforts were made to organize further military expeditions. The practical results were negligible; yet the fact that serious discussions and preparations went forward attests to the continuing vitality of the ideal. As for pilgrimage, it continued until the Reformation and, in Catholic territories, beyond it up to the present day.

The interconnectedness of pilgrimage and crusade, and the central role of these enterprises for the history of European society and thought, prompted the choice of this topic for a Symposium held at the University of Pittsburgh on 27-28 October 1988 and organized by the Medieval and Renaissance Studies Program. Of the papers presented at that time, twelve have been selected for this volume. Some of these treat primarily of pilgrimage or crusade as historical events, with preparation and aftermath. Some stress the ideology that under-girded these undertakings and served to motivate the participants. Certain essays concentrate on eyewitness accounts, or the interpretations of contemporary events and ideas as voiced in literature. A brief précis of each may demonstrate the range of perspectives from which pilgrimage and crusade are explored in this collection; at the same time it may help the reader who has a specialized interest to identify the contribution(s) of greatest potential value in that area.

The first essay, by J. G. Davies, was also the first keynote address in the Symposium. While dealing primarily with pilgrimage literature, it emphasizes the overlap of the multiform genre with crusading literature and points out that in this respect the written accounts mirror the thought of the medieval period. Much the same spirit informed these enterprises, so that the Crusades had a pronounced pilgrimage aspect—with the additional elements of armed conflict and official sanction. Consequently, writings for and by pilgrims—itineraries, diaries, letters, books of indulgences, aids to devotion, guidebooks, travel accounts, maps and plans—were also useful to crusaders both en route and when they arrived at their destinations. Writings generated by the Crusades fall into similar categories (with the additional one of crusading songs and epic poems).

Some of the following essays also pay attention to the spiritual and intellectual impulses giving rise to such mass movements. Robert Worth Frank, Jr., examines pilgrimages within Europe, with particular attention to the miracle narratives they engendered; these in turn served as powerful inducements for subsequent pilgrimages. Dorothea R. French concentrates on one distant pilgrimage, the greatest of all—that to the Holy Land and more specifically to Mount Calvary, taken by Christian intellectuals and cartographers to be the center of the earth and so represented on *mappae mundi*. The subject of Gary Dickson's essay is the so-called Children's Crusade of 1212, undertaken not by armed nobles but by mobs of adolescents and young people of the peasant class who hoped both to reach the pilgrim goal of the Holy Land and to succeed in liberating it where rulers and knights had failed.

A number of the contributions to this collection take up works of literature embodying medieval ideas on pilgrimage and crusade. Horst Richter deals with medieval German literature; he discusses the idea of *militia Dei* as expressed in the twelfth-century *Rolandslied* of Pfaffe Konrad, tracing Konrad's crusading zeal back to some of the more militant passages of St. Paul and the early Church Fathers. An approach to the Crusades from the direction of Spain comes in the essay by Donna M. Rogers; the thirteenth-century poem *¡Ay Jherusalem!* (unusual in that it has to do with Palestine rather than the Iberian peninsula) depicts the opposition of Christians and Moors. Another document, this one in French, is presented by Jeanette M. A. Beer: the letter containing an account of the taking of Damietta in 1249; its author, Jean Sarrasin, was eyewitness, crusader, and chamberlain to Louis IX. The Crusades formed the subject not only of prose letters and chronicles but also a very substantial corpus of *chansons de geste* grouped in two cycles of rhymed formulaic verse; these cycles (which began in the late twelfth century and continued into the fourteenth) are discussed as vehicles of propaganda for the First and Third Crusades by Robert Francis Cook. The Third Crusade also inspired a fourteenth-century alliterative poem in Middle English, *The Siege of Jerusalem*; as Mary Hamel points out, this gruesome pseudo-historical work has the Roman siege of A.D. 70 as subject but is informed by late-medieval attitudes (including a particularly violent anti-Semitism). Rounding out the literary part of this collection, Susan Stakel's essay explores the convergence of pilgrimage and dream-vision in the French prose and verse of Christine de Pizan, writing in the first years of the fifteenth century.

That the idea of crusade survived and indeed revived in the fifteenth century, and that one was even attempted by Isabel of Portugal after the fall of Constantinople, is set forth in the last essay in this collection, that of Charity Cannon Willard.

The editor of this volume is much obliged to the other members of the Executive Committee of the Medieval and Renaissance Studies Program at the University of Pittsburgh for the time they devoted to the organization of the Symposium and to the selection of abstracts and finished papers. These colleagues are: Professors Klaus Conermann, Mary Elizabeth Meek David (who also assisted in editing this volume), Bernard Goldstein, Richard Landes, Daniel Russell, and David Wilkins. Professor Thomas H. Seiler of the Medieval Institute, Western Michigan University, has been extremely helpful at all stages of the preparation of these studies for publication. Praise is also due to Ms. Candace Porath, copyeditor at Medieval Institute Publications; and, at the University of Pittsburgh, to Ms. Mary Jo Lazar for secretarial work and to Ms. Linda Rouillard for bibliographical checking.

BARBARA N. SARGENT-BAUR

PILGRIMAGE AND CRUSADE LITERATURE

†J. G. Davies

Pilgrimage literature is a somewhat imprecise designation because it refers to a multiform genre that includes many diverse types of documents. Obviously it must be understood to cover those that have been written by, for, and about pilgrims, but if its richness and variety are to be appreciated the works have to be more clearly distinguished than by the use of three different prepositions. Nor is a categorization in the terms of the language employed very helpful towards appreciating the genre as a whole. It is not uninteresting, but is scarcely illuminating, to note that the earliest Western texts, invariably from the pens of clerics, were in Latin, and that the use of the vulgar tongue began towards the end of the twelfth and the beginning of the thirteenth centuries with works in French, the opening of the fourteenth century witnessing the appearance of Italian and German texts with contemporary translations into other languages.[1]

It is equally beside the point to consider the distinction between the fictional and the non-fictional, important though this is to the historian. A document can be assigned to a particular literary type without the question of its veracity affecting the classification. A letter, for example, may be a forgery, or it may be

1

wholly what it purports to be—in either case it is still a letter, and the question of its authenticity is secondary when one is seeking to establish a typology.

As a step towards devising a more acceptable and comprehensive typology I would propose for consideration the following nine categories, the nature of each one of which I shall then proceed to sketch while directing attention to specific examples. Under the first heading may be grouped itineraries; under the second, pilgrim diaries; and under the third, letters. Fourth, there are lists of indulgences; then follow aids to devotion. Guidebooks come next, and these are to be seen as a development of Type One and often contain Type Four. In the seventh place there are travel accounts, which from time to time included maps and/or illustrations. Finally, as the Church sought to regulate the rapidly increasing pilgrimage movement, conciliar canons were produced, and these constitute a category of their own. These nine types are, of course, not discrete; they could and did merge into one another, as will be evident when they are examined further.

TYPES OF PILGRIMAGE LITERATURE

1. Itineraries

Amongst the military equipment discovered during the excavations at Dura Europos on the Euphrates was the shield of a soldier who had perished there defending the city from attack shortly after A.D. 256. He had previously served beside the Black Sea, and he had carefully noted on his shield distances and stopping places on his march from there to Syria.[2] In effect, therefore, he had kept a log and had transcribed it on one of his most precious possessions. Such an itinerary is little more than a list of stations en route and a record of the mileage between them. This particular example was individual, but there existed public ones, copied and circulating freely. Such are the two Antonine itineraries that contain lists of ways by land and sea throughout the Roman Empire. First produced in the early third century, these have survived in an edition produced a hundred years later.[3]

Having an identical format but specifically devoted to travel as a Christian is the list produced by the Bordeaux pilgrim to Jerusalem in the year 333.[4] From then on such short documents were in continuous and widespread use. Several of them from the period of the Crusades have been assembled recently by J. D. Wilkinson, although he mistakenly calls them guidebooks, and these include the one attached to the *Gesta Francorum et aliorum Hierosolymitanorum* ca. 1101, the one linked to the *History* of Baudry of Dol (1099-1103), and, of the same date, the one preserved in the *Codex Ottobonianus latinus* 169 of the Vatican Library.[5] Each one lists the places to be visited *seriatim* and indicates the distances to be traversed, sometimes expressed as so many days' journey, sometimes in miles or leagues, and, in and around Jerusalem, even in feet, stones' throws, and bow shots.

The necessity for pilgrims—whatever their destination, be it the Holy Land, Compostela, or Rome—to possess one of these itineraries ensured their continuous production, and it is not surprising to find that they were eventually incorporated into devotional manuals and also formed a standard section in complete guidebooks.

Needless to say, such brief lists seldom bore the names of their authors; but there is at least one, compiled by Belard of Ascoli ca. 1155.[6]

2. Pilgrim Diaries

These rather stark road-books soon developed into pilgrim diaries simply by the addition of details and personal comments recorded en route. One has only to contrast any passage in the Bordeaux pilgrim's itinerary with what the Piacenza pilgrim (ca. 570) has to say about the same place, to perceive the elaboration.[7] Or, from a later period, there is Sigeric's terse register of 990 to set over against that of the Anglo-Saxon merchant Saewulf who in 1102-03 filled out his itinerary with many personal observations, noting such incidents as storms at sea and the deaths of some companions.[8] Although personal and individual, such diaries could provide source material for guidebooks and be easily expanded into full-length travel accounts.

3. Letters

One of the earliest accounts of a pilgrimage is that which Egeria wrote towards the end of the fourth century. This took the form of a letter to her sister nuns back home in Galicia. She reported that she was sending it from Constantinople, whence she was setting out to visit Ephesus and other centers, and in due course, so she stated, "I will either tell you about them face to face (if God so wills), or at any rate write to you about them if my plans change."[9] An equally famous description of a pilgrimage, also epistolary, is contained in Jerome's 108th letter, but this was not penned in the course of a journey but is part of a panegyric on the scholar's lamented longtime friend, the Roman matron Paula.

Pilgrims, often away from their native lands for months and even years, were accustomed to keep in touch with those they had left behind and they recount, often with vivid touches, some of their experiences. Such was Brother John of Canterbury, who wrote from the Great St. Bernard in February 1188 and gave a spine-chilling account of the hazards of seeking to pass the Alps in winter.[10]

4. *Libri indulgentiarum*

Just over a century after Brother John, the quest for indulgences was in full cry; and this promoted another type of pilgrimage literature, books of indulgences, which listed holy places and the corresponding benefits to be obtained if they were visited. In effect, therefore, since the information had to be related to specific locations, these books were a form of itinerary but with additional emphasis on the remission of sins.

The earliest example to survive relates to the shrines of Acre and was written ca. 1280, if the dating of its editors be accepted, but they acknowledge that this is by no means certain,[11] and in fact all other documents of this type are post-1300. It was then that Boniface VIII gave an immense impetus to this kind of pilgrimage literature, linked as it was to indulgences by his declaration of the first Jubilee year.[12] Indeed, the first known table of undisputed date is that in the *Peregrinationes et indulgentiae Terre Sancte* by Giacomo de Verona of 1335.[13] Since the catalogue of indulgences could be long and memories fallible, sometimes the facts were presented in rhyming form, the easier to learn; such is the Vernon manuscript (1370), which includes a section entitled *The Stacyons of Rome*.[14] Summaries were also prepared, such as the broadsheet preserved in the Bodleian and printed by Pynson early in the sixteenth century.[15]

5. Aids to Devotion

In intention, a pilgrimage was a protracted spiritual exercise, and many of those who took the scrip and the staff carried with them devotional manuals. The clergy took breviaries and mass books. In addition to these, Frescobaldi (1384) records that he had with him some of the books of the Bible, that is, parts of the Old Testament and the Gospels, together with the *Moralia* of Gregory the Great.[16] Since Frescobaldi was going via Cairo and Sinai the first item must have included at least Exodus and Numbers; but of the third work, originally issued in six volumes, he probably took an epitome.

Almost exactly a century later Felix Fabri took to the road, and in his voluminous *Wanderings* he refers frequently to a *Processional for Pilgrims to the Holy Land*. "These processionals," he explains, "are little books wherein are marked all the versicles, collects, responses, hymns, psalms and prayers which ought to be

5

said or sung at all the holy places throughout the course of a pilgrimage beyond the seas."[17] Their exact contents can be ascertained because at least three copies have been preserved. One of these, of the fourteenth century, is in the Colombina Library, Seville; another is in the University Library at Würzburg; and the third was incorporated as a separate section in a complete pilgrim guide of 1471. All of these are versions of the same original, which must have emanated from the Franciscan monastery on Mount Sion in Jerusalem, since there is a note in the 1471 guide to the effect that it was transcribed there on 21 January of that year.[18]

The devotions each follow an identical pattern, as described by Fabri. They open with an antiphon, a verse from Scripture relating to the place and to the event that is believed to have occurred where the pilgrims are gathered. This is followed by a versicle and response, also from the Bible and similarly related to the location. A collect sums up the hopes and aspirations of the pilgrims who then, if the distance between one station and another warrants it, go in procession singing a prescribed hymn.

Amongst other aids to devotion are what are best described as prayer-cards. One example, used by Christians going to Bromholm, where they venerated pieces of the True Cross, has been preserved in Lambeth Palace Library. It depicts Jesus crucified. Along the upper edge there is written in Latin: "Jesus of Nazareth the King of the Jews," while an inscription on the sides reads: "This cross yat here peynted is / Signe of ye cross of Bromholm is." Within the outline of a heart, which itself frames the drawing of the Crucifixion, is a prayer for the pilgrims to use. The card is in fact not only an aid to devotion but also a token of a completed pilgrimage to take back home.[19]

6. Guidebooks

If all the information distributed between the several types of literature surveyed so far is brought together in a single work, then the guidebook emerges as a further type in its own right, more comprehensive than any of its predecessors.[20] The earliest example extant to which this designation can be properly applied is the fifth part of the *Liber Sancti Jacobi* or the *Codex Calixtinus*, the latter name deriving from an apocryphal letter of Pope Calixtus II that stands as its preface.[21] Its author, writing ca. 1145, was a Frenchman full of devotion for James. The simplest way to convey an idea of what this work is about is to reproduce its table of contents:

  I.   The Road to Santiago
 II.   The Days' Journeys on the Road of the Apostle
III.   The Names of the Towns on His Road
 IV.   The Three Good [Religious] Houses of This World
  V.   The Names of the Overseers of St. James's Road
 VI.   Bitter and Fresh Waters on His Road
VII.   The Characteristics of the Countries and People on His Road
VIII. The Bodies of the Saints to Be Visited on the Way and the Passion of St. Eutropius
 IX.   The Characteristics of the City and Church of Santiago
  X.   How the Offerings at the Altar of St. James Are Disposed Of
 XI.   How the Pilgrims of St. James Should Be Properly Received

The documentation relating to Santiago must be regarded as somewhat meager when it is compared with that generated by Rome. Amongst the works devoted to this latter pilgrimage center, the most important were entitled *Mirabilia*. Dating from the mid-twelfth century, they had at first no general title, but by the thirteenth some were known as *Graphia aureae urbis Romae*, and then in the fourteenth and fifteenth centuries simply as *Mirabilia urbis Romae*. These guides could cover pagan Rome, with accounts of such antiquities as the Colosseum and the Pantheon; but when qualified by the words *Romanarum ecclesiarum*, then churches and relics were their subjects. Such a work was published in 1375.[22] This was widely popular; Martin Luther was but one who made use of it, some years before the development of his ideas led to his wholesale repudiation of all pilgrimages.[23] The majority of versions were in Latin, but there were also several in German, at least four in French, three in Italian, and one in Spanish.[24]

Guidebooks to Jerusalem and the Holy Land, however, were the ones most in demand. Their comprehensiveness can be gauged from the one transcribed on Mount Sion in 1471, previously mentioned in connection with devotional aids. This has been preserved with its original binding of sheep leather on pressboards with brass fastenings; it measures only 125/99 mm. and consists of five distinct and self-contained sections that deal successively with historical, geographical, doctrinal, liturgical, and linguistic data.[25]

Similarly all-embracing was the *Information for Pilgrims unto the Holy Land*, the first edition of which was published by Wynkyn de Worde ca. 1498. It was based upon a journey made a decade before and also drew upon the accounts of others, such as *The Itineraries of William Wey*, a Fellow of Eton who made his first visit to Jerusalem in 1458 and his second four years later.[26]

A description of the contents of the *Information*, of which a second edition was issued in 1515, will show the extent of the practical advice deemed necessary. After specifying a number of alternative itineraries, the author lists the rates of exchange from England to France and to Venice. Advice follows about how to choose a galley at Venice and how to select a place on board. The pilgrim is warned not to travel on the lower deck, as it will be stinking; he is told to buy a padlock to keep the door of his cabin safe, as well as a chest to hold personal possessions. Various herbs and spices, cookery utensils, crockery, and so forth are itemized; indeed, no detail is too insignificant to mention, and even the requirement of a barrel in case of seasickness is stressed.

The advice given about arrival at Jaffa is to select a mule quickly, as the best beasts are soon snapped up. From that port of entry into the Holy Land the distances are given in miles, the holy places are named one by one, and those carrying indulgences are indicated. In this way an itinerary has been combined with a *liber indulgentiarum*. The last few pages are taken up with short vo-cabularies in Greek and Turkish, with a list of Stations at Rome and a final note on the symbolism of the several parts of a church. This was of course in the vernacular, as was also the *Pilgerbuch* from which Arnold von Harff copied several pages (1496-98); this had been printed in Rome by Stephen Planck in 1489.[27] Simi-lar guides have survived and include another to Palestine, ca. 1350, which opened its tour at Nazareth because "it is fitting we should commence our pilgrimage where were the beginnings of our redemption."[28]

Most guidebooks have no name attached to them, but there is one that does, by Peter the Deacon. He was the librarian of Monte Cassino, and in 1137 he compiled a work for his abbot, who was about to set off on a pilgrimage. In his prologue he acknowledges that he has "collected the material from all the books," and these included Bede's work on the Holy Places, together with the letter of Egeria.[29]

7. Travel Accounts

Those pilgrims who completed their journeys and returned safely to their own countries, especially if they were of a literary turn of mind, often committed their experiences to writing. The number of such authors was considerable; it has been calculated that between 1100 and 1500 some 526 writers produced works of this kind.[30] They strove to make their accounts as accurate as pos-sible: Niccolò of Poggibonsi, for example, who visited the Holy Land in 1346-50, states that he had with him two measuring rods and that all he saw and touched he noted on "two small tables."[31]

These narratives have a uniform plan in that their sequence rests upon and is determined by a more or less identical itinerary, but it is often interrupted by insertions; for instance, the Italian notary Nicholas di Martoni (1394-95) incorporated information of all kinds, introducing each item with its own preface. Descrip-

9

tions of places are given at the appropriate point in the journey, while an account of the different denominations of Christians existing in the Middle East, which is regularly provided, is usually linked to a verbal portrayal of the Holy Sepulchre where they each had a stake. Inevitably these reports were personal, as contrasted with the impersonality of the guidebooks, and consequently this type of pilgrimage literature can be subdivided according to the intentions of its authors.

In the first place are those narratives that are to provide information for those who would follow the same pilgrimage road; in effect, therefore, while cast in an autobiographical mold, they are alternatives to guidebooks—which they unashamedly plagiarized. So Richard Torkington, rector of Mulberton in Norfolk, who set sail from Rye on 20 March 1517, not only repeated passages from *Information for Pilgrims unto the Holy Land* but also took verbatim the descriptions of Venice, of the voyage to Jaffa, and of the sites throughout Palestine from *The Pylgrymage of Sir Richard Guylforde to the Holy Land, A.D. 1506*, written by Sir Richard's chaplain.[32] Much of what every pilgrim needs to know was summarized by Niccolò of Poggibonsi in his preface to *A Voyage beyond the Seas (1346-50)*.[33] "I am going to provide you," he writes, with "all the indulgences in order, and the distances, and the dimensions of the holy places, and also what things are within them and how they are arranged." Other accounts included expenses as well as word lists in different languages.

The second motive that inspired some of these writers was the desire to stir up others to imitation; on occasion they even named the particular individuals they had in mind. So von Harff mentions Duke William of Julich and his wife.[34] Such works have a hortatory character.

In the third place, some pilgrims penned their stories to provide themes for meditation for those who could not make similar journeys. Abbot Daniel, who travelled from Russia to Jerusalem in 1106-07, says that his record is "for the faithful, so that, in hearing the description of the holy places, they might be mentally transported to them, from the depths of their souls, and thus obtain from God the same rewards as those who have visited them."[35] In similar vein Burchard of Mount Sion, who lived for several years in Palestine, states (1280) that he is writing to help others picture the holy places in their minds when they cannot behold them with their eyes.[36]

In the fourth instance, some narratives of a biographical nature include accounts of pilgrimages to affirm the sanctity of their heroes. Such is the *Hodoeporicon* (i.e., a book for a journey) in which a nun told of St. Willibald's passage to the Holy Land ca. 754.[37]

As the Middle Ages move towards their end, a fifth intention is discernible, that is, to cater for *curiositas*. This concept had been condemned by writers widely separated in time, such as Augustine and Aquinas; they did so because they held that curiosity about the universe could prevent concentration on the world to come. To pursue knowledge under the impetus of curiosity was to be like Adam in the garden—and his knowledge was indeed disastrous. But in time curiosity ceased to be regarded as a vice; a desire to know the world at large was emerging and travel could be undertaken as a proper human pursuit for those concerned to learn more about God's creation. As early as ca. 1322, John Maundeville, while still providing a pilgrimage itinerary, could combine it with an account of worldly exploration.[38] A similar desire to satisfy *curiositas* is to be found expressed in a book by the Irish Franciscan Simon Semeonis (1323-24), who describes his journey onwards from Great Britain with infinite detail relating to women's clothes, the practices of customs officials, natural products, etc.[39] There is then a shift in motivation that was eventually to distinguish the Renaissance voyager from the medieval pilgrim.

8. Maps, Plans, and Illustrations

Maps, plans, and illustrations are perhaps more correctly styled documentation than literature, but since they often accompany works by or for pilgrims they need to be noticed in this context. Certainly their benefit to travelers is too obvious to require demonstration; an itinerary is more helpful if it is pictorial than if it is simply a list of places and distances—hence the illustrated example drawn up or copied by Matthew Paris in 1253 showing the route to Rome and the Holy Land.[40]

As early as the fourth century Eusebius of Caesarea had devised a map showing the divisions of the twelve tribes of Israel with a representation of the Jerusalem temple. He was followed by Jerome, whose version (ca. 385) has been preserved in a twelfth-century copy.[41] From Jerome onwards there is a continuous history of Holy Land cartography; this includes the grid maps of Marino Sanuti, who added three to his account of his journey in 1321.[42] Other examples accompanied the narratives of Gabriele Capodilista and William Wey of the spring voyage of 1458,[43] and the former reproduced drawings of the monuments he had seen. Bernhard von Breydenbach, dean of Mainz, took an artist with him in 1483-84; that was Erhard Reuwich of Utrecht, who produced panoramic views of the places visited that are so detailed as to be virtually city plans.[44]

9. Canons

Chaucer's Wife of Bath was interested in "daliaunce," and she was by no means untypical. Consequently, the Church authorities, while happy to encourage pilgrimages, sought to institutionalize and regulate them. As one example of the type of literature to which this endeavor gave rise, canon 45 of the Council of Châlons in 813 may be cited. This condemns numerous categories of so-called pilgrims, who are very precisely defined:

> 1. Clerks who think they can purge their sins by going on a pilgrimage and at the same time escape from their pastoral duties.
> 2. Laity who think they can sin with impunity simply by frequenting such places of prayer.

3. Powerful folk who exact payment from the rest of the company en route under pretence of protecting them.
4. Poor folk whose sole motive is to have better opportunities for begging.

And so the list continues.[45]

THE CRUSADES AND PILGRIMAGE

That under the heading of pilgrimage literature is also to be included the writings generated by the Crusades necessarily follows, if those who participated in these campaigns are correctly to be identified as pilgrims. The Crusades can of course be considered from the perspective of political history or military history, as well as that of social and/or economic history; but if their true nature is not to be obscured they also have to be studied in relation to the medieval understanding of pilgrimage.

Although the precise words of Urban II at the Council of Clermont in 1095, when he sounded the call to the First Crusade, are uncertain, it is generally accepted that he envisaged the enterprise as a pilgrimage.[46] Moreover, the crusaders themselves accepted that this was precisely what they were engaged in. Fulcher of Chartres in his prologue to the *Historia Hierosolymitana* (1105-06) states that the Franks "made a pilgrimage in arms to Jerusalem in honour of the Saviour" and he notes that "many men in this our pilgrimage burned with zeal for God."[47] William of Tyre, who began his history ca. 1170, uses the same vocabulary in his preface,[48] and so also does Caesarius of Heisterbach ca. 1223.[49] That *peregrinus* and its cognates do refer to pilgrims and pilgrimages by this time is evident from a bas relief of 1085-1100 in San Domingo de Silos near Burgos that illustrates Jesus meeting the two disciples on the road to Emmaus. According to the Vulgate, Luke 24.18, they think he is a *peregrinus*, and the sculptor has represented Jesus in pilgrim dress, carrying a scrip that bears the cockleshell of St. James.[50] Vernacular accounts support the same understanding of the crusader. Robert de Clari's *Conquête de Constantinople* refers to *li pelerin*,[51] as does Villehardouin (ca. 1215),[52] while Joinville (ca. 1290) speaks of the "pelerinaige de la croiz."[53]

A comparison of the activities of ordinary pilgrims and of crusaders further endorses their identification. Before setting off, one and all took steps to discharge their debts—as did Margery Kempe on the one hand[54] and Louis IX on the other.[55] Next, they were invested with the insignia of their new profession, that is, with a scrip and a staff, at the prescribed pilgrim mass; these tokens were equally sought by would-be crusaders such as Louis IX of France, who received them at an episcopal mass in Paris.[56] In addition, they all were said to be "taking the cross," which was then marked on their garments.[57]

Once en route, pilgrims made use of rallying cries: those on the way to Compostela shouted "Deus adjuva" or "Sancte Jacobe."[58] The crusaders were no less pious in their imprecations; according to the *Gesta Francorum* their constant battle cry was "God's will, God's will, God's will."[59] The chanting of psalms was common to all: Roberto de Sanseverino (1408) found the seven penitential psalms of great help,[60] while those on the First Crusade who besieged Antioch were instructed to say each day the response, "For lo, the kings were assembled" (Ps 47.5), together with the doxology.[61]

Every opportunity was taken to attend mass and to hear sermons, to visit shrines and adore relics. So Sir Richard Torkington (1517) enjoyed an audio-visual presentation at Chambéry,[62] while pilgrims to Compostela halted at St. Gilles to kiss the saint's altar and tomb.[63] The crusaders were equally devout, fasting and scourging the body (William of Tyre),[64] observing the great festivals of the Church's year (the *Gesta Francorum*),[65] listing the relics they had seen (Robert of Clari at Constantinople).[66] Everyone was similarly moved on reaching Mountjoy and beholding the Holy City for the first time, as witnessed by John Maundeville in 1322[67] and previously by Ambrose the Minstrel, who was in the train of Richard Coeur de Lion.[68]

Arrived at their destinations, pilgrims and crusaders alike discarded their footwear and made a round of the holy places, expressing their devotion with tears, frequent prostrations, and kissing. To Albert of Aix, Godfrey of Boulogne was the ideal crusader because upon the capture of Jerusalem in 1099, unlike his companions, he did not seek loot but processed round the walls in pilgrim's dress and then entered the city to give thanks at the Holy Sepulchre with weeping and prayers.[69] A visit to the Jordan and a swim in it were regarded as compulsory for all, pilgrims and crusaders alike: so, among many, Sigurd of Norway, 1109,[70] while Fulcher of Chartres records how he bathed and collected palm branches near Jericho.[71]

Not only did ordinary pilgrims and crusaders engage in the same practices but they also shared many of the same motives. They all set out in search of indulgences; many were moved by a desire to "worship in the places where his feet stood"—this is from the seventh verse of Psalm 131, and it is significant that it is quoted both by Paulinus of Nola in his forty-ninth epistle and, seven hundred years later, by Fulcher of Chartres to describe the intention behind a visit to the Holy Land.[72] Both pilgrim and crusader often took to the road in fulfillment of a vow, and in either case a substitute was permissible, as early as the tenth century for the former and by the time of the Third Crusade for the latter.[73] Also common to the two categories were the privileges they enjoyed while undertaking their tasks. They were assured that any lands or possessions seized by others during their absences would be returned to them; they could demand hospitality from the Church authorities; in theory they were immune from arrest and exempt from tolls and taxes.[74]

Despite these parallels, ordinary pilgrimages and crusades were not at all points identical. A crusade was an official expedition, usually initiated by a pope; an ordinary pilgrimage did not have this character. Consequently, crusader literature includes some types that are not exactly paralleled by those of the ordinary pilgrimages; in particular, there are papal encyclicals, decretals, and the commentaries of canon lawyers. Further, a crusade involved armed conflict with an enemy of the Church—in the case of the Holy Land this meant, of course, with the Muslims. Right up to the end of the thirteenth century, however, the narratives of ordinary pilgrims, even when they are not completely indifferent to the conflicts between the rival faiths, appear very much detached from them. Crusader accounts are naturally full of such events. Moreover, the devotions of the two groups, while similar in form, are often different in intent: the pilgrim sought spiritual development; the crusader, divine aid for victory in battle. Nevertheless, there is sufficient of the pilgrimage concept within that of a crusade to explain that the literature emanating from both has many types in common.

TYPES OF CRUSADER LITERATURE

Insofar as the crusaders were pilgrims, it is to be expected that the typology of their literature would correspond with that already reviewed. As will become apparent, this was often the case, although within the types there are some dissimilarities to be noted.

1. Itineraries

Several itineraries for crusader use have survived, and among these is the document entitled *Descriptio sanctorum locorum* that was appended to the *Gesta Francorum et aliorum Hierosolymitanorum* ca. 1101.[75] Another example that was probably in circulation at the same time was included in the history of Bishop Baudry of Dol and claims to have been written by an eyewitness.[76] Chapters 31 to 33 of the *Gesta Francorum Jherusalem expugnantium* constitute another itinerary, ca. 1109,[77] and the first four sections of the eighth book of William of Tyre's history are also an itinerary that has been slightly expanded by the insertion of descriptive material.[78]

The relatively simple lists of places and distances that were of help to pilgrims as individuals or in groups were, however, scarcely sufficient for large armies advancing through hostile territory. The crusaders sought to supplement them by employing local guides; Alexius I Comnenus so appointed one Taticius.[79] Later, having taken Tripoli, the crusaders were poised to advance on Jerusalem and sought the advice of some Syrian Christians about "the safest and easiest road," and the town governor detailed some members of his household to lead the way.[80] Nevertheless, reports William of Tyre, they were "anxious over their ignorance of the country"[81] and leaders were appointed for each day's march, their duty being to plan the route to be followed, the mileage to be covered, and the eventual location of the camp.[82] Without guides they were apt to wander about entirely uncertain of where they were[83]—they were in fact in dire need of another type of document, maps (see sect. 8 below).

2. Crusader Diaries

One of the earliest crusader diaries is that of Fulcher of Chartres, who states that he went on the First Crusade with the other pilgrims and "collected all this in my memory for the sake of posterity."[84] From the same campaign comes the diary of Raymond of Aguilers.[85] It is from documents such as these that it is possible to obtain some idea of what P. Alphandéry has called "the interior life" of the crusades,[86] for they reveal the feelings of their authors, describe their devotions, and tell of their religious preparation before a battle.

3. Letters

In addition to papal letters and encyclicals, individual crusaders wrote a considerable number of letters of their own. These obviously constitute a discrete type. A comprehensive inventory was drawn up by P. Riant[87] and a collection of those written during the century from 1088 to 1188 has been edited by Heinrich Hagenmeyer.[88] Further comment would appear to be unnecessary.

4. Indulgences

The *libri indulgentiarum* that became such a feature of pilgrimage literature in general do not figure in that of the Crusades. The reason for this is twofold. First, each Crusade in itself was regarded as earning plenary indulgence. Second, it was only with the opening of the fourteenth century, and therefore after the end of the epoch of the Crusades, that the *libri* came to the fore.

5. Aids to Devotion

Whereas individual pilgrims, as noted previously, could take with them a variety of books for their private devotions, the nature of the Crusades was such that they were scarcely deemed necessary by those bearing arms. Each campaign was an official event, usually accompanied by a papal legate with large numbers of archbishops, bishops, and priests in attendance, each with his breviary and mass book; and they saw to it that the crusaders observed a regular round of devotions. There were frequent sermons. On 8 July 1099, immediately before launching their opening attack on the Holy City, "our bishops and priests preached to us, and told us to go in procession round Jerusalem to the glory of God, and to pray and give alms and fast, as faithful men should do."[89] Earlier, prior to a sortie from Antioch, the men had spent three days in fasting, had confessed their sins, and received absolution and communion.[90] Whenever there were main festivals and saints' days, on the First Crusade for example, celebrations were the order of the day—Candlemas at Kephalia and Whitsunday near Caesarea.[91]

The regular round of services constituted so many liturgical assurances of the divine collaboration that would lead to victory,[92] but individual nobles also had their own clerics to see to their spiritual welfare. When Joinville fell sick in mid-Lent 1250 he reported, "my priest came to sing mass for me at my bedside, in my pavilion."[93] He provides the further information that "I had two chaplains who recited my Hours to me. One chanted mass for me as soon as dawn appeared, the other waited till my knights and those attached to my battalion had arisen."[94]

In these ways devotion was sustained and the spirit of the crusaders supported so that they might be reminded constantly, in the words of Bohemond to his troops, that "this is no war of the flesh, but of the spirit."[95]

6. Guidebooks

This heading is included here in order to preserve uniformity with the list of pilgrimage literature, but it is not a type that found a place amongst that generated by the Crusades. Although guidebooks to Rome and Compostela predated or were contemporary with them, the Holy Land examples were the end product of a long development that did not reach its culmination until after the Crusades had come to an end. Guides were in demand by the crusaders, but guidebooks were scarcely what they needed.

7. Travel Accounts

A. *Histories.* This type of crusading literature is abundant, but it differs in several important respects from the corresponding pilgrimage travel accounts. In the first instance, the basic structure is not that of an itinerary but of a sequence of events of a military character: sieges, battles, etc. It scrupulously follows a chronological order and so belongs to the type best designated an historical narrative or chronicle. It is punctuated by a series of struggles that mark the stages of an army's advance, for instance, the investing and eventual capture of a city such as Antioch. These are not the stations that are prominent in the records of non-crusading pilgrims, who laid greater stress on arriving at Venice, beholding the coast of Palestine, venerating the footprints of Jesus in the Church of the Ascension on the Mount of Olives, and so on. Moreover, the personal note of the pilgrims' descriptions relating to individual devotions and emotions is largely lacking. Indeed, comprehensive accounts cannot be firsthand, and so William of Tyre properly distinguishes between the first fifteen books of his work, which he states he has assembled from previous writings, and the remainder, which relate what he has himself witnessed.[96]

Despite these differences, some of the intentions behind the histories are identical to or at least parallel with those that motivated the pilgrims' accounts before them. First, there is the desire to provide information for those who would follow after. Such was the purpose of William Adam's *De modo Saracenos extirpandi* and Raymond Etienne's *Directorium passagium faciendum*.[97] Also illustrative of this category is the very lengthy record by Sir Gilbert de Lannoy of his tour in 1422, a report of the situation in the Near East drawn up at the request of Henry V. The king was contemplating a crusade and wanted exact information about cities, ports, and rivers.[98]

A second intention was to stir the readers to imitation, and this literature of crusading projects developed greatly after the fall of the Latin Kingdom during the last third of the thirteenth century. So Bertrand de la Brocquière's book is both an itinerary for a prospective pilgrim and a source of information for any prince or king who would undertake the conquest of Jerusalem.[99] Other works stressed the value of hearing about the wonders of divine justice, examples of the punishment of the wicked and the triumph of the righteous, which were noble themes for contemplation. Parallel to the *Hodoeporicon* of St. Willibald is Joinville's study of St. Louis, in that both works were intended to affirm the sanctity of their heroes, each one being a perfect pilgrim.

One other motive is peculiar to a group of three crusader historians: the desire to produce an account that would be based upon the *Gesta Francorum* but would improve upon it. These men were Robert the Monk, Guibert de Nogent, and Baldwin of

Bourgueuil. Each regarded the work from which he started as uncouth and crude; each sought to give the subject "proper" literary treatment, and this involved paying attention not only to grammar and style but also to theological analysis.[100]

B. *Poems*. The subjects of the prose narratives just noticed could equally well be treated in a different manner, that is, in verse. The Crusades did in fact generate poems written by the troubadours. The earliest of these minstrels were to be found in Languedoc ca. 1100, but the heyday of the movement was between 1150 and 1250. They flourished throughout Europe, some of them composing songs known as *sirventes*; the crusading *chansons* are of this type, a number of their authors having accompanied the soldiers as they went East.[101] Such was Ambrose the Minstrel, who composed *L'Estoire de la guerre sainte* ca. 1196. He indicates that his work was prompted by the example of the epics relating the exploits of Tristan and of Arthur and his knights, and he compares the valor of one crusader with that of Roland and Oliver, although, he adds, what he records is true, unlike "the ancient gests which minstrels do so celebrate."[102] Collections of these songs in French and German have been published.[103] However, most of them are epics, not chronicles; they recount the exploits of heroes; they sing of battles and victories; they present the ideal of the holy warrior; they have something of a hortatory character, being to a certain degree propaganda to encourage others to take the cross. They seldom reflect direct experience; they are, rather, literary works that seek to create myths.

8. Maps

The crusaders' difficulties in finding their way through Asia Minor and Syria, noted above in connection with the itineraries, resulted in a great development of cartography. One of the first maps produced for and by the crusaders was the *Situs Hierusalem*, which was included in the *Gesta Francorum*; indeed, it was incorporated into many manuscripts of the historical narrative type.[104] It introduced a significant change in layout because the Holy Land was moved to the center of the world. One famous example, the so-called Byzantine-Oxford T-O map, was brought back to England or Ireland after the First Crusade.[105] Without question, the greatest cartographer of the period was Matthew Paris; witness his map in the St. Albans Bible, of ca. 1252, now in Oxford.[106]

9. Canons

A link between the Crusades and ecclesiastical councils was forged from the outset, since it was at the one meeting in Clermont that the first call to take up the cross was sounded. Not many canons were promulgated over the years relating to campaigns against the Saracens; but there were exceptions to this, such as those issued by the Council of Lyons in 1274, which attempted unsuccessfully to promote another expedition to deliver the Holy Land.[107]

CONCLUSION

The typology suggested in this essay is more comprehensive and pays greater attention to the differences within and among the several items than that formulated in 1981 by Jean Richard in *Les Récits de voyages et de pèlerinages*.[108] Moreover, the presentation *seriatim* of the principal types of pilgrimage literature and of crusader writings facilitates a comparison between them.

Of the nine types generated by the non-crusading pilgrims, six were also produced by and for the crusaders. The same itineraries appear; pilgrim diaries correspond to those by crusaders; all wrote letters; travel accounts are abundant; maps were cherished by everyone; and canons were promulgated.

The absence of *libri indulgentiarum* and of guidebooks from the crusader corpus finds its explanation in the fact that these productions appear only after the ending of the ill-fated Eighth and last Crusade, when St. Louis died on St. Bartholomew's Day 1270. The crusaders had their devotions supervised by the clergy who accompanied them, and so they did not need the range of manuals used by the private pilgrims; in any case, the *Processional for Pilgrims to the Holy Land* was not drawn up until ca. 1340 by the Franciscans, after their return to Jerusalem in 1335.[109]

When there are types in common, some differences have to be acknowledged. The pilgrims' travel accounts, for example, are more personal that the scholarly histories, although all were promoted by identical motives. In fact, there is a sufficient overlap to endorse or reinforce the correctness of three separate but connected observations:

(1) The Crusades are properly to be interpreted as pilgrimages.
(2) To neglect the pilgrimage aspect of the Crusades is to do less than justice to the subject as a whole and to risk obscuring their true nature.
(3) Crusading literature in particular has to be considered as a subdivision of pilgrimage literature in general.

NOTES

[N.B.: Professor Davies was unable to make final corrections to his essay and notes.—Ed.]

[1] J. Richard, *Les Récits de voyages et de pèlerinages*, Typologie des sources du moyen âge occidental, 38 (Turnhout, 1981), p. 44.

[2] C. Hopkins, *The Discovery of Dura Europos* (New Haven and London, 1979), pp. 20-21.

[3] O. Cuntz, ed., *Itineraria Romana* (Leipzig, 1929).

[4] J. D. Wilkinson, ed. and trans., *Egeria's Travels* (London, 1971), pp. 153-63.

J. G. DAVIES

[5]J. D. Wilkinson, ed. and trans., *Jerusalem Pilgrims 1099-1185*, Hakluyt Society, 167 (1988), pp. 87-93. For the *Gesta Francorum* see *Gesta Francorum et aliorum Hierosolymitanorum. The Deeds of the Franks and Other Pilgrims to Jerusalem*, ed. and trans. R. Hill (London, 1962).

[6]Belard of Ascoli, *Descriptio Terrae Sanctae*, in S. de Sandoli, *Itinera Hierosolymitana Crucesignatorum*, vol. 2 (Jerusalem, 1980), pp. 42-49.

[7]Wilkinson, ed. and trans., *Egeria's Travels*, p. 162; idem, *Jerusalem Pilgrims before the Crusades* (Warminster, 1977), p. 85.

[8]T. Wright, *Early Travels in Palestine* (London, 1848), pp. 31-50.

[9]Wilkinson, ed. and trans., *Egeria's Travels* 23.10.

[10]*Epistolae Cantuariensis.*

[11]H. Michelant and G. Reynaud, eds., *Itinéraires à Jérusalem* (Geneva, 1882), pp. 235-36.

[12]J. G. Davies, *Pilgrimage Yesterday and Today. Why? Where? How?* (London, 1988), p. 8.

[13]R. Röhricht, "Le pèlerinage du moine augustin Jacques de Vérone," *Revue de l'Orient Latin* 3 (1895): 155-302.

[14]F. J. Furnivall, ed., *The Stacyons of Rome*, EETS, o.s., 25 (1867).

[15]E. G. Duff, ed., *Information for Pilgrims unto the Holy Land (1498)* (London, 1893), p. xiii, n. 1.

[16]Frescobaldi, Gucci, and Sigoli, *Visit to the Holy Places of Egypt, Sinai, Palestine and Syria, in 1384*, ed. and trans. T. Bellorini and E. Hoade, Studium Biblicum Franciscanum, 6 (Jerusalem, 1948).

[17]*The Book of the Wanderings of Brother Felix Fabri*, ed. and trans. A. Stewart, Palestine Pilgrims' Text Society (hereafter PPTS), vols. 7-10 (London, 1892-93; all 13 PPTS vols. rept. New York, 1971), 7:290.

[18]M. de Castro, "Dos itinerarios de Terra Sante de los siglos xiv y xv," *Hispania Sacra* 10 (1957): 451-70; A. Bernouilli, "Ein Reisebüchlein für Jerusalemspilger," *Zeitschrift für Kirchengeschichte* 28 (1930): 79-86; R. Pernoud,

Un guide de pèlerin de Terre Sainte au XVe siècle, Cahiers d'histoire et de bibliographie, 1 (Mantes, 1940), pp. 41-67.

[19]W. Purcell, *Pilgrims' England* (London, 1981), pp. 37-40.

[20]Hence the need to distinguish clearly between guidebooks and itineraries.

[21]*Liber sancti Jacobi, Codex Calixtinus,* ed. W. M. Whitehill, vol. 1 (Santiago de Compostela, 1944); French text, *Le Guide du pèlerin de Saint-Jacques de Compostelle,* trans. J. Vieillard, 2nd ed. (Macon, 1950); an English edition by G. Gerson, J. Krochalis, A. Shaver-Crandell, and A. Stones is forthcoming.

[22]F. M. Nichols, *Mirabilia urbis Romae. The Marvels of Rome or A Picture of a Golden City* (London, 1894), pp. 120-54.

[23]J. G. Davies, *Pilgrimage Yesterday and Today,* pp. 96-100.

[24]H. W. Davies, *Bernhard von Breydenbach and His Journey to the Holy land, 1483-4. A Bibliography* (London, 1911), p. 37.

[25]Pernoud, *Un guide de pèlerin.*

[26]Duff, ed., *Information for Pilgrims*; William Wey, *The Itineraries of William Wey,* Roxburghe Club (London, 1857).

[27]*The Pilgrimage of Arnold von Harff,* ed. and trans. M. Letts, Hakluyt Society, n.s. 94 (1946), p. xviii.

[28]Anon., *Guide Book to Palestine, c.1350,* trans. J. H. Bernard, PPTS, 6:1.

[29]Wilkinson, ed. and trans., *Egeria's Travels,* p. 179. For the works of Peter the Deacon see *PL* 173.

[30]D. R. Howard, *Writers and Pilgrims* (Berkeley, 1980), p. 17.

[31]Niccolò da Poggibonsi, *A Voyage beyond the Seas (1346-50),* ed. and trans. T. Bellorini and E. Hoade, Studium Biblicum Franciscanum, 2 (Jerusalem, 1945), p. 11.

[32]R. Torkington, *Ye Oldest Diarie of Englysshe Travell,* ed. W. J. Loftie (London, 1884); anon., *The Pylgrymage of Sir Richard Guylforde to the Holy Land, A.D. 1506,* ed. H. Ellis, Camden Society, Ser. 1, 151 (1851).

[33]See n. 31 above.

[34]*Pilgrimage of Arnold von Harff*, ed. and trans. Letts, p. 2.

[35]*The Pilgrimage of the Russian Abbot Daniel in the Holy Land 1106-1107 A.D.*, ed. and trans. C. W. Wilson, PPTS, 4:2.

[36]Burchard of Mount Sion, *The Holy Places*, ed. and trans. A. Stewart, PPTS, 12:4.

[37]Anon. [Roswida of Heidenheim Abbey?], *The Hodoeporicon of St Willibald*, ed. and trans. the Rev. Canon Brownlow, PPTS, 3:1.

[38]J. G. Davies, *Pilgrimage Yesterday and Today*, pp. 85-86. See *Mandeville's Travels*, ed. M. Letts, Hakluyt Society, Ser. 2, vols. 101, 102 (1953).

[39]*Itinerarium Symonis Semeonis ab Hybernia ad Terram Sanctam*, ed. M. Esposito, Scriptores Latini Hiberniae, 4 (Dublin, 1960).

[40]G. B. Parks, *The English Traveller in Italy*, vol. 1 (Stanford, 1954), pp. 179-84.

[41]K. Nebenzahl, *Maps of the Bible Lands* (London, 1986), p. 19.

[42]Nebenzahl, *Maps of the Bible Lands*, figs. 9, 10.

[43]Nebenzahl, *Maps of the Bible Lands*, plates 17, 18.

[44] H. W. Davies, *Bernhard von Breydenbach*, p. 23.

[45]J. D. Mansi, *Sacrorum Conciliorum Nova et Amplissima Collectio*, vol. 14 (Graz, 1961), col. 103.

[46]T. Merton, *Mystics and Zen Masters* (London, 1967), pp. 103 ff.; J. Riley-Smith, *The First Crusade and the Idea of Crusading* (London, 1986), pp. 22-23.

[47]Fulcher of Chartres, *A History of the Expedition to Jerusalem, 1095-1117*, trans. F. R. Ryan, ed., with intro. by H. S. Fink [Knoxville, 1969], II.xxvii.10 (pp. 57, 179). Original text, Fulcherii Carnotensis, *Gesta Francorum Iherusalem peregrinantium*, *PL* 155.821-940; also in *Recueil des historiens des croisades. Historiens occidentaux*, vol. 3 (Paris, 1866), pp. 48-543 (hereafter, *RHC Hist. occ.*).

[48]William of Tyre, *A History of Deeds Done beyond the Sea*, ed. and trans. E. A. Babcock and A. C. Krey, 2 vols. (New York, 1943), 1:57. Text in *RHC Hist. occ.*, vol. 1, pt. 1 (1844), pp. 1-702: *Historia rerum in partibus transmarinis gestarum a tempore successorum Mahumeth usque ad annum Domini MCLXXXIV*, edita a Venerabili Willermo Tyrensi Archiepiscopo, Prologus, pp. 3-6.

[49]Caesarius of Heisterbach, *Dialogus miraculorum*, ed. J. Strange, 2 vols. (Cologne, 1851), I.6.

[50]H. W. Davies, *Bernhard von Breydenbach*, plate 4.

[51]*The History of Them That Took Constantinople*, in *Three Old French Chronicles of the Crusades*, trans. E. N. Stone (Seattle, 1939), p. 176. Text in Robert de Clari, *La Conquête de Constantinople*, ed. P. Lauer, 1924), X, XI (pp. 9-10).

[52]*Memoirs of the Crusades, by Villehardouin and de Joinville*, ed. and trans. F. T. Marzials (New York, 1958), p. 39.

[53]*Villehardouin and Joinville*, ed. and trans. Marzials, p. 346.

[54]J. G. Davies, *Pilgrimage Yesterday and Today*, p. 42.

[55]Joinville, in *Villehardouin and Joinville*, ed. and trans. Marzials, p. 192. For other examples see Riley-Smith, *First Crusade*, p. 37 n. 45.

[56]Anon., *The Chronicle of Reims*, in *Three Old French Chronicles*, ed. Stone, XXX, p. 334. Text in *Récits d'un ménestrel de Reims au treizième siècle*, ed. N. de Wailly, Société de l'Histoire de France (Paris, 1876), XXX, pp. 189-90. [The marking of the garments is not mentioned here.—Ed.]

[57]J. G. Davies, *Pilgrimage Yesterday and Today*, p. 17.

[58]J. G. Davies, *Pilgrimage Yesterday and Today*, p. 49.

[59]*Gesta Francorum et aliorum Hierosolymitanorum* I.3 (*Deeds*, ed. and trans. Hill, p. 7).

[60]Roberto de Sanseverino, *Viaggio in Terra Sante (1408)* (Bologna, 1888), p. 37.

[61]*Gesta Francorum* IX.23 (*Deeds*, ed. and trans. Hill, p. 58).

[62]Torkington, *Oldest Diarie of Englysshe Travell*, p. 3.

[63]*Liber Sancta Jacobi*, ed. Whitehill, 1:361.

[64]William of Tyre, 4.22 (*History*, ed. and trans. Babcock and Krey, 1:220).

[65]*Gesta Francorum* I.3 (*Deeds*, ed. and trans. Hill, p. 8).

[66]Robert de Clari, *History of Them*, LXXXIII in Stone, *Three Old French Chronicles*, pp. 227-28. Text in Robert de Clari, *Conquête*, ed. Lauer, pp. 82-83.

[67]Wright, *Early Travels in Palestine*, p. 175.

[68]Ambrose, *History of the Holy War*, in Stone, *Three Old French Chronicles*, pp. 156-57. Text in *L'Estoire de la guerre sainte: histoire en vers de la troisième croisade* (1190-92) par Ambroise, ed. and trans. G. Paris (Paris, 1897), cols. 322-27 (lines 12013-195).

[69]Albert of Aix/Aachen. Text in *RHC Hist. occ.*, vol. 4 (Paris, 1879), III: Alberti Aquensis *Historia Hierosolymitana*, III, XLV, p. 463.

[70]J. G. Davies, *Pilgrimage Yesterday and Today*, p. 57.

[71]Fulcher of Chartres, I.xxxii.1 (*History,* Ryan and Fink, p. 128).

[72]Fulcher of Chartres, I.vi.10 (*History,* Ryan and Fink, p. 74).

[73]J. Riley-Smith, *What Were the Crusades?* (London, 1971), p. 47.

[74]Riley-Smith, *What Were the Crusades?*, p. 47.

[75]*Deeds*, ed. and trans. Hill, pp. 98-101.

[76]Wilkinson, ed. and trans., *Egeria's Travels*, pp. 90-91.

[77]Wilkinson, ed. and trans., *Egeria's Travels*, p. 11. [This *G. F. J. e.* is a précis of the account of Fulcher of Chartres; text in *RHC Hist. occ.* 3:48-543. See n. 47 above. Subsequent references to the *Gesta Francorum* are to the *Gesta Francorum et aliorum Hierosolymitanorum*; see n. 5 above.—Ed.]

[78]William of Tyre, 8.1-4 (*History*, ed. and trans. Babcock and Krey, 1:339).

[79]William of Tyre, 4.21 (*History*, ed. and trans. Babcock and Krey, 1:218).

[80]William of Tyre, 7.21 (*History*, ed. and trans. Babcock and Krey, 1:330).

[81]William of Tyre, 16.21 (*History*, ed. and trans. Babcock and Krey, 2:170).

[82]William of Tyre, 16.25 (*History*, ed. and trans. Babcock and Krey, 2:175).

[83]William of Tyre, 16.26 (*History*, ed. and trans. Babcock and Krey, 2:178).

[84]Fulcher of Chartres, I.v.12 (*History*, Ryan and Fink, p. 71).

[85]Raimundi de Aguilers canonici Podiensis, *Historia Francorum qui ceperunt Iherusalem*, in *RHC Hist. occ.* 3:231-309.

[86]P. Alphandéry, *La chrétienté et l'idée de croisade* (Paris, 1954), p. 186.

[87]P. Riant, *Inventaire critique des lettres historiques des croisades*, Archives de l'Orient latin, 1 (1881), pp. 1-224.

[88]*Kreuzzugsbriefe (1088-1108)* (Innsbruck, 1901).

[89]*Gesta Francorum* X.37 (*Deeds*, ed. and trans. Hill, p. 90).

[90]*Gesta Francorum* 9.29 (*Deeds*, ed. and trans. Hill, pp. 67-68).

[91]*Gesta Francorum* 10.33, 36 (*Deeds*, ed. and trans. Hill, pp. 82, 87).

[92]Alphandéry, *La chrétienté et l'idée*, p. 129.

[93]Joinville, in *Villehardouin and Joinville*, ed. and trans. Marzials, p. 239.

[94]Joinville, in *Villehardouin and Joinville*, ed. and trans. Marzials, p. 291.

[95]*Gesta Francorum* VI.17 (*Deeds*, ed. and trans. Hill, p. 37).

[96]William of Tyre, 16.1 (*History*, ed. and trans. Babcock and Krey, 2:136).

[97]Richard, *Les Récits*, p. 70.

[98]Sir Gilbert de Lannoy, "A Survey of Egypt and Syria Undertaken in the Year 1422," ed. and trans. and with an introduction by the Rev. J. Webb, *Archaeologia* 22 (1827): 281-444.

[99]*The Travels of Bertrandon de la Brocquière* A.D. *1432, 1433*, in Wright, *Early Travels in Palestine*, pp. 283-382.

[100]Riley-Smith, *First Crusade*, pp. 135 ff.

[101]E. Siberry, *Criticism of Crusading 1095-1274* (Oxford, 1985), p. 5.

[102]Ambrose, *L'Estoire*, in Stone, *Three Old French Chronicles*, p. 63. [Text in Ambroise, *Estoire*, ed. Paris, col. 112, lines 4179-94. What Ambroise actually says is that he cannot either confirm or deny the tales about Alexander, Balan, Tristan, Paris, Helen, Arthur and his brave company, Charles, Pippin, Agoland, Wittikind, nor the old *chansons de geste* so celebrated by the *jugleur*. What he is sure of, and will narrate truthfully, is the suffering of the army before Acre. (No one crusader is singled out, nor compared with Roland and Oliver, and no inspiration from the epics is mentioned.)–Ed.]

[103]J. Bédier and P. Aubry, eds., *Les chansons de croisade* (Paris, 1909); M. Colleville, ed., *Les chansons allemandes de croisade en moyen haut-allemand* (Paris, 1936).

[104]Nebenzahl, *Maps of the Bible Lands*, p. 32.

[105]Nebenzahl, *Maps of the Bible Lands*, p. 33. [A T-O or O-T (for *orbis terrae*) map consisted of a circle with an inscribed T dividing the earth's land masses into Asia at the top, Europe in the lower left and Africa in the lower right segments. See the essay by D. French in the present volume.–Ed.]

[106]Nebenzahl, *Maps of the Bible Lands*, p. 36. [MS in Corpus Christi College, Oxford, MS 2, fol. 2ᵛ. See Richard Vaughan, *Matthew Paris* (Cambridge, 1958; rept. with bib. supp. 1979), plate 17.–Ed.]

[107]Mansi, *Extractiones de libro*, caps. vi-xxvii *(Sacrorum Conciliorum*, vol. 24, cols. 111-19).

[108]See n. 1 above, Richard, *Les Récits*. I was unable to consult this work until I had almost completed this paper. It is a study to be commended but it does not affect the conclusions given here.

[109]J. G. Davies, "A Fourteenth Century Processional for Pilgrims in the Holy Land," *Hispania Sacra* 41 (1989): 421-29.

PILGRIMAGE AND SACRAL POWER

Robert Worth Frank, Jr.

In an essay on the skeptic philosopher Demonax, the Greek satirist Lucian reports with obvious relish Demonax's response when asked to accompany a friend to the temple of Asclepius to make a prayer for his son. "Poor deaf Asclepius!" he exclaimed. "Can he not hear at this distance?"[1]

Demonax's skeptical jibe would have fallen on deaf ears indeed in twelfth-century France. The visit of a petitioner to the shrine of the sacral figure being petitioned was normally part of the process in securing miraculous assistance. It was not a case of the saint's or the Virgin's not "hearing." The Virgin of Rocamadour, for example, "heard," and answered, a prayer in Asia Minor by a man buried in an earthquake, and the plea of a pregnant woman in Jerusalem suddenly struck blind.[2] But the shrine or church where the saint or the Virgin was venerated was the dynamic center at which divine power was concentrated and from which it flowed. The pilgrim travelled to this dynamic center in the conviction that the journey was an integral part of the process of miracle.

To be sure, the specific motives of pilgrims in making the journey were varied. Some were seeking divine aid at the shrine, miraculous cure or intervention in crisis. The prayers of others had already been answered and they were fulfilling a compensatory vow of pilgrimage to render thanks and praise and, perhaps, to offer an *ex voto*. Some were travelling under duress, ordered or sentenced to make the pilgrimage as an act of penance.[3] Some may have been seeking diversion, the excitements of travel—new scenes and famous places; for these, pilgrimage was the medieval equivalent of two weeks in Hawaii or a trip to Disneyland. Most pilgrims, however, had more modest though serious goals: to give thanks for survival through past troubles and to ask for continued protection. For some, the difficulties and dangers of travel in themselves endowed their pilgrimages with a penitential character. All were journeying in the knowledge that pilgrimage was a meritorious act from which benefits accrued in the hereafter.

At the shrine the pilgrim might make his or her confession and would in all likelihood attend mass. Who was without sin? As a center of sacral power the shrine was especially efficacious in the restoration and strengthening of grace. Thus the familiar, quotidian miracles of removal of mortal sin and of transubstantiation were ratified by the dramatic evidence of extraordinary miracle surrounding the worshipper.

From the custodians the pilgrims would hear accounts of past wonders and could gaze at *ex voto*s memorializing them: wax limbs, candles the height of a man, silver teeth, discarded crutches, a wax ship. Pilgrims coming in payment of a vow had their stories to tell: escape from an enemy prison, a wasting illness suddenly lifted, relief from possession by an evil spirit. Clustered around the shrine or statue were men and women seeking cures, weeping, praying, imploring. When from time to time a miraculous cure occurred, there would be an explosion of excitement—a scream of joy; a press of worshippers crowding to see; townspeople rushing in from shops, homes, taverns, summoned by the ringing of the church bells; a Te Deum sung. The shrine was the magnetic center: there the pilgrims came into the immediate presence of sacral power.

But what of the act of pilgrimage itself? Was it merely pragmatic, a business of getting to the shrine and back? Or, if made to honor a vow, was it thought of in legalistic or mercantile terms, fulfillment of promise or payment of debt, part of that "relation d'échange" of which Pierre-André Sigal speaks?[4] Did no element of the sacral attach to it? The penitential dimension of pilgrimage and its value as a meritorious act in itself push in that direction. We can reconstruct the pilgrim's apperception of the shrine experience. Can we not reconstruct the apperception of the journeying experience? That is what I shall attempt here.

There have been some efforts in this direction. The anthropologists Victor and Edith Turner have analyzed the total experience of pilgrimage as "liminoid." This they define as like liminal experiences (rites of passage) in some respects but unlike them in being voluntary. Liminal experience is characterized by release from mundane structure; homogenization of status; communitas; healing and renewal; ordeal; removal from a mundane center to a sacred periphery.[5] But this focuses on the communal and, furthermore, is tainted for our purposes by the conflation of shrine experience with the journey. Alphonse Dupront, in "Pèlerinages et lieux sacrés," speaks of "a spiritualization of the pilgrim life." This he sees as a consequence of the passage through space, which by involving the pilgrim in changes makes him a stranger, first to others and finally to himself. The pilgrim experiences "space therapy," powerful enough to effect a deliverance of soul, to create a new universe. Dupront's approach is phenomenological and highly abstract. His analysis of the fundamental elements of pilgrimage as religious man, space, and the sacred preserves a complete dichotomy between pilgrimage and shrine.[6]

I shall argue here that a sacral character inheres in the very act of pilgrimage. It is intermittent, it is nowhere near so pervasive as at the shrine, it is probably not perceived by all pilgrims, but it is always potentially present. The pilgrim travelled to and from the shrine in a kind of "force field."[7] This is the conclusion that emerges when we examine the twelfth-century pilgrimage narratives from the shrine of Notre-Dame de Rocamadour in southwestern France, near Cahors. They reveal clearly the insistent and complex entanglement of the pilgrimage act itself with manifestations of the shrine's power.

The Rocamadour narratives were written down in the year 1172 by an unknown recorder, probably one of the monks from the monastery.[8] The recorder says he will limit himself to miracles he has either seen or learned from the true report of informed persons ("a certis personis certa relatione"). Although a few of the narratives must date from before 1150, he may well be speaking truly concerning most of them.[9] The Rocamadour collection is apt for our purposes. It is apparently the largest surviving collection of local miracles of the Virgin in France, 126 separate narratives involving at least 134 miracles. (Counting miracles is not always a simple matter. There is, for example, the peasant, bedridden, suffering terrible leg pains, who promised his goods to the Virgin of Rocamadour if he were cured. He was cured, immediately, but then he reneged, claiming the medication was responsible. The pains returned, even more severe. He was finally persuaded to offer her all his money and was completely relieved [II.21 (215-18)]. Cure, punishment by relapse, second cure: how many miracles do we have: one? two? three?[10])

Nonetheless, when we group the miracles in categories according to place of occurrence certain surprises await us. The first is the small percentage of miracles that occur at the shrine itself: nineteen (14.4%), or, if we count four punishment miracles, twenty-three (17.4%).[11] Some 80% occurred either at the scene of need or in the course of pilgrimage. This is especially surprising because the narratives, for Rocamadour and other shrines as well, generally convey the impression that presence at the shrine is obligatory. Consider, for instance, the dramatic story of Stephana of Rouergue, carried off into the forest one cold night by two wolves and savagely mauled. She was found at last, but was horribly disfigured. Her wounds began to suppurate, and their foul odor was so disgusting that her fellow villagers put her into a cart one night and dumped her by the entrance to a neighboring village. She was no more welcome there but was tied like a faggot on the back of a donkey and sent packing—loosely tied, it appears, for when the beast clambered down a ravine to drink poor Stephana slid off its back into the stream. Instead of drowning she drifted along until she was rescued. A kindly local lord took pity on her, gave her shelter in a stable, and paid a herdsman to bathe her wounds with wine and oil. Although she had now been rescued on two occasions by the Virgin of Rocamadour, she was not finally relieved from her horrible suffering and isolation until she could scrape together enough money to make the pilgrimage to the shrine itself (II.15 [200-06]). The miraculous rescues are reported fully and vividly, but it is the visit to the shrine that is the culmination of the narrative and seems to be the necessary act. The fact remains, however, that comparatively few miracles occurred there.

The pilgrimage road itself is the scene of almost as many miracles as the shrine: seventeen by my count, twenty-one if we include four that occurred after the return home. A recent book on Chaucer says, "a pilgrimage . . . was declared over at its destination; the return home was a contingency, not part of the ritual act."[12] That may have been true of the long pilgrimage to Rome or Jerusalem, but it was not true for Rocamadour. The monks there told a mother seeking relief for her insane son that the Virgin often worked her miracles upon return. They may simply have wished to rid themselves of the son, a screaming nuisance who insulted people coming to the sanctuary, and the mother also, a nag who begged pilgrims to pray for her poor boy. But as they reached the oratory at the highest point above the town of Rocamadour, she looked back and uttered a prayer, and her son began to speak to her with an unaccustomed mildness and his expression, once so terrible, became agreeable and pleasant (II.10 [190-93]).

There is also the knight, Geraud Tosez, suffering from a life-threatening tumor on his throat, who came to Rocamadour, prayed all night, and left the next morning without having recovered his health but still confident and untroubled. "What happened on the way? What did the Lady of Mercy do for this suffering one?" the narrator asks. Before he reached home the tumor burst and disappeared (I.48 [154-55]).

The pilgrimage could even extend its protection after the journey. With houses all around afire after a lightning strike and with flaming brands dropping on his roof, a desperate knight cried to the Virgin, "Didn't I visit your sanctuary and put myself under your protection, and my goods too? My clothes are burning. How can I alone escape?" The answer came. Rain fell and extinguished the fire (I.9 [90-92]). Again, two young men returning from Rocamadour crowded into a boat at a river crossing and fell into a raging torrent. Though fishermen whose job it was to rescue persons crossing there searched in vain and finally gave up hope, suddenly the two men were seen on the river bank, dry and unharmed. The Virgin had sheltered them under the water and led them to safety (I.1 [70-71]).

Just to begin a pilgrimage was sometimes enough to evoke divine power. Although only a few narratives tell of cure on the journey to the shrine, several of them are among the most striking. A son born in answer to a petition to the Virgin of Rocamadour was blind at birth. The mother grieved but nursed him and raised him. Finally she set out with her child to seek for him the gift of sight at Rocamadour. Arriving at the village of Hermet just as the bells were summoning the faithful to prayer, at a crossroad before an image of the Savior, she fell to her knees and prayed passionately. A profusion of blood poured from the child's eyes, and he could see (I.23 [112-14]). Even more mysterious and suggestive is the account of Bernarde, a woman weakened and emaciated by a tumor of the breast that the doctors feared to lance. On her way to Rocamadour to seek relief she met another pilgrim, an old man, who asked her where she was going and why. When she told him, the venerable pilgrim revealed that he was a messenger of the Virgin, the mediator of God and mankind. Thereupon he perforated the tumor, pus burst out, and she was cured.

He put a plaster on the wound, bound it, bid her farewell, and disappeared. Bernarde went on to the church, showed her scar, and told her story (I.43 [145-46]).[13]

Another category of miracles relates exclusively to the process of pilgrimage: protection miracles, miracles whose specific effect was to guard or give remedy to pilgrims on the journey to or from the shrine. The miraculous rescue from drowning of the two young men returning home, told above, should perhaps be so classified. Of the seven such miracles in the Rocamadour collection, six occur on the journey to the shrine. In them pilgrims are protected against abuse, thieves, or loss of money. An early "detective story" tells of three women on pilgrimage to Rocamadour who were set upon by robbers in the depths of the forest of Limousin. One woman, Constantina of Auxerre, fought back fiercely. Three times a thief stabbed at her throat yet failed to cut so much as a thread of her garment. At last, at her friends' urging, she gave up, and the robbers made off with their few possessions. But the dog of one of the thieves, though "an animal without reason," was revolted by their cruelty and remained with the three women. They made their way back to civilization, where the dog was recognized. The thief his master, thus identified, was ultimately caught and brought to justice. The miracle was the escape from stabbing: Constantina brought the knife to Rocamadour. But the action of the dog seems equally remarkable (I.47 [150-54]).

The protection miracles offer particularly vivid glimpses of the pilgrim experience. Rocamadour was situated in rugged territory, which heightened the penitential value of the pilgrimage there. Robert de Torigny, describing the visit of King Henry II of England to Rocamadour in 1170, spoke of it as a place surrounded by mountains and frightful solitude ("locus . . . montaneis et horribili solitudine circumdatur").[14] Our narrator exclaims rhetorically at one point, "Considering the ruggedness of the place and its geographical location (*asperitatem loci situmque considerans*), who would not wonder at so much divine power and such radiance of graciousness (*tanto numine tantoque lumine venustatum*).[15]

Robbers were a frequent danger. We hear of one man who, to baffle thieves pursuing him, hid his money by the roadside. Having eluded them, he reached Rocamadour. On his return he could not locate his cache because the road had been badly trampled by travelers and animals. Only after berating the Virgin soundly for failing so faithful a servant did he find his money (II.44 [254-58]). Surprisingly, we hear of some pilgrims travelling alone. One was abused by a knight who took a fancy to his wonderfully warm hat and kicked him to the ground, injuring him, when he refused to sell it (after two offers, the second lower than the first). The knight was punished by a frightful attack of *mal d'ardents* (ergot poisoning) (I.24 [114-16]). More frequently we hear of groups of three, as in the account of three pilgrims traversing the solitude and wastes of St. Guilhem-le-Desert who were stopped by thieves and forced across mountains and valleys, the while being frightfully mistreated. The Virgin rendered the thieves blind and paralyzed, with only their tongues free to move, to beg for mercy and forgiveness (II.9 [189-90]).

Among the many Rocamadour miracles are two that can only be described as reporting metaphorical pilgrimages. They seem especially suggestive of pilgrimage's sacral power because of their symbolic content. One is of a priest of Chartres (a noteworthy detail, for Chartres had its own miracle-working shrine of the Virgin), ill for some weeks, about to die (he had already been placed on the ground three times). In desperation his mother called on the Virgin of Rocamadour for aid and pinned on her son the pilgrim badge of Rocamadour. At that very moment the priest ceased to feel ill and recovered his health (I.37 [135-36]). The other tells of Hathvide, a young and beautiful woman, rich and well-born, who for seven years had suffered from dropsy (a pathological accumulation of diluted lymph in body tissues and cavities). Doctors could do nothing. Although everyone else despaired, Hathvide, night and day, with sighs and prayers, begged the Virgin to cure her. Since she lived in Valenciennes, a great distance from Rocamadour, and could not travel, she would prostrate herself in prayer and position herself in the direction of the shrine. One day when she went out to pray, staggering and tottering on one foot ("titubans et uno pede labens"), the humors, internal and subcutaneous, began to pour forth like a fountain through the natural passages. Though previously two people could scarcely get their arms around her, she was now so thin that her navel seemed to stick to her spine (I.20 [107-08]).

A pilgrim badge employed as the catalyst for cure, the pilgrimage route travelled metaphorically by gesture in quest of aid—here we see the elevated status of pilgrimage clearly revealed and see it sharing the miraculous power of shrine and Virgin.

The pragmatic and self-serving reasons why attendants at the shrine should encourage pilgrimage are too obvious to need mention. They are of course not the only reasons. But what is really significant is the attitude of layfolk, the pilgrims especially, that these narratives reveal in varying degrees and in varying ways. The gesture of the priest's mother, pinning the pilgrimage badge on her dying son; Hathvide, grotesque and cumbersome, coming as close to pilgrimage as she can manage; and the hundreds of pilgrims travelling to and from Rocamadour because of a cure or a vow or a need of aid, certain that the action of *going* was essential, telling their stories and talking of miraculous protection, of cures en route or upon return—the Rocamadour narratives suggest no sharp and absolute separation between journey and shrine in the matter of sacral power. For all the climactic awareness of divine presence at the shrine, the pilgrims' own narratives told them that divine presence might be manifest along a whole spectrum: from the moment of beseeching through the whole pilgrimage experience. The sacral power that flowed mysteriously through the shrine flowed also along the pilgrim way.

ROBERT WORTH FRANK, JR.

APPENDIX: ROCAMADOUR MIRACLES BY CATEGORY

The Roman numerals (I, II, III) refer to the particular "partie" or main division (three in all) in which the miracle appears in Albe, ed. and trans., *Les Miracles* (see n. 2 below); the Arabic numerals refer to the "chapter" number assigned to a specific miracle in that "partie."

A. Miracles at scene of need, pre-pilgrimage, with pilgrimage vow:

   I.3 (2), 8, 10, 12, 13, 14, 15, 17, 18, 19, 25, 27, 40, 41, 42, 45, 49, 52.

   II.4, 8, 12, 13, 14, 18, 19, 20, 21 (2), 24, 37, 41, 42.

   III.3, 4, 8, 10, 12, 13, 15, 16, 21, 23, 24.

B. Shrine miracles, after pilgrimage to shrine:

   I.2, 6, 11, 21 (2), 22, 26, 28, 33, 35, 38, 53.

   II.5, 15, 16, 24, 36.

   III.19.

C. Post-pilgrimage miracles:

   I.1, 4, 9, 21, 29, 30, 48.

   II.10, 39.

D. Miracles at scene of need, no pilgrimage vow, pilgrimage of thanks:

   I.5, 50, 51.

   II.2, 28, 29, 35, 38, 45, 49.

E. Miracles at scene of need, no pilgrimage reported:

   (a) *Ex voto* reported:

   I.7, 31, 36.

   II.1, 31, 32, 33, 40, 46, 47.

   III.9.

(b) Prayer for help, no *ex voto* reported:

I.32, 46.

II.3, 7, 17, 22, 23, 43, 48.

III.1, 5, 6, 17, 18, 20, 22.

F.   Miracles en route to shrine:

I.16, 23, 43, 44.

III.2.

G.   Protection miracles, during pilgrimage:

I.24, 47.

II.9, 11, 30, 44.

III.7.

H.   Punishment miracles:

I.3, 6.

II.6, 21, 24, 25, 26, 27, 30.

III.11, 14.

I.   Symbolic pilgrimage miracles at scene of need:

I.34, 39.

NOTES

[1]*Works of Lucian of Samosata*, trans. H. W. and F. G. Fowler, 4 vols. (Oxford, 1905), 3:7.

[2]*Les Miracles de Notre-Dame de Roc-Amadour au xii*[e] *siècle*, ed. and trans. Edmond Albe (Paris, 1907), II.20 [213-15]; II.19 [212-13]. References to the miracles of Rocamadour will be to this edition and will be given hereafter in the text as above: the Roman numeral identifies the "partie" or main division (there are three in all) in Albe's *Les Miracles* in which the miracle appears; the Arabic numeral immediately following refers to the "chapter" number assigned the miracle in the "partie" (a "chapter" for each miracle). The Arabic numerals in brackets are page numbers. In *L'homme et le miracle dans la France médiévale*

(xie-xiie siècle) (Paris, 1985), Pierre-André Sigal cites Dieter Harmening's study (which I have not seen) of Frankish miracles where he defines degrees of sacrality determined by relative proximity to the sanctuary and the relic "sous forme d'une série de cercles concentriques dont la sacralité croissait de la périphérie vers le centre" (p. 61). No such pattern appears in the Rocamadour collection. (The Harmening reference is to *Fränkische Mirakelbücher, Würzburger Diözesan-Geschichtsblätter* 28 [1966]: 105-06.)

[3]On penitential pilgrimage see Jonathan Sumption, *Pilgrimage: An Image of Medieval Religion* (Totowa, N.J., 1975), pp. 98-113.

[4]Sigal, *L'homme et le miracle*, pp. 80-116.

[5]Victor Turner and Edith Turner, *Image and Pilgrimage in Christian Culture: Anthropological Perspectives* (New York, 1978), pp. 34-39, 249-50, and passim.

[6]Alphonse Dupront, in *Méthodologie de l'histoire et des sciences humaines (Mélanges en l'honneur de Fernand Braudel)* (Toulouse, 1973), pp. 189-206.

[7]I borrow the phrase from Aron Gurevich, *Medieval Popular Culture: Problems of Belief and Perception*, trans. Janos M. Bak and Paul A. Hollingsworth (Cambridge, 1988), p. 42.

[8]The narrator, at the conclusion of the story of Stephana of Rouergue (II.15 [200-06]), told above, pp. 34-35, says it occurred in the year 1166 and he is writing about it six years later. See also *Les Miracles*, ed. Albe, p. 12.

[9]*Les Miracles*, ed. Albe, pp. 61-62 and pp. 12, 13.

[10]A number of miracles tell of two or three events, each of which seems miraculous but is part of a continuous narrative, such as escape from an enemy. Most of these I count as a single miracle. I list here the narratives with multiple miracles, placing in parentheses the number of "events" and in brackets those narratives whose multiple miracles I have counted separately: I.[3 (3)], [6 (2)], 10 (2), 11 (3), 13 (2), [21 (3)], 32 (2), 40 (2), 53 (2); II.9 (2), 15 (3), 17 (2), [21 (3)], [24 (3)], 34 (2), 49 (2); III.14 (2), 17 (2).

[11]Sigal (*L'homme et le miracle*, pp. 60-68) discusses the subject of miracles occurring at a distance from the relics or shrine and finds that in the eleventh and twelfth centuries most miracles occurred near the relics. This changes toward the end of the thirteenth century, and in the fourteenth century most occur at a distance. The Rocamadour miracles, of course, are of the twelfth century. Sr.

Benedicta Ward (writing before Sigal) said that the many miracles occurring away from the shrine differentiated Rocamadour from other shrines (*Miracles and the Medieval Mind: Theory, Record and Event, 1000-1215* [Philadelphia, 1982], p. 148). Ronald Finucane says that out of some three thousand miracles (English and French) half occurred at the shrine, half at home (*Miracles and Pilgrims: Popular Beliefs in Medieval England* [London, 1977], pp. 69-70).

Ward's figures for Rocamadour are puzzling: eleven miracles at the shrine, forty-eight elsewhere, five on the journey. None of these figures agrees with what is found in Albe's *Les Miracles.*

[12]Donald R. Howard, *Chaucer: His Life, His Works, His World* (New York, 1987), p. 405.

[13]A few years later there were a number of miracles on the road, the Chartres wagon miracles, as materials were brought to rebuild the cathedral after the disastrous fire of 1194 (*Miracles de Notre Dame de Chartres*, ed. Antoine Thomas, *Bibliothèque de l'école des Chartes* 42 [1881]: 505-06, 508-09; and see miracles 3, 4, 5, 9, 10). See also Léopold Delisle, ed., "Lettre de l'Abbé Haimon sur la construction de l'église de Saint-Pierre-sur-Dive en 1145," *Bibliothèque de l'école des Chartes*, 5th ser., 1 (1860): 115-21.

[14]*Les Miracles*, ed. Albe, p. 15 n. 1.

[15]*Les Miracles*, ed. Albe, p. 63.

JOURNEYS TO THE CENTER OF THE EARTH:

MEDIEVAL AND RENAISSANCE

PILGRIMAGES TO MOUNT CALVARY

Dorothea R. French

In 1484, Felix Fabri "faithfully recorded" an account of his two pilgrimages to the Holy Land for his brothers in the Dominican convent in Ulm.[1] *The Wanderings of Felix Fabri* contains the most elaborate and highly developed discussion of Mount Calvary as the allegorical Center of the Earth to appear in pilgrimage literature between the fourth and fifteenth centuries.[2] Pilgrims to Palestine and Jerusalem from Late Antiquity to the Renaissance had visited Mount Calvary not only because they believed it was the actual place where Christ had been crucified, *sensus literalis*, but also because of its symbolic meaning for the salvation of the world, *sensus allegoricus*.[3] These two perceptions of Mount Calvary existed in pilgrims' guides, iconography, and Christian cartography. The allegorical meaning of Mount Calvary, however, came to exert an enormous appeal as a sacred *omphalos*, or navel, the symbolic center of the earth out of which all creation and redemption sprang.[4] This essay will examine the way in which the allegorical concept of Mount Calvary gradually merged with the cartography of the High Middle Ages to become both the literal and allegorical Center of the Earth. As the inheritor of a tradition that identified Mount Calvary as both the symbolic and literal center of the earth, Felix Fabri faced a dilemma in a period of increasing knowledge about the known world. His creative resolution of this dilemma illustrates the power of the allegorical meaning of a sacred center.

Fig. 1 Claudius Ptolemy (ca. A.D. 90–168). World Map compiled ca. A.D. 150. Florence, 1474; manuscript on vellum (MS. Vat. Lat. 3811, fols. iv–3). Photography by Foto Biblioteca Vaticana. Reproduced by permission of the Biblioteca Apostolica Vaticana.

LATE ANTIQUITY AND THE EARLY MIDDLE AGES

One of the fundamental motivations for Christian pilgrimages to the Holy Land has always been a desire to visit the "actual" places where significant sacred events had occurred. On a literal level the physical remains in Palestine served as a readily observable and historically verifiable proof of the claims of the Bible. The Bible acted as the guidebook for the itineraries of Mileto of Sardis, the Bordeaux pilgrim, St. Jerome, Paula, and Egeria, all of whom made a circuit of the notable sites associated with both the Old and New Testaments. Everything that Egeria saw was in response to her demand to be shown the literal settings of biblical events.[5]

Fig. 2 Claudius Ptolemy. Tabula Asia iv, ca. A.D. 150. Florence, 1474; manuscript on vellum (Ms. Vat. Lat. 3811, fols. 45ᵛ–46. Photography by Foto Biblioteca Vaticana. Reproduced by permission of the Biblioteca Apostolica Vaticana.

There is no evidence in the pilgrimage literature from the second through the fourth centuries that Mount Calvary was accorded any more reverence than other biblically significant places. Every stop on the pilgrimage circuit throughout Palestine validated the historical truth of the Scriptures to the early pilgrims. In an important sense, the ritual journeys helped to claim all of Roman and Jewish Palestine for Christianity. By visiting the ancient sites long venerated by Jews, Christians began the long, slow process of transforming Palestine into a Christian rather than a Jewish sacred center.[6]

Biblical map-making, or Christian cartography, beginning with Eusebius and Jerome in the fourth century, parallels the effort of Christian pilgrims to claim Palestine for Christianity. It is clear that Eusebius and Jerome were familiar with classical map-making. There were two major classes of maps circulating in Late Antiquity: the practical or thematic, and the schematic. The finest example of the first class is Ptolemy's second-century *Geographia*, the earliest known atlas of the world. It includes not only a map of the world but also ten maps of Europe, twelve of Asia, and four of Africa.[7] Figures 1 and 2 illustrate the high standard Ptolemy set for practical maps. The cartography of Eusebius and Jerome falls into the practical tradition. Their maps of Palestine demonstrate the way in which Christian scholars with roots in classical learning took old models and infused them with new meaning.[8] On the one hand, Jerome sketched the Roman province of Palestine; on the other, he utilized biblical place-names rather than those of contemporary Palestine. By superimposing the biblical setting (as represented by its place-names) on the organization of the Roman province in which he lived, Jerome transformed profane into sacred space.

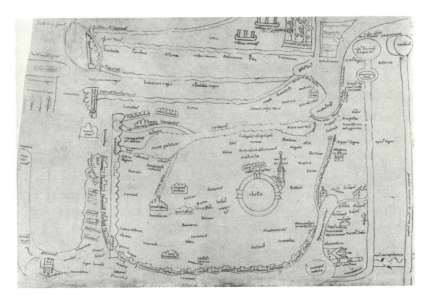

Fig. 3 Jerome (ca. 348–420) and Eusebius of Caesarea (ca. 260–340). Latin copy (ca. 1150) of a map of Palestine compiled ca. 385; manuscript on vellum (British Library ADD. MS. 10049, fol. 64ᵛ). Reproduced by permission of the British Library Board.

His map shown in Figure 3 demonstrates many of the characteristics of biblical cartography. The maps are oriented to the East (associated with the Garden of Eden); the scale is extremely variable and gives prominence to Palestine and Jerusalem; topographical detail is limited to important mountains, lakes, and rivers. Thus both the Christian ritual activity associated with places linked to the Old and New Testaments and the cartography of Eusebius and Jerome emphasized the *sensus literalis* of Palestine.

In contrast, some Church Fathers, particularly in the Greek East, stressed the allegorical meaning of biblical sites. Gregory of Nyssa, touring Palestine in the early fourth century, wrote a letter to three women of his congregation, interpreting for them the significance of what he had seen. For Gregory, the leading New Testament sites were symbols of the salvation that lay in Christ. To follow Christ anywhere was to be born with him in Bethlehem, to be crucified with him on Golgotha, to roll away the stone from the tomb of mortal life, and to rise with him to life immortal. According to Gregory, Bethlehem, Golgotha, the Mount of Olives, and the

Fig. 4 Lambert of St.-Omer, *Liber Floridus*, twelfth century. The emperor's orb is a spherical T-O map. (Fol. 138ᵛ of Ghent, University Library MS. 92). Reproduced by permission of Ghent University Library.

empty tomb should always stand before the true Christian's eyes as spiritual pointers to the godly life. For Christian pilgrims Palestine existed on both the literal and allegorical levels simultaneously. Although there is perhaps a tendency of such Latin writers in this period as Jerome to stress the *sensus literalis* and of the Greeks to stress the *sensus allegoricus* of biblical sites, it would be misleading to emphasize a sharp distinction between East and West. Both Greek and Latin Fathers accepted both meanings of pilgrimage sites.[9]

The impulse to universalize the biblical message, to see the cosmic implications of Christianity, found expression in the Christian adaptation of the schematic T-O maps, which reflected the classical conception of the *oikumene*, or known world, and were not intended for—nor used by—government officials or travelers.[10] These schematic maps depict the world, encircled by an ocean, as divided into three parts, with Asia occupying the upper half of the world and Europe and Africa the lower half (fig. 4).

Like Eusebius and Jerome, Christian scholars such as Orosius and Isidore of Seville adapted this classical model to fit their conception of the world. Orosius's *Historia* and Isidore's *Etymologiae* included biblically-oriented T-O maps in which each of the continents was assigned to one of the three sons of Noah: Ham, Shem, and Japhet (fig. 5).[11] Both of these Fathers were widely read and quoted by almost every Christian encyclopedist down to the fourteenth century. Their alteration of the classical schematic style of cartography further demonstrates the tendency of Christians in Late Antiquity and the Early Middle Ages to sacralize profane space. It also complemented their allegorical view of the world.

Christianity developed within a society that had a long-standing and carefully articulated set of ideas regarding the allegorical meaning of place. The pagan and Jewish traditions viewed a sacred center as the center of creation—the umbilicus of the world. There existed living organisms linked to the cosmos by natural cyclic time, physical "openings" in the three cosmic zones of Heaven, Earth, and Hell. The "openings" might occur in

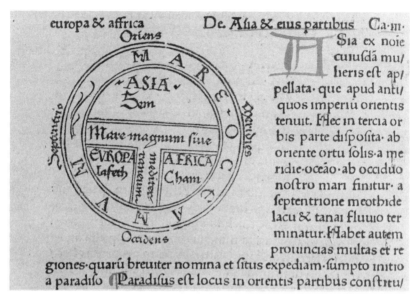

europa & affrica

Oriens

MARE

ASIA

Sem

Septentrio

Mare magnum siue

Pachdies

EVROPA

Iafeth

mediterraneum

AFRICA

Cham

Occidens

De. Asia & eius partibus Ca·m·

Sia ex noie cuiusdã mu/ lieris est ap/ pellata· que apud antí/ quos imperiũ orientis tenuit. Hec in tercia or bis parte disposita· ab oriente ortu solis·a me ridie·oceão·ab occiduo nostro mari finitur· a septentrione meotbide lacu & tanai fluuio ter minatur. Habet autem prouincias multas et re giones·quarũ breuiter nomina et situs expediam·sũpto initio a paradiso Paradisus est locus in orientis partibus constitu/

Fig. 5 The earliest printed map, published at Augsburg in 1472. Reproduced courtesy of The Newberry Library, Chicago.

the depths or on the heights. The center of the earth might be con-cretized as a hole if it arose from the depths; if from the heights, as a mountain, a tree, a pillar, or a temple. For the Jews, Jeru-salem and the Temple had become saturated with the symbols of a sacred center. According to Rabbi ben Gurion, the Rock of Jerusalem "was called the Foundation Stone of the Earth, which is to say the Earth's umbilicus, because it is from there that the entire earth unfurled."[12] Apocalyptic Judaism and the *Midrash* specify that Adam was made in Jerusalem and therefore at the Cen-ter of the World. The fountain of Jacob, according to one Jewish tradition, was a kind of cosmic pillar. On the day of the summer solstice the sun cast no shadow on the fountain, and for that rea-son it was called the "umbilicum terrae nostrae habitabilis."[13]

Just as they had absorbed and changed the classical carto-graphic tradition, Christians gradually created a new sacred topography for Jerusalem and Palestine. They did this first by discovering the exact location of caves associated with Christ's birth, passion, and ascension; second, by erecting basilicas over the newly defined Christian sites; and finally by encrusting these new shrines with layer upon layer of legitimizing ancient associations or legends. This process is particularly clear in the slow development of Mount Calvary as the literal and symbolic Center of the Earth for Christians.[14]

The emperor Constantine played a significant role in helping to create a Christian "Holy Land" carefully laid over the Jewish sacred center of Jerusalem and interacting with it in complex ways.[15] Book 3 of Eusebius's *Vita Constantini* describes the close collaboration between the emperor and Macarius, bishop of Jerusalem. Macarius eagerly searched Jerusalem to discover the precise loci of significant biblical events. According to tradition a temple of Venus had been erected by the emperor Hadrian over the exact location of the Holy Sepulchre. Constantine, "acting under the guidance of the divine spirit," called for the destruction of the temple. As soon as it, and the ground upon which it had stood, had been removed, the excavators discovered the Holy Sepulchre. Constantine called for the immediate construction of a splendid complex of shrines, called the Church of the Holy Sepulchre, to be erected over the sacred cave.[16] Eusebius tells us that at a later date St. Helena, Constantine's mother, went on a pilgrimage to Palestine, during which she dedicated other churches that had been erected over sacred caves identified with the birth and ascension of Christ.[17] By the early fourth century, then, Christians had churches that could not have been built elsewhere. They had to correspond to the topos of the gospel narratives or to the actual location of caves, mountains, or other natural phenomena. Their "locative specificity and thick associative content" guaranteed the sites' power and religious function.[18] Annual rituals in Jerusalem helped to forge strong bonds between sacred space and sacred time. Pilgrims commented on the appropriateness of the biblical passages that were part of the liturgical reading in situ.[19] Thus the liturgy tended to emphasize the symbolic importance of the exact place where an event had occurred.

Once Christians had the Church of the Holy Sepulchre as their pre-eminent sacred center, comparable to the Temple, the slow and deliberate encrustation of the sacred site with venerable relics, additional legends, and ancient symbolism began. In effect, the *sensus allegoricus* came to dominate the *sensus literalis*. Mount Calvary was located within the precincts of the Church of the Holy Sepulchre. In the course of the sixth century it acquired enormous prestige with the circulation of stories regarding the *inventio*, or discovery, of the True Cross. The Cross, or Cosmic Tree, is an archetypical symbol of the center. All sacred trees are thought of as situated in the Center of the World, with roots that reach down into Hell and branches that reach into Heaven.[20] From the sixth century onward numerous legends emerged that helped to strengthen Mount Calvary's symbolic significance. One legend that gained wide circulation by the sixth century linked the *inventio* of the True Cross on Mount Calvary with St. Helena's pilgrimage to Palestine in the early fourth century. In the course of her pilgrimage she reportedly found on Golgotha the three crosses, which the Jews had covered with earth.[21] In order to discover which was Jesus', Helena commanded that each cross be laid in turn on a dead man, and the one on whom Christ's cross was laid came to life again.[22] It is interesting that this legend, and many others that flourished in the sixth century, linked the *inventio* of a number of sacred places in Jerusalem with the fourth-century pilgrimage of St. Helena. The developing pilgrimage sites gained authenticity and prestige when their foundations were grafted onto older roots and consecrated by the association with a holy woman.[23]

There were two traditions concerning the literal place where the miracle of the discovery of the True Cross had occurred. A sixth-century Breviarius advertising the major attractions of the pilgrimage circuit in Palestine says, "there is an exedra at the place where the man was brought back to life and proved which was the cross of Christ."[24] The context of the account suggests that the exedra was located in the Church of the Holy Sepulchre near Mount Calvary. By the seventh century, however, the pilgrim Adoman states that a "very tall column" marked the spot where the miracle had taken place. According to Adoman the column was located in the middle of the city "to the north of the holy places, where it is seen by every passer-by."[25] The importance of this column is that it is a cosmic pillar, or obelisk, of the type that was widely known in the classical world.[26] The legend associated with the cosmic pillar parallels that of the fountain of Jacob. Again according to Adoman, "proof" that the pillar in Jerusalem marked the exact literal center of the earth was irrefutable and cosmic: "during the summer solstice at noon the light of the sun in mid heaven passes directly above this column, and shines down on all sides, which demonstrates that Jerusalem is placed at the center of the earth."[27] He enlarges,

> This [solar phenomenon] explains why the psalmist uses these words to sing his Prophecy of the holy places of the Passion and Resurrection which are in the Aelia, "Yet God, our King, of old worked salvation in the midst of the earth." This means "in Jerusalem", which is called the "Mediterranean", and "Navel of the Earth".[28]

The pillar, not Mount Calvary, says Adoman, marked the literal place where the Cross, symbol of both life and death, demonstrated its cosmic power.

The appropriation of numerous legends, iconography, and Old Testament symbolism formerly associated with the Temple helped to resolve the conflict between the competing traditions for the precise locus of the "Miracle of the True Cross." The miracle later became associated with Mount Calvary, the physical location of the most important rupture or opening in the cosmic levels. It was Christ's sacrifice on the Cross that had brought redemption to mankind and had broken the power of the grave. Mount Calvary and the very socket in the rock where the Cross had been inserted were located within the Church of Mount Calvary, which was itself located within the sacred precincts of the Church of the Holy Sepulchre. To emphasize the centrality and antiquity of the place of Christ's crucifixion, sacred events previously associated with the Temple were gradually transferred to the Mount.[29] It was Mount Calvary, not the Temple, that became the birthplace of Adam, the spot where Abraham was prepared to sacrifice Isaac, and the place where Melchizedech offered sacrifice.[30] Jesus' death was seen as the fulfillment of the messianic prophecy of suffering and an atonement for human sin. Mount Calvary's links to the Old Testament exhibit the continuity of the history of salvation and make Christ the high priest, whose sacrificial death represents the culmination of Old Testament sacrifices. New Testament references (1 Cor 15.20-23, Rom 5.12, 18) and later legends further developed the Adam-Christ typology, which rests upon the antithesis Fall-Death and Death-Resurrection.[31]

Iconography, ritual, and legend strengthened the allegorical significance of the Cross and Mount Calvary and helped to intensify the Adam-Christ link. On a sixth-century paten from Siberia the Cross stands on the mount of Paradise, from which four rivers flow. It rests on a starry disc symbolizing the cosmos[32] (fig. 6). The sun and moon, symbols of Christ's eternal mastery of the world, are engraved at the top, on either side of the cross; they underline the universal significance of the event at Golgotha and its timeless truth.

The veneration of the Cross became a significant pilgrimage ritual in the sixth century. The iconography on numerous lead ampullae, used as souvenirs, depicts pilgrims venerating the Cross[33] (fig. 7).

Fig. 6 Embossed silver paten, end of the sixth century. Berezov, Siberia. Leningrad, the Hermitage.

A number of early eastern legends centering on the connection between Adam and Jesus through the medium of the Cross found expression in Christian iconography and pilgrimage literature.[34] A particularly potent series of legends stressed the belief that Mount Calvary was the burial place of Adam. The exact place where the Cross had stood was thought to be the place where Adam had implored God to allow him to be buried. According to one version of this legend, "When the Messiah gained victory by the lance, blood and water flowed from his side, ran down into Adam's

Fig. 7 Lead relief, end of the sixth century. Palestine. Ampulla, 11 Monza, obverse. Photograph by Denise Fourmont. Taken from André Grabar, *Ampoules de Terre Sainte (Monza-Bobbio)* (Paris: Librairie C. Klincksieck, 1958), planche 18. © Editions Klincksieck. Reproduced by permission.

mouth and was his baptism and thus he was baptized."[35] The monk Epiphanius, writing in the eighth century, states, "In the middle of the Holy city is the holy tomb of the Lord, and near the tomb the place of the skull. There Christ was crucified. . . . And beneath the crucifixion there is a church, the tomb of Adam."[36] Figure 8, an illumination from the Khludov Psalter, depicts the skull of Adam in a little cave underneath the cross.[37] This topic, rendered in this way, becomes fairly standard crucifixion iconography after the sixth century.

Fig. 8 Manuscript illumination, second half of the ninth century. Constantinople. Khludov Psalter. Moscow (Historical Museum, Cod. gr. 129, fol. 45ᵛ). Copyright Photooptik, Paris.

DOROTHEA R. FRENCH

In summary, while the Cross and Mount Calvary acquired enormous symbolic importance between the fourth and tenth centuries, pilgrimage literature suggests that Mount Calvary itself was not yet perceived to be the literal center of the earth. Jerusalem certainly held that position in the *sensus allegoricus*, less definitely in the *sensus literalis*. Adoman's cosmic pillar suggests that the spot that marked the power of the Cross demonstrated the cosmic importance of Jerusalem and the Crucifixion. The development that played the largest role in the evolution of Jerusalem as the literal center of the earth, however, was the blossoming of the art of sacred cartography.

Christian map-makers began to alter the way in which individuals conceptualized the literal world. The eighth-century *mappa mundi* illustrating St. Beatus's *Commentary on the Apocalypse* marks an important transition in biblical cartography, since it combines the characteristics of the broad, schematic T-O maps with the practical, thematic maps of Late Antiquity (fig. 9). It identifies all of the Roman provinces and their capitals, and a number of important cities.[38] The cartographer's real interest in the literal world, however, was biblical—and he effectively appropriated all of the world into sacred space. He, and others who followed his paradigm, viewed sacred geography as the only kind that is effectively *real*, as opposed to profane geography. According to Mircea Eliade profane geography is "objective" and, as it were, abstract and non-essential, "the theoretical construction of a space and a world that we do not live in, and therefore do not *know*." Sacred cartography delineates the only *real space*, for it is concerned with the only indubitable reality—the sacred.[39]

The Beatus map-maker's primary concern was to represent the spread of Christianity throughout the known world as it was described in the Acts of the Apostles. At the top of the map, in the extreme east, is the Garden of Eden. Christians believed in the terrestrial paradise in both the *sensus literalis* and *sensus allegoricus*. The creation of mankind was an historical event, but because of the Fall mankind was prohibited from regaining entry into the Garden.

Fig. 9 Beatus of Liebana and Valcavado (ca. 730–98). World Map, compiled ca. 776; manuscript on vellum, ca. 1060 (Bibliothèque Nationale, Paris, Ms. lat. 8878, fols. 45ᵛ–46ʳ). Phot. Bibi. Nat. Paris. Reproduced by permission.

The cartographer therefore painted flames of fire surrounding the physical location of Eden. It is important to note that Jerusalem is not yet located in the exact center of the Beatus world map, although Palestine is dramatically oversized to stress its symbolic importance. Many features of the Beatus map would become conventional in the High Middle Ages when sacred geography completely displaced profane or classical cartography.

THE ELEVENTH THROUGH THE FOURTEENTH CENTURIES

The influence that religion exerted on medieval culture resulted in the loss of profane geography; this fact in turn had a dramatic impact on the way in which people viewed the literal world.

Since the only known maps were sacred maps, the *sensus allegoricus* dominated men's perception of the world. Abelard wrote, "The soul of the world is found at the middle of the world; consequently, Jerusalem from whence comes salvation, is found at the center of the world."[40] Medieval *mappae mundi* dealing with the *real* or sacred sphere place Jerusalem in the exact "literal" center of the world. This convention applied to both schematic T-O and thematic maps.

The Byzantine-Oxford T-O map is an excellent example of the schematic variety of map that placed Jerusalem at the center of the world (fig. 10). Brought back to England or Ireland in 1110 after the First Crusade successfully recovered Jerusalem and the Holy Land for Christendom, this T-O map departs in several significant respects from traditional T-O maps.[41] The copyist or a later hand has added Brittania, Hibernia, and the northern island of Thule in the margin, and recent political boundaries are indicated. For instance, the domain of Europe is extended across the Mediterranean to the southern and eastern coasts, where the crusaders had made inroads. The Holy Land dominates the center of the map, with Jerusalem replacing the bodies of water as the dividing line between Asia and Europe-Africa. The Cross, symbol of the salvation of mankind, is placed at the exact literal center of the world. Ludolph von Suchem, a fourteenth-century pilgrim, describes the world as it was familiar to Christians from such *mappae mundi*:

> The mediterranean Sea is that over which one sails to the Holy Land and is called the mediterranean Sea because it has to the East Asia whose frontier it forms, to the West and North Europe, and to the South Africa, which countries it separates by its arms.[42]

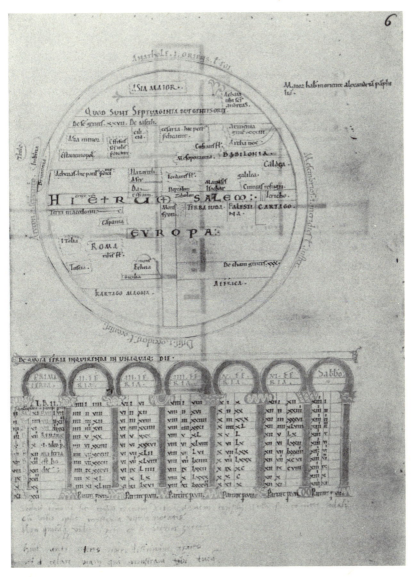

Fig. 10 The Byzantine-Oxford T-O map of the habitable world. Great Britain, 1110, from a Byzantine prototype; manuscript on vellum (The Library of St. John's College, Oxford, MS. 17, fol. 6^r). Reproduced by permission of The President and Fellows of St. John's College, Oxford.

Mappae mundi, art, and pilgrimage literature indicate that medieval people visualized centers within centers—that sacred space itself was centered. Thematic *mappae mundi* dramatically illustrate this concept. One excellent example is the way in which the imagery of the Ebstorf map highlights the cosmic importance of the crucifixion in the scheme of salvation of the world (fig. 11). Christ himself is integrated into the very structure of the world. His head emerges at the east, his wounded hands from the north and south, and his feet protrude from the edge of the world in the west. His body is comprised of the entire world. He also is shown rising from the tomb in a centrally-placed Jerusalem. The cartographer placed illustrations of both Old and New Testament stories, including Adam and Eve in the Garden, the Tower of Babel, and the story of Abraham, directly on the map.[43] At the same time, however, the map lists a large number of contemporary place-names, including monasteries and pilgrimage shrines.

Unlike the more schematic Byzantine-Oxford T-O map, the Ebstorf map was based upon Roman geography and was designed to be useful to travelers. The Ebstorf map and others of its kind (such as the Hereford and "Psalter" *mappae mundi*) also depict the integration of the literal and allegorical worlds.[44] The "real" world of sacred cartographers in Late Antiquity had become the literal world of Christian cartographers in the High Middle Ages. This world was infused with multiple levels of meanings that drew one into the center in ever-smaller concentric rings.

Another example of the medieval love of visualizing centers within centers is the appearance in the twelfth and thirteenth centuries of mazes or labyrinths within cathedrals. These labyrinths, similar to Oriental mandalas, are generally circular, have a cruciform axis, and are set in the nave pavement.[45] One of the functions of the mandala and the labyrinth, according to Eliade, is to help neophytes to concentrate, to find their own "center[s]."[46] By entering into the maze in Chartres, for example, Christians began the process of centering spiritually. Since the cathedral was seen as a microcosm of the world, believers who found themselves at the

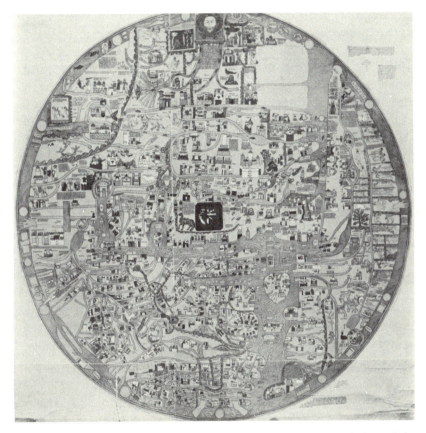

Fig. 11 The Ebstorf World Map, ca. 1235. Reprinted by permission of the publishers from *History of Cartography* by Leo Bagrow edited by R. A. Skelton, Cambridge, Mass.: Harvard University Press. Copyright © English edition 1964 by C. W. Watts & Co., Ltd, London.

center of the maze found themselves at the symbolic Center of the Earth and ultimately in union with Christ.[47]

Pilgrimage literature in the High Middle Ages reveals Jerusalem and Mount Calvary as dramatically affected by the desire to center sacred space. Pilgrims visited sacred places in the Holy Land before they reached Jerusalem, the goal of their pilgrimages. Within Jerusalem itself there were a number of shrines that were part of every pilgrim's itinerary. The premier pilgrimage goal in Jerusalem, however, was the Church of the Holy Sepulchre, which had been rebuilt in the first half of the twelfth century, and which enclosed the remains of several Byzantine shrines. Beneath the great dome of the church was the holy of holies, the Sepulchre. Every Christian sect (Greeks, Armenians, Jacobites, and Copts) tried to secure some space in its vicinity and a fixed time for divine service.[48] Close to the Holy Sepulchre and still under the dome was the Church of Calvary, which had two levels. Within the choir was Mount Calvary, "where the Lord was crucified ... and beneath it is Golgotha where the precious blood of our Savior fell on the head of Adam."[49] The levels of shrines in the Church of the Holy Sepulchre were like a three-dimensional labyrinth with ever-smaller concentric circles leading the devout down to the sacred center, or the navel of the earth.

The *omphalos* of the world, the precise literal center of the earth in the High Middle Ages, came to be associated with a dramatic crevice in the rock located deep within the Church of Calvary, itself located within the Church of the Holy Sepulchre in Jerusalem. This rupture was thought to have occurred after the crucifixion of Christ, and therefore it was intimately connected with the Cross.[50] Pilgrimage literature contains descriptions of the hole itself and the rituals associated with it. Burchard of Mount Sion says that the rent in the rock "is as large as my head and extends lengthways 18 feet."[51] Theoderich tells us that "into this hole pilgrims, out of the love and respect they have to him who was crucified, plunge their head[s] and face[s]."[52] John of Würzburg observes that the faithful cast offerings into the opening.[53] Devout pilgrims wanted to get as physically close as possible to the source of divine energy emanating from this opening in the cosmic zones and to leave some personal belonging behind in the center. Both Burchard of Mount Sion and Joannes Phocas describe the stains of blood on the rock. Burchard says that "even today the color of the blood of our Lord Jesus Christ may be seen in the rent of the rock."[54]

Once again legends developed, not only to lend authenticity and antiquity to the literal place but also to stress its allegorical meaning. A widely-circulated Syrian legend weaves together the earlier Adam-Christ theme with the new emphasis on the rupture in the earth. According to John of Würzburg,

> As our lord was dying on the cross . . . the veil of the temple was rent from the top to the bottom and the rock in which the cross was fixed was split through the midst, in the place where it was touched by his blood; through which rent the blood flowed to the lower parts wherein Adam is said to have been buried, and who was thus baptized in the blood of Christ. It is said to be in commemoration of this that a skull is always represented in paintings at the foot of the Cross.[55]

A mosaic from the second half of the eleventh century from Daphni illustrates the iconography described by John of Würzburg (fig. 12). It graphically depicts the baptism of Adam with the blood of Christ through the rent in the rock of Mount Calvary.[56] This iconography becomes conventional throughout the High Middle Ages and the Renaissance. It emphasizes both the *sensus literalis* and *sensus allegoricus* of Mount Calvary. The actual place where the earth had opened after Christ's crucifixion was also a symbolic *axis mundi*. Here God had opened the three cosmic zones. Through the First Man, Adam (buried in this precise place), sin and death had entered into the world. But with the death and resurrection of the Second Man, Christ (also in this very place), eternal life was offered to mankind.

To summarize, the sacred and the profane merged in the cartography of the High Middle Ages. The confluence of the *sensus literalis* and the *sensus allegoricus* had a major impact on the medieval imagination with regard to the perception of the world and of Mount Calvary. Both became highly concentrated, sharply focused sacred centers with multiple levels of meaning. The preoccupation of Christendom with the recovery of Jerusalem and the Holy Land no doubt reinforced the attitude that Jerusalem was the center of the world in this time period.[57]

Fig. 12 Mosaic, second half of the eleventh century. Daphni, Attica. Monastery church. Part of the cycle of the twelve feasts in the dome. Copyright Meletzis, Athens.

THE RENAISSANCE

Paradoxically, the interest in Jerusalem fostered by crusaders, pilgrims, and merchants resulted in ever more precise knowledge of the physical world.[58] The long experience of navigators in the Mediterranean resulted in the appearance of portolan charts, which accurately fixed knowledge of the slant of coastlines and maintained a fairly accurate scale. The combination of portolan charts and the travels of men such as Marco Polo and Friar Odoric helped cartographers in the fourteenth century to gain a much more accurate picture of the world than that presented by the schematic and biblically oriented T-O maps. The Holy Land began to assume its proper dimensions with respect to the rest of the world because of the growth of European geographical knowledge. Nevertheless, geography continued to be dominated by biblically-oriented cartographers until in the fifteenth century Ptolemy was rediscovered and his maps were published.[59]

The rediscovery of Ptolemy completely revolutionized cartography, because his outlook was classical and secular. His *Geographia* is a complete cartographer's handbook. It specifies the need for precise astronomical measurements and correct mathematical construction in preparing a scientific map. It describes a method of making a terrestrial globe and of projecting maps on a plane surface. Finally, in an extensive set of tables it gives the location, expressed in latitude and longitude, of over eight thousand places in the *oikumene*. The *Geographia* provided all the elements from which scientific maps could be, and were, constructed.[60] Unlike the T-O maps, Ptolemy's maps were all oriented to the north. His goal was to portray the physical world as clearly and accurately as possible. He was not concerned with abstract concepts of the *oikumene* or with mapping sacred space. On these maps Jerusalem was not the literal center of the physical world nor did it dominate the earth's surface (figs. 1, 2). Ptolemy's maps made it abundantly clear that the biblically-oriented sacred T-O maps of the High Middle Ages did not represent the literal world. His geography raises the question of what was *real*—the sacred or the profane.

The world map illustrated in Figure 1 comes from a manuscript of Ptolemy's maps compiled in 1474 by Donnus Nicholaus Germanus, a German Benedictine working in Florence. Nicholaus began printing his manuscript in 1477, and his ideas quickly reached a wider audience.[61] Felix Fabri, writing in 1484, was intimately familiar with the Renaissance copies of Ptolemy's *Atlas*. He specifically mentions Ptolemy's maps of Africa and Maps 6, 9, 10, 11, and 12 of Asia. The significance of the complete remapping of the physical world as it appeared on Ptolemy's maps had a tremendous impact upon Fabri. His discussion on the Center of the Earth must be examined against the revolutionary divorce in the Renaissance between sacred and secular geography.

The growing precision in the mapping of the actual world had a counterpart in the mapping of the sacred space within the Church of the Holy Sepulchre in the fifteenth century. Various sects competed fiercely with one another to establish control over meticulously defined space.[62] The basilica was so dense with holy places that Fabri sheepishly confesses a *faux pas* on his first pilgrimage to Jerusalem in 1482. He had entered the basilica and was standing gazing up at the vault when, much to his amazement, two women pilgrims fell down before his feet and lay weeping and sobbing and kissing the stone upon which he was standing. When he asked them why they were behaving in this manner, they pointed out to him that he stood on the very place where Joseph and Nicodemus had laid the body of Christ when he was taken down from the Cross, where they had anointed him and wrapped him in his shroud. Horrified, Fabri fell down upon the earth and fervently prayed that God would forgive his irreverent footsteps.[63] With so many venerable places crammed into the Church of the Holy Sepulchre, first-time pilgrims often rushed helter-skelter from one shrine to the next. Fabri urges the thoughtful pilgrim to progress methodically from shrine to shrine, and to complete the proper rituals at each stop.

The second most important site within the basilica after the Sepulchre was, according to Fabri, the Church of Mount Calvary. Within the chapel pilgrims found the actual socket hole of the Cross. They placed their faces, eyes, and mouths over the socket hole and put their arms and hands into it.[64] Fabri does not question the authenticity of this site. He accepts the socket hole in the *sensus literalis*. At the same time, however, venerable Old and New Testament associations tended to stress the *sensus allegoricus* of the place. According to Fabri, "Here Cain killed his brother Abel; here Adam died, and his skull was found in this place; in this place Abraham was blessed by Melchizedech, to it Isaac was brought to be sacrificed, the brazen serpent was set up; and here God was slain by man."[65] On the left side of the socket there was a great rent in the rock that "is believed to have been made after Christ's death."[66] Once again pilgrims kissed the place and put as much of their bodies as they could into the chasm. Fabri appears to be a little uncertain about the authenticity of this rupture in the ground but he does not dispute it. Underneath the chapel of Mount Calvary there was another chapel, said to be the place where Christ was nailed to the Cross.

The Chapel of the Place of the Nailing of the Cross exemplifies the tendency to refine the sacred geography within the Church of the Holy Sepulchre. Fabri explains,

> For if the rock were there as it is at this day, Christ could not
> have been nailed to the cross upon it, but at its foot, and this
> must needs have been the place of the nailing of the cross.[67]

There was no scriptural "or certain proof" that the chapel marked the literal place of the event, "except that the shape of the ground seems to prove it."[68] Against the rock of Calvary "on the right hand side" Fabri saw the rent in the rock, which "reaches from the top of it quite down to the earth." Legends and the authority of Ambrose, Athanasius, Chrysostom, and Jerome authenticated this spot also as the burial place of Adam. The chapel belonged to the

Nubian Christians, who based their claim to this plot of ground on a legend according to which one of the Three Magi was a Nubian king who had been entertained near Mount Calvary.[69] A possible conflict over the exact location of the skull of Adam and the rupture in the earth had been resolved by the two-tiered chapels on Mount Calvary, each controlled by competing sects. In the High Middle Ages it was this locality that had marked the center of the earth in the *sensus literalis*.

By the fifteenth century the eastern Christians had successfully appropriated that nomenclature for a spot they controlled within the church of Golgotha, "which is the choir" of the whole Church of the Holy Sepulchre. In the middle of the choir there was a round stone with a hole in the middle "into which a man could put his . . . clenched fist."[70] According to a legend promulgated here, before his Passion the Lord Jesus had stood in this place with his disciples and pointed to this spot with his finger, saying, "Lo, here is the middle of the world."[71] Fabri refers to this locus as the place where the central point of the whole world "is said to be."[72] There appeared to be physical, cosmic "proof" that the hole in the church of Golgotha was indeed the center of the world in the *sensus literalis*.

Fabri describes a great round opening in the lofty vaulted dome in the Church of the Holy Sepulchre directly over the hole in the church of Golgotha. Light streamed down through the hole and lit the interior of the church.[73] There was a way to the top of this dome from the outside of the church. At the top of the vault there was a platform built out over the hole, where adventurous pilgrims could stand to verify the claim that their bodies would cast no shadow when the sun shone directly overhead. A member of Fabri's party eagerly conducted the experiment and solemnly declared that when he had stood in the exact center of the platform he had not cast a shadow.[74]

Such "proof" might suffice for less sophisticated pilgrims than Felix Fabri. He wrote,

> But I do not see that the fact that the sun shines at mid-day so
> directly above men's heads that their bodies cast no shadow is
> any true and certain proof that the spot where it does so is the
> middle of the earth, for I have read in several books about
> many places where at certain times men's bodies cast no
> shadow.[75]

He cites a number of both classical and Christian authorities to substantiate his claim. Foremost among his examples is the third book of Dionysius's *Antiquities*, where a similar phenomenon is said to occur on a "certain island which lies in the ocean towards the southward . . . and yet this island is a very long way from Jerusalem."[76] Peter de Abano, a well-known philosopher and physician of Padua in the Middle Ages, says the same phenomenon took place in the city of Athens where he himself had proved it by experiment. "At the city of Syene, too, upon the Nile, the same thing is said to happen when the sun is in the summer tropic."[77] The ultimate proof that neither Jerusalem nor the hole in the church of Golgotha was at the center of the earth in the *sensus literalis* was Ptolemy's *Atlas*. Fabri says that in Maps 3 and 4 of Africa Ptolemy "brings in many regions where the noonday sun stands directly overhead: and what is more than this, in the same map many places are noted where twice in the year the sun stands overhead without casting any shadow."[78] Fabri says there are many such places also in Asia, "as may be seen in the sixth map, in the ninth, tenth, eleventh, and twelfth: and it is well known that these places are not in the middle of the world."[79]

Fabri was wrestling not only with the new discoveries in cartography and science but also with the pre-Christian idea of sacred centers. He was confronting a problem that other thinkers would also have to resolve: the discrepancies between secular science and sacred geography. All of the Oriental civilizations recognized an unlimited number of "centers," each of which was called the "Center of the World." Within a single inhabited region the plurality of Centers of the Earth presented no problem.[80] Each one was a place where the divine had been manifested and might be marked by such natural phenomena as trees, mountains, caves, rivers, or solar activity, for instance, the absence of a shadow when the sun stood directly overhead. In the classical and pre-Christian cultures these centers represent the only essentially *real space*, for in the archaic world the myth alone is real.[81]

The existence of multiple "Centers of the Earth," as evidenced by solar activity, did pose a problem for Felix Fabri. He had inherited a tradition in which the physical world, as portrayed in the *mappae mundi*, was completely integrated into the spiritual world. For him there could be only one Center of the Earth—Jerusalem. The new geography, however, had completely transformed and rotated his physical world. His reasoned and scientific approach to solar activity demonstrates that he could not accept the idea that there was one literal center of the physical world. He not only had to face the question of what was real, the profane or the sacred, but also what "proof" was valid.[82] His discussions about whether or not solar activity marked Jerusalem as the center of the physical world, the authenticity of the sepulchre, and what constituted the precise location of Mount Calvary all illustrate that Fabri was aware of a rising skeptical "scientific" attitude not only toward the world but also to the long-venerated but perhaps inaccurately-located places associated with the Old and New Testaments. Were the shrines visited by pilgrims located in the precise, actual places where the events they commemorated occurred? Was there any historical truth to the legends associated with various places of worship in Jerusalem?

It is perhaps not surprising to learn that when Fabri had compiled all of the conflicting evidence relating to each of these questions from various sources he concluded that the sacred alone is real. He does not reject the "new" geography or the scientific approach, but he recognizes that the *sensus allegoricus* is ultimately more important than the *sensus literalis*. While the actual physical locus of a significant event may not be identified, the spiritual or allegorical meaning associated with it transcends time and space. It is therefore the only reality. For example, Fabri goes into an elaborate review of all the conflicting descriptions of the Sepulchre in pilgrimage guides from the seventh through the fifteenth centuries.[83] He concludes that whether or not the present sepulchre was to any degree identified with the real Sepulchre "matters very little either one way or the other, because the main fact connected with the place abides there and cannot by any means be carried away or demolished."[84]

For Fabri proof for the sacred meaning of place is not physical phenomena but Scripture and the authority of Christian writers. For that reason he can still state that Jerusalem was in the middle of the world, since "the infallible truth of Holy Scripture proves by its testimonies that Jerusalem is in the middle of the world . . . and tells us that our saviour worked out our salvation in the midst of the earth."[85] It was the Center of the Earth because of the activity of the Cross. Fabri quotes Hilarius as an authority to explain the allegorical significance of Jerusalem: "The place where the cross stood is, as it were, a point in the center of the earth, in order that all men might have equal opportunities of obtaining knowledge of God."[86] Fabri concludes,

> As then Christ is the central person in the Trinity, and the mediator between God and man, as he holds the middle position in the scheme of the Redemption of the world, even so He chose the middle point of the world and set up His cross in the same.[87]

Jerusalem and Mount Calvary would remain the Center of the Earth for Christian pilgrims in the *sensus allegoricus*. It is the archetypical *axis mundi*, the place where God worked out the redemption of mankind. Its meaning for the world transcended secular time and space. Modern cartography and science could never disprove the enduring truths of sacred authority. The only reality for Fabri was the sacred.

NOTES

[1]Felix Fabri, *The Book of the Wanderings of Brother Felix Fabri*, trans. Aubrey Stewart, Palestine Pilgrims' Text Society (hereafter PPTS), 13 vols. (London, 1887-97; rept. New York, 1971), 7:364-69, 376-77; 8:416-18.

[2]See the pilgrimages of Paula, the Piacenza Pilgrim, and Adoman in John Wilkinson, *Jerusalem Pilgrims before the Crusades* (Warminster, 1977), pp. 47-52, 70-89, 93-111; The Bordeaux Pilgrim, *Itinerary from Bordeaux to Jerusalem*, trans. Aubrey Stewart, PPTS, 1:1-35; St. Silvia of Aquitania, *Pilgrimage to the Holy Places*, trans. John H. Bernard, PPTS, 1:1-77; Fetellus, *Description of Jerusalem and the Holy Land*, trans. James Rose MacPherson, PPTS, 5:1-58; John of Würzburg, *Description of the Holy Land*, trans. Aubrey Stewart, PPTS, 5:1-72; *The Pilgrimage of Joannes Phocas in the Holy Land*, trans. Aubrey Stewart, PPTS, 5:1-36; *Anonymous Pilgrims I.-VIII.*, trans. Aubrey Stewart, PPTS, 6:1-77; *The City of Jerusalem and Ernoul's Account of Palestine*, trans. C. R. Conder, PPTS, 6:1-69; anon., *Guide-Book to Palestine*, trans. J. H. Bernard, PPTS, 6:1-40; Burchard of Mount Sion, *A Description of the Holy Land*, trans. Aubrey Stewart, PPTS, 12:1-136; Marino Sanuto, *Secrets for True Crusaders to Help Them to Recover the Holy Land*, pt. 14 of Bk. 3, trans. Aubrey Stewart, PPTS, 12:1-63; Ludolph von Suchem, *Description of the Holy Land, and of the Way Thither*, trans. Aubrey Stewart, PPTS, 12:1-136; Theoderich, *Guide to the Holy Land*, trans. Aubrey Stewart, 2nd ed. (New York, 1986). Please note: pagination within PPTS volumes is not consecutive.

[3]Edward Kennard Rand, *Founders of the Middle Ages* (New York, 1957), pp. 85-87.

[4]Mircea Eliade, *The Sacred and the Profane: The Nature of Religion*, trans. Willard R. Trask (New York, 1961), pp. 42-47.

[5]E. D. Hunt, *Holy Land Pilgrimage in the Later Roman Empire A.D. 312-460* (Oxford, 1982), pp. 86-89.

[6]Jonathan Z. Smith, *To Take Place: Toward Theory in Ritual* (Chicago, 1987). Smith's thesis is that ritual activity transforms space into place. See esp. ch. 5, "To Take Place."

[7]Kenneth Nebenzahl, *Maps of the Holy Land: Images of "Terra Sancta" Through Two Millennia* (New York, 1986), pp. 16-17.

[8]George H. T. Kimble, *Geography in the Middle Ages* (London, 1938), p. 16. Peter Brown, *The World of Late Antiquity AD 150-750* (London, 1971; rept. 1978), ch. 7, "The Conversion of Christianity, 300-363," also deals with this theme.

[9]Hunt, *Holy Land Pilgrimage*, pp. 88-93.

[10]Nebenzahl, *Maps*, p. 40.

[11]Nebenzahl, *Maps*, p. 10. John Kirtland Wright, *The Geographical Lore of the Time of the Crusades* (New York, 1965), pp. 45-52.

[12]As cited in Eliade, *Sacred and Profane*, p. 44.

[13]As cited in M. Eliade, *The Myth of the Eternal Return*, trans. Willard R. Trask (Princeton, 1971), p. 13.

[14]Victor and Edith Turner, *Image and Pilgrimage in Christian Culture* (New York, 1978), pp. 25-29, discuss the theory of the phases of development of pilgrimage sites. See a discussion of this in my forthcoming article "Mapping Sacred Centers: Pilgrimage and the Creation of Christian Topographies in Jerusalem and Roman Palestine" in the proceedings of the 12. Internationaler Kongress für Christliche Archäeologie, Bonn, September 1991, to be published as supplements to *Jahrbuch für Antike und Christentum* published by Aschendorffsche Verlagsbuchhandlung Münster.

[15]Smith, *To Take Place*, p. 78; Hunt, *Holy Land Pilgrimage*, chs. 1, 2, for the development of the Holy Land under Constantine.

[16]Eusebius, *The Life of Constantine*, ed. Philip Schaff and Henry Wace, in *Nicene and Post-Nicene Fathers*, vol. 1 (New York, 1890), pp. 526-29.

[17]Eusebius, *Life of Constantine*, pp. 530-31.

[18]Smith, *To Take Place*, p. 86.

[19]Smith, *To Take Place*, pp. 89-95; Hunt, *Holy Land Pilgrimage*, ch. 5, passim.

[20]Mircea Eliade, *Images and Symbols: Studies in Religious Symbolism*, trans. Philip Mairet (New York, 1969), pp. 44-47.

[21]Smith, *To Take Place*, p. 82; Hunt, *Holy Land Pilgrimage*, pp. 28-35; Gertrud Schiller, *Iconography of Christian Art*, trans. Janet Seligman, vol. 2 (Greenwich, Conn., 1971), pp. 12-14.

[22]Schiller, *Iconography*, p. 13.

[23]Smith, *To Take Place*, pp. 84-85; Eliade, *Images and Symbols*, pp. 41-46; Hunt, *Holy Land Pilgrimage*, ch. 2, passim.

[24]Anon., *Breviarius*, trans. John Wilkinson, 2 in idem, *Jerusalem Pilgrims before the Crusades*, p. 59.

[25]Adoman, *the [sic] Holy Places*, trans. Wilkinson, 11.1 in idem, *Jerusalem Pilgrims before the Crusades*, p. 99.

[26]Mircea Eliade, *Symbolism, the Sacred and the Arts*, trans. Diane Apostolos-Cappadona (New York, 1985), pp. 99-100, 137-38.

[27]Adoman, *Holy Places*, trans. Wilkinson, 11.2 in idem, *Jerusalem Pilgrims before the Crusades*, p. 99.

[28]Adoman, *Holy Places*, trans. Wilkinson, 11.4 in idem, *Jerusalem Pilgrims before the Crusades*, p. 99.

[29]Smith, *To Take Place*, pp. 84-85.

[30]Smith, *To Take Place*, pp. 84-85.

[31]Schiller, *Iconography*, p. 93.

[32]Schiller, *Iconography*, p. 8.

[33]Schiller, *Iconography*, p. 8; André Grabar, *Ampoules de Terre Sainte (Monza-Bobbio)* (Paris, 1958), plate 8; Gary Vikan, *Byzantine Pilgrimage Art* (Washington, D.C., 1982), pp. 22-26.

[34]Schiller, *Iconography*, p. 93.

[35]Schiller, *Iconography*, p. 12-13.

[36]Epiphanius the Monk, *The Holy City and the Holy Places*, trans. Wilkinson, I.10-12 in idem, *Jerusalem Pilgrims before the Crusades*, p. 117.

[37]Schiller, *Iconography*, p. 97.

[38]Nebenzahl, *Maps*, pp. 26-27.

[39]Eliade, *Images and Symbols*, pp. 39-40.

[40]As cited in Eliade, *Symbolism*, p. 109.

[41]Nebenzahl, *Maps*, p. 33.

[42]Ludolph von Suchem, *Description*, PPTS, 12:11.

[43]Leo Bagrow, *History of Cartography* (Cambridge, Mass., 1966), pp. 49-50, 72.

[44]G. R. Crone, "New Light on the Hereford Map," *The Geographical Journal* 131 (1965): 447-62.

[45]Eliade, *Images and Symbols*, p. 52; Jocelyn and Ed Badovinac, "The Chartres Labyrinth," *Medieval Studies* 3/1 (January 1988); Penelope Reed Doob, *The Idea of the Labyrinth* (Ithaca, 1990), p. 118.

[46]Eliade, *Images and Symbols*, p. 53.

[47]Georges Duby, *The Age of the Cathedrals: Art and Society 980-1420*, trans. Eleanor Levieux and Barbara Thompson (Chicago, 1981), p. 123; Doob, *Labyrinth*, pp. 128-33.

[48]Joshua Prawer, *The Crusaders' Kingdom: European Colonialism in the Middle Ages* (New York, 1972), p. 209.

[49]Theoderich, *Guide*, p. 20.

[50]Ludolph von Suchem, *Description*, PPTS, 12:103; *Pilgrimage of Joannes Phocas*, PPTS, 5:19; John of Würzburg, *Description*, PPTS, 5:32.

[51]Burchard of Mount Sion, *Description*, PPTS, 12:76.

[52]Theoderich, *Guide*, p. 20.

[53]John of Würzburg, *Description*, PPTS, 5:32.

[54]John of Würzburg, *Description*, PPTS, 5:32; *Pilgrimage of Joannes Phocas*, PPTS, 5:19.

[55]John of Würzburg, *Description*, PPTS, 5:32.

[56]Schiller, *Iconography*, pp. 10-14, 97.

[57]John B. Friedman, *The Monstrous Races in Medieval Art and Thought* (Cambridge, Mass., 1981), pp. 219-20, n. 23.

[58]Nebenzahl, *Maps,* pp. 42-43; see the maps of Marino Sanuto and Petrus Vesconte.

[59]Boies Penrose, *Travel and Discovery in the Renaissance 1420-1620* (Cambridge, Mass., 1952), p. 255.

[60]Dana Bennett Durand, *The Vienna-Klosterneuburg Map Corpus of the Fifteenth Century* (Leiden, 1952), p. 13.

[61]Nebenzahl, *Maps*, pp. 14-15.

[62]Fabri, *Wanderings*, PPTS, 8:413, explains that when the Latins lost control of Jerusalem the eastern Christians entered into negotiations with Saladin and secured the right to control access to the Holy Sepulchre. Other Christian sects apparently followed the same method of purchasing rights to specific areas within the basilica. Fabri, ibid., pp. 350-51, tells us that the chapel commemorating the place where the miracle of the True Cross occurred was controlled by the Latins and "no nation has any right therein save only the Latins, and the guardians of the holy sepulchre, who represent the Latins, perform service therein."

[63]Fabri, *Wanderings*, PPTS, 8:343-44.

[64]Fabri, *Wanderings*, PPTS, 8:365.

[65]Fabri, *Wanderings*, PPTS, 8:365.

[66]Fabri, *Wanderings*, PPTS, 8:365.

[67]Fabri, *Wanderings*, PPTS, 8:369.

[68]Fabri, *Wanderings*, PPTS, 8:369.

[69]Fabri, *Wanderings*, PPTS, 8:373.

[70]Fabri, *Wanderings*, PPTS, 8:374.

[71]Fabri, *Wanderings*, PPTS, 8:374.

[72]Fabri, *Wanderings*, PPTS, 8:374.

[73]Fabri, *Wanderings*, PPTS, 8:424.

[74]Fabri, *Wanderings*, PPTS, 8:375.

[75]Fabri, *Wanderings*, PPTS, 8:375.

[76]Fabri, *Wanderings*, PPTS, 8:375.

[77]Fabri, *Wanderings*, PPTS, 8:375-76.

[78]Fabri, *Wanderings*, PPTS, 8:376.

[79]Fabri, *Wanderings*, PPTS, 8:376.

[80]Eliade, *Images and Symbols*, pp. 39-40.

[81]Eliade, *Images and Symbols*, pp. 39-40.

[82]Conal Condren, "Authority, Emblems, and Sources: Reflections on the Role of a Rhetorical Strategy in the History of History," *Philosophy and Rhetoric* 15 (1982): 170-86. Condren addresses the problem of the attitude of writers in the late-medieval and early-modern periods toward what he calls "authority clusters." Fabri's use of authorities in many ways parallels the rhetorical devices Condren identifies.

[83]Fabri, *Wanderings*, PPTS, 8:408-15. He elaborately reviews all of the conflicting descriptions of the Sepulchre in pilgrimage guides from the seventh through the fifteenth centuries.

[84]Fabri, *Wanderings*, PPTS, 8:415.

[85]Fabri, *Wanderings*, PPTS, 8:376-77.

[86]Fabri, *Wanderings*, PPTS, 8:376-77.

[87]Fabri, *Wanderings*, PPTS, 8:376-77.

STEPHEN OF CLOYES, PHILIP AUGUSTUS,

AND THE CHILDREN'S CRUSADE OF 1212

Gary Dickson

Of the names or phrases used by the thirteenth-century chroni-clers to describe the popular enthusiasm of 1212, *peregrinatio puerorum*, the pilgrimage or crusade of the *pueri*, is probably the least contentious.[1] Now universally known as the Children's Cru-sade, it was the most important peasant revival between the cru-sade of Peter the Hermit's *pauperes* of 1095-96 and the crusade of the *pastores* of 1251, although, quite unlike either of these popular crusades, it appears to have massacred no Jews.[2] Stephen of Cloyes's movement, the first in the medieval West to arouse the shepherds, was wholly confined to the Ile-de-France, and it constituted a more or less self-contained episode within the broader enthusiasm of 1212. As such it can be examined from its inception to its dispersion.

Taken in its several phases, the *peregrinatio puerorum*, as a peasant-led, unoffical crusading enthusiasm, was (strictly speak-ing) unprecedented. Jonathan Riley-Smith has argued convincingly that the so-called peasants' crusade of Peter the Hermit actually had significant contingents of knights and feudal captains in its ranks.[3] Moreover, Peter himself, whatever his personal charisma and popular appeal, owed much of his success to his recognized eremitical status.[4] All of these elements were entirely lacking in 1212. Besides, Peter the Hermit's crusade had occurred more than a century earlier: none of the chroniclers of 1212 so much as allude to it. In fact, one reason why the chroniclers of the time found themselves bewildered by the crusade of the *pueri* was that they were unable to cite any past collective behavior comparable to it; and to a certain extent this helps us to understand why some of them should have regarded it as astonishing, and even miraculous, and why others should have discovered strange parallels to it in nature or folklore.[5] Modern historians, believing they can do better, have listed their own precursors of 1212; but these supposed prefigurations depend upon superficial resemblances commonly encountered in movements of religious enthusiasm.[6]

Nearly all we know about Stephen of Cloyes's pilgrimage to Saint-Denis during June of 1212 comes from one source, the anonymous chronicle of Laon.[7] We know from the incidents he reports that the Laon Anonymous had a considerable interest in the popular religious events of his day. Wonders and the workings of providence fascinated him. Provided that we keep his perspective in mind, his information is of real value. He mentions, for example, the death of that miraculous non-eater, a true medieval hunger-artist, Alpais of Cudot (d. 1211).[8] He also reports the death of "that lover of voluntary poverty," the holy woman Matilda, as occurring in the same month as what he calls the "puerilis illa devocio" of Stephen. By so characterizing Stephen of Cloyes's movement the Laon chronicler applies to it the crusading and Bernardine concept of *devotio*, which already before the second half of the thirteenth century was coming to denote collective enthusiasm or "revival."[9] Then, too, our chronicler is well informed about the heretical Amalricians, burnt at Paris in 1210, and particularly about one of that sect's most prominent leaders, Master Godin, who was incinerated at Amiens probably not more than two years afterwards. We perhaps should recall that the eponymous founder of this Paris-based group of dissident clerical intellectuals, whose heresy was a potent mixture of pantheism, antinomianism, and Joachite prophecy, was Amalric of Bène (d. ca. 1206). Amalric, like Stephen of Cloyes, was a native of the diocese of Chartres.[10]

The chronicle of the Laon Anonymous terminates in 1219. Such a proximate date strengthens Peter Raedts's verdict that as a source for the unauthorized crusade of the *pueri* the chronicle is "extremely accurate and important."[11] Indeed, two entries, one for Stephen and one for the holy woman Matilda, each separately dated as occurring in the same month, June 1212, give us good reason to believe that the anonymous chronicler was jotting down his notes or making his entries that very month. Finally, it has to be said that one scholar's suspicions that the Laon chronicler's account of Stephen was contaminated by hagiographic motifs previously related in his description of the career of the youthful bridge-builder St. Bénézet are entirely misconceived, and utterly without foundation.[12]

The fact that Laon is much nearer to where Stephen's enthusiasm effectively came to an end, in the town or territory of the French royal abbey of Saint-Denis outside Paris, than it is to the village of Cloyes, not far from Châteaudun, from where Stephen himself was said to hail, is mirrored in the anonymous chronicler's account of the movement.[13] Whoever the informant of the Laon chronicler was—another Premonstratensian, perhaps, or even another Englishman—there can be little doubt that the information that the Anonymous received, came to him if not from Saint-Denis, then from Paris. For it is noteworthy that the Laon Anonymous does not tell us explicitly *where* Stephen had his vision of Christ, though it may well have been near Cloyes. Nor does he mention the place from which his pilgrimage actually began. Hence the chronicler's narrative emphasizes the period *after* the arrival of Stephen's peasant multitude at Saint-Denis, rather than their departure *for* Saint-Denis. Moreover, the key line in the opening section of the Anonymous's brief report, which tells of the apparition of Christ to Stephen and the handing-over of the celestial letters, is attributed to the protagonist himself: it states what he (is alleged to have) said. The line of text reads as if it could have derived from an oral source, as if it summarized a story that Stephen himself oftentimes told.[14] And this is plausible because the story both established and legitimized his mission. Taken together, his story, his letters from Christ, and his miracle-working abilities constituted his charismatic credentials.[15]

Closely paraphrased, the incident related by the Laon chronicler is this: A certain *puer* named Stephen, a shepherd of Cloyes, near Vendôme, gave bread to and received letters from a poor pilgrim who was actually the Lord appearing to him in this guise. The letters were intended for the king of the French. When Stephen came to an unspecified locality, nearly thirty thousand[16] of his fellow shepherds, his contemporaries, coming from diverse parts of Gaul, rallied round him. Then, while he waited at Saint-Denis, the Lord caused many miracles to happen through him, in the presence of many witnesses. Elsewhere, in other localities, other *pueri* too were being held in great veneration as miracle-workers by crowds of common people. These attracted additional multitudes of *pueri*, who seemingly wished to journey under their authority to the holy *puer* Stephen. All recognized Stephen as their master and prince. Finally, the king consulted the Paris masters about this multitudinous congregation of *pueri*. Thereafter, on his instructions ("ex eius precepto") the *pueri* returned to their homes.[17]

From this account, despite much that is obscure, several things are clear. Like the later shepherds' crusade of 1251, which, proposing to come to the aid of Louis IX, arrived in Paris and was initially well-received by Queen Blanche,[18] Stephen's movement was also captivated by the mystique of the Capetian monarchy.[19] Furthermore, Stephen of Cloyes's unique charismatic authority over his fellow *pueri*, well-publicized by his wonder-working powers, was allegedly sealed by the possession of celestial letters addressed to Philip Augustus. Just as Stephen's story was presumably known to all his followers, so too, presumably, was the fact that he claimed to possess such letters. These heaven-sent epistles were entrusted to him by a poor pilgrim, revealed as Christ. (At that time, of course, *peregrinus* might just as properly have designated a crusader.)[20] George Z. Gray once speculated that in reality the "pilgrim" was "undoubtedly a disguised priest" intent upon manipulating Stephen![21] Yet, whoever he was, if he existed at all, it was this pilgrim (or crusader) Christ who, as Stephen himself apparently claimed, instigated the mass pilgrimage of the shepherds to the king at Saint-Denis.

Such letters from Heaven[22] figured in medieval sabbath-observance campaigns, for instance, Eustace de Flay's of 1200-01,[23] as well as in the Crusades. One was even popularly associated with Peter the Hermit.[24] At the time of the Second Crusade a prophetic letter was directed to Louis VII that, as cited by Otto of Freising, begins: "I say to you L[ouis], *shepherd* of bodies, whom the spirit of the time of *the pilgrim God* has inspired . . ." (italics mine).[25] In this Sibylline prophecy, addressed over sixty years earlier to the father of Philip Augustus, tantalizingly similar motifs can be discerned. Celestial letters renewed the providential contact between God and man, the precondition for all prophecy and the miraculous. Like the tau cross carried by the leader of the Rhenish *pueri*, Nicholas of Cologne, Stephen's letters functioned as the attribute of a distinctive behavioral iconography,[26] in addition to serving as the emblem of collective charismatic fascination.

Now, if Stephen was eventually forced to surrender his Christ-given letters to one of Philip Augustus's royal officials or, in any case, suffer the loss of his claim to possession of them, did the act of handing them over (or the loss of his claim—both amount to the same thing) thereby break the necessarily precarious hold of his power over his fellows and—his charisma now at the mercy of the king, and hence of the king's decree—simultaneously terminate his mission and assure the collapse of his movement? The extremely limited scope of Stephen's providential mission, at least as it was publicly articulated, allowed him to fulfill it success-fully, but at the cost of bringing to a speedy dead-end whatever his wider prophetic ambitions may have been. One must imagine that the divine letters (or his exclusive claim to possess them) in-corporated some broader prophetic commission, or animating spir-itual concern, which the king's judgment, given in some form, ef-fectively nullified.

Apart from the Laon Anonymous, four other French chron-iclers, three of them in virtually identical words, speak of a move-ment of *pueri* also beginning near Vendôme that same year, al-though none of them refers to a leader, much less names him.[27] In addition, the English "Barnwell" chronicle, which terminates in 1225, gives Paris as the point of arrival for a single stream of *pueri* then flowing through France.[28] But from that distance Paris might have been substituted for Saint-Denis, or indeed have been cor-rectly picked out as the metropolis where some of the *pueri* did eventually choose to settle. These chroniclers, while not corrob-orating the report of the Laon Anonymous, nevertheless lend sup-port to his testimony.

Still another chronicler may have a further clue to offer us, even though Peter Raedts rejects him out of hand.[29] At first glance, dismissing him without comment seems perfectly sensible. Jean le Long or Jean d'Ypres, author of the *Chronica monasterii sancti Bertini*, died in 1383. Not a contemporary, he was perforce a re-tailer of stolen goods. His editor has helpfully labelled the source of each of his plagiarized paragraphs. That the following para-graph has not been so identified could mean that its source has not been traced or, worse, that its author stands guilty of manu-facturing the past:

> When at that time processions were being made throughout France to plead for God's grace against the infidels [the chronicler is here referring to the Iberian crisis of 1212, pro-voked by the invading Muslim Almohads from Berber North Africa, a crisis resolved by the Christian victory at Las

> Navas da Tolosa, on 16 July], it came into the mind of a shep-
> herd of the diocese of Chartres, that he would go to the pro-
> cession, and he went. Returning, he found his sheep almost
> consuming the grain, and when he wanted to drive them
> away, they kneeled to him, as if begging pardon. When news
> of this reached the common people, he was honoured exces-
> sively. In a short space of time, from every part of the king-
> dom, there came to him . . . (etc.) [the rest of this is taken
> from William of Andres; it is at this juncture that the shep-
> herd acquires his following, his flock].[30] (brackets mine)

Léon van der Essen has confirmed that, in order to compose
his chronicle of Saint-Bertin, Jean le Long carried out genuine research into the history of the monastery of which he was then abbot. Jean consulted "antiquities," older chronicles, and even archives and official documents. Moreover, his *Vita Erkembodonis*,
which concerns a saint who died in the eighth century, provides
more reliable historical information that do the bulk of the saint's
contemporary hagiographers.[31] So is it valid to ask: Could this
late-fourteenth-century chronicler have had sources at his finger-
tips that have not come down to us? That his account is necessarily derivative might go without saying—but from whom did he
borrow?

As for the seemingly bizarre incident of the kneeling and
repentant sheep, should this alert us to a purely hagiographic
motif (Alphandéry thought so),[32] and convince us that the chronicler was far too credulous to be credible? Not at all. There is a
well-attested and well-known physical circumstance in which
sheep do in fact appear to "kneel" as they graze. This occurs
when they suffer from foot-rot, a relatively common disease af-
flicting sheep that was widespread in the past.[33] Furthermore,
what appears to be ripening grain in the fields nearby would be
seasonally appropriate. What this chronicler has done is supplied
us with a spiritual gloss on a natural phenomenon and so transformed it into the first sign of a leader's charismatic recognition.
The story also signals a prophetic calling, although its nature is
left completely obscure. Indeed, Jean le Long neither names

Stephen nor knows anything about any putative visitation by, or vision of, the pilgrim-crusader Christ. Jean le Long, therefore, supplements the Laon Anonymous without contradicting him. Nor does he evidence the slightest indebtedness to him. This adds further weight to the basic reliability of our main sources. Their mutual independence does not subvert their compatibility.

Jean le Long's chief contribution to our understanding of the enthusiasm is the connection of a leader of the subsequent *peregrinatio* to the processions ordered by Innocent III on behalf of the endangered Spanish church, processions that were held in Rome on 16 May 1212, and that (we have every reason to suppose) were held elsewhere as well. Most authorities now accept that the origins of the Children's Crusade must be sought in two areas: the crisis of the Spanish church, and continuing recruitment to the crusade against the Cathars.[34] What Jean le Long enables us to do is link the earliest "unled" processions associated with the very beginnings of the movement to the later pilgrimage to Saint-Denis led by Stephen of Cloyes. It is not particularly important whether or not Jean le Long's shepherd is identified with Stephen. It is the connection itself, between two phases of the movement, that is truly indispensable. Without reference to Stephen of Cloyes or his fellow shepherds, France's pioneering crowd psychologist Gustave LeBon once pronounced that "a crowd is a servile flock that is incapable of ever doing without a master." He then immediately offered the far more valid and much more astute comment that "the leader has most often started as one of the led."[35] The latter dictum would certainly pertain to Stephen.

Stephen most likely participated in special diocesan processions inspired by papal anxiety concerning the impending battle in Spain between Christians and Saracens. It is probable that these were held during the octave of Pentecost, the last day of which was 20 May.[36] Chartres, the only cathedral complex in a vast diocese and the center of a rich area for cereal grains, was a pilgrimage shrine that drew visitors from all over its territory. The pride of its relic collection was probably the *sainte chemise*,

the Virgin's shift or tunic.[37] Mary was also celebrated in Jean le
Marchant's vernacular *Miracles de Notre-Dame de Chartres*, written towards the mid-thirteenth century but based upon an earlier
(ca. 1225) Latin version. Of considerable significance here is the
fact that people from Stephen's Dunois are referred to in these miracle stories, which demonstrates that they were accustomed to visit
Chartres on pilgrimage.[38] Miracle stories such as these include al-
lusions to the famous "cult of carts" of 1144, when from all over
the diocese pilgrims, in a spirit of devotion, converged on Chartres
to help in the building of the cathedral.[39] Decades before 1212,
consequently, Chartres had already witnessed scenes of collective
zeal. At Chartres Stephen would have been able to gaze at the
sculpted Annunciation to the Shepherds adorning the south portal's
tympanum on the cathedral's west façade. Seeing the shepherds
whom angels were summoning to the Nativity of the *Christus puer*
may well have contributed to his, and his workmates', sense that
their unique calling gave them an assured place in Christendom's
providential destiny.[40]

Nor can it be forgotten that in the history of the Crusades the
diocese of Chartres was, to employ a term from American revivalism, a "burned-over district,"[41] having sent out crusaders—
barons, knights, and clerics—from the First Crusade on.[42] Renaud
de Mouçon, Chartres's bishop in 1212, a veteran of the crusade of
Philip Augustus, had already taken part in the Albigensian crusade.[43] Innocent III's letter, prompting an awareness of the
Spanish danger, would naturally have provoked a liturgical response. After all, medieval Chartres was an accomplished pro-
ducer of dramatic ecclesiastical rituals. Delaporte's edition of
Chartres's thirteenth-century *ordinaire* shows that Pentecost was
solemnly celebrated at Chartres: flower petals were gently floated
down from the vaults of the choir to symbolize the descent of the
Holy Spirit.[44] According to Berlière, during the octave of Pentecost or thereabouts priests and parishioners from diocesan churches
would assemble at their mother church with crosses, banners, and
relics, in order to present their offerings there.[45] Hence shepherds

from the Dunois, including Stephen of Cloyes, might have visited Chartres along with their priests during that Pentecostal season of 1212, simply as a matter of annual festal obligation. If we accept Jean le Long's report, however, it seems much more likely that they went on pilgrimage to Chartres, the religious capital of their diocese, because of the extraordinary processions that were being performed there on behalf of the threatened Spanish church. Let us note, however, that the papally-instituted liturgy of crisis would almost have coincided with the annual diocesan gathering, and the venue would have been the same for both rites.

After Chartres, and possibly a return to the Dunois, why Saint-Denis? Apart from the question of Capetian messianism and Stephen's celestial letters, there were secular rhythms and routines that might have helped to make the idea of such a journey congenial. Rural overpopulation in the thirteenth century necessitated some emigration from the region, and we know that peasants throughout the Chartrain and Dunois found Paris, and also Saint-Denis, attractive places for immigration.[46] Accordingly, they were already familiar destinations. André Chédeville informs us, furthermore, that sheep-shearing in the region usually took place between Easter and Pentecost.[47] That task now completed, there would have been an interval of relative calm. Just then, during that same interval, the town of Saint-Denis and its great abbey held famous fairs, the Lendit fairs, which lasted for about ten to sixteen days, concluding on St. John's Eve, 23 June.[48] In fact, a fourteenth-century poem places Dunois merchants from Bonneval and Châteaudun there.[49] With reasonable confidence, we may therefore situate the large crowds and the miracle-working performances of the *pueri* within the well-attended, public setting of the Lendit fair. This fair provides us with the perfect backcloth, at once social and religious, against which to see the pilgrimage of Stephen's shepherds.

The links between the royal abbey of Saint-Denis and the ruling dynasty were especially important. The abbey's patron saint, Saint Denis, increasingly in this period became the protector of all

France; its abbots were the counsellors of kings; its historiography chronicled Capetian achievements and yielded ideological propaganda; as a Capetian royal burial place its cultic position was unequalled.[50] Besides its fairs, which attracted many merchants, Saint-Denis was a pilgrimage center, and not only because of the relics of its esteemed titulary. It claimed important relics of the Passion, and such claims were enhanced by gifts from Philip Augustus of numerous exotic items, including hair from the Christ Child, which had been taken from the relic spoils of Constantinople in 1204 and sent to the French king by the Latin emperor, Baldwin.[51] Rejoicing in the Christocentric mementoes of the Holy Land, the abbey church attempted to inculcate the heroic virtues of the crusading movement directly and visually. Iconography taught a lesson from which Stephen and his followers might have derived inspiration: the abbey church of Saint-Denis exhibited a great window celebrating Jerusalem and Charlemagne and depicting the battles and heroes of the First Crusade.[52]

Saint-Denis without a doubt had profound crusading associations. It had a particularly significant part to play whenever the king heeded a papal summons to the Crusade. It was from this royal abbey that Louis VII received the oriflamme at the time of the Second Crusade.[53] Likewise, his son, Philip Augustus, received his pilgrim's staff there at the start of the Third Crusade.[54] Often enough it has been assumed that Philip got such a bad press as a result of his precipitous return to France after his sojourn in *outremer* that the prestige of crusader status eluded him. Yet who can say how far the negative after-image of 1191, when he left the Holy Land, still clung to him amongst countryfolk in 1212? The king had nonetheless been a crusader. He had worn the cross, gloriously or not. Although he habitually turned down new offers to serve in further crusades, these continuing appeals, which came to him from others besides Innocent III, indicate that he was still perceived as a potential crusading leader. Above all, he was the king.[55] Recent crusades had attracted sharp criticism, but the crusading movement itself remained a focus for dreams of Christian renewal. So, too, the king, whatever his personal shortcomings, could serve as a messianic figure of the prophetic imagination. In 1210 the Amalricians had gone to the stake believing in their own sinlessness and professing faith in the providential destiny of the French royal house. For the Amalricians as well as for Stephen's movement, learned Parisian ecclesiastics were invited to come to a decision.[56] In contradistinction, Stephen's *pueri* were not accused of any heresy, nor, apparently, were they subjected to a clerical inquisition.

These *pueri* of 1212, by making their way to the holiest shrine of Capetian kingship, were both testifying and paying tribute to the power of the sacral-royal myth. Of Stephen's reputedly Christ-given commission, and what it might have entailed, nothing is known. One might, in fact, have expected the contemporary royal annalist, Guillaume le Breton, to have referred to Stephen's movement.[57] Guillaume, however, was not a monk of Saint-Denis. Moreover, he wrote up the years 1209-14 as a period culminating in Philip's victory at Bouvines. Indeed, 1212 sees Philip starting on the road to that decisive battle.[58] Now, the Laon chronicler contains no hint of any face-to-face meeting between Stephen of Cloyes and Philip Augustus, a climactic scene that no teller of tales would have omitted. Once again, the Anonymous appears to be fundamentally reliable, because the documents do *not* place Philip Augustus at Saint-Denis while the *pueri* were there, although from what can be determined from his itinerary he was near enough to the abbey to have been readily contacted about matters requiring a decision.[59] When the king ordered the *pueri* to return home Stephen's pilgrimage came to an abrupt end. From its pre-history in the Chartres processions (no later than 20 May?) to its dispersal at Saint-Denis (probably no later than the end of Lendit, 23 June), the prophetic mission of Stephen of Cloyes had been remarkable, if also remarkably short. Some existing reports from non-German chroniclers referring to bands of *pueri* may well signal groups originating from this dispersal; but to speculate about their route or destination would lead us to another phase of the revival. And it is at this point that Stephen of Cloyes entirely disappears from view.

Who, then, were Stephen's *pueri*? The term has given rise to controversy. Raedts has maintained, on the basis of Georges Duby's research, that these *enfants de paradis* of 1212 were not children at all but peasants of indeterminate years, and indeed not considered to be part of any age-group as such. According to him, they belonged to an agricultural proletariat, a landless peasant workforce—poor, socially marginal, agrarian laborers who, lacking the wherewithal, were unable to marry.[60] That such a group existed in thirteenth-century peasant society can easily be documented.[61] At this point an American analogue to the shepherd—the cowboy—might suggest itself; for in what sense were American cowboys "boys"? Indeed, how youthful were the shepherds depicted at Chartres? Of course, it is equally undeniable that among those tending the flocks belonging to parents or employers were youthful shepherd boys.[62]

So far as Stephen's movement is concerned, we must note that Chédeville, the leading expert in the agrarian history of the medieval Chartrain, has never come upon the term *puer* in the archival documents of that region—notably in the subscription lists of witnesses—to mean other than child or young man.[63] The *pueri* summoned to Stephen were thought of as belonging to a common generation. The Laon Anonymous speaks of Stephen's *coaevi*: his contemporaries, or age-mates. Their relative youthfulness therefore must have been a category of his perception. This is further reinforced by his remark about the "puerilis illa devocio."[64]

The *pueri* (or "the lads"?) also may have constituted a group of workmates, occupational comrades, associated with stockraising, for so we find them in the thirteenth-century tale of *Aucassin and Nicolette*. Nicolette encounters the *pastoriaus* or shepherds eating together in a group. Such close comradeship was obviously a key to their collective recruitment in movements like Stephen's, or that of the *pastores* of 1251. *Bel enfant* is Nicolette's mode of addressing them. At least some of these young men must have been

post-pubescent, for they react strongly to Nicolette's beauty.[65]
Still, the Laon chronicler describes the *pueri* as "innocents."[66]
Now, by this he was alluding to a Bernardine concept of spiritual
purity and innocence, as an exemplum by the thirteenth-century
preacher Jacques de Vitry makes clear. Vitry says: St. Bernard
had the custom, when he rode along in the morning and saw *pueri*
tending the sheep in the fields, of proclaiming to his monks: "Let
us salute these *pueri* so that they respond by blessing us, and we
may ride on safely, protected by the prayers of these innocents."[67]
Bernardine spiritual innocence would definitely seem to imply
sexual purity, a topos of medieval childhood.

Limiting our discussion to Stephen's phase of the 1212 enthusiasm, it appears that Raedts's reading of *pueri* goes much too
far. Contemporaries perceived a relative youthfulness about the
shepherds that cannot be abandoned. While nothing suggests that
the *pueri* were little children, Rodney Hilton observes that
"herdsmen would very likely be the younger and more mobile of
the rural population."[68] At the same time, to equate the *pueri* with
the social identity of a particular deprived stratum in the peasant
world is not warranted by the evidence. Nonetheless, must there in
every case have been a necessary divergence of meaning between
puer as applied to relative age and also to social status? In reality,
there was frequent overlap and crossover, in which both categories tended to converge. This allowed the term itself to retain its
ambiguity, and its theological and mythical resonances. Whatever
the biological age of these shepherds (and a good many of them
must have been youths), childhood, in its social meaning, was
their lot. Unable to marry, they were denied that full attribution
of adulthood that in peasant society came only through marriage.
Unmarried, they were regarded as pre-sexual, as innocent youths,
socially dependent and dependent on parents, juniors. Hence the
medieval agrarian *puer*, in a floating but nevertheless definite
sense similar to the American "kid" or "youngster," could not escape from a social childhood.

The conventional judgment of historians is that the enthusiasm of 1212 vanished without creating a lasting monument. Unlike such medieval revivals as that of the flagellants of 1260, the crusade of the *pueri* failed to institutionalize its spiritual aspirations. And that is not all it failed to do. According to the Laon Anonymous, the movement heightened prophetic expectations. To "many," he says, it appeared that through the *pueri* "the Lord would accomplish something great and new upon the earth."[69] What this may have been, we can only guess. But we can assume that amongst those stirred by the spirit of prophecy the excitement created by Stephen's shepherds led to disappointment when those prophetic hopes failed to materialize.[70] In sharp contrast, scholars have argued that Innocent III took the revival of the *pueri* as a positive sign of popular support for a new crusade to rescue the Holy Land, a Crusade that he launched the next year.[71] Quite apart from this question, there is a wider issue. If the outstanding consequence of the centuries of crusading was the idea or myth of the crusade, the same could be said for this popular movement.[72] The myth of a children's crusade, an idealistic but pathetically foredoomed venture, has become part of the historical bric-à-brac that furnishes the civilized consciousness. For an enterprise that altogether lasted no more than around five months over 750 years ago, this is no mean achievement.

NOTES

I wish to dedicate this, the sixth of my Studies in Medieval Revivalism (SMR, 6), to the memory of my very dear friend Professor Harry Singer of the School of Education, University of California at Riverside.

A discussion of "The Genesis of the Children's Crusade" (SMR, 5) is now in preparation, and, as this is a subject that requires much detailed and rather technical argument, I do not propose to do more than touch upon it here, especially as Stephen's movement can be treated somewhat independently of the controversial issues it raises.

[1]What the term *pueri* may signify (for Stephen's movement alone) is best left to the close of this essay. To pursue this question across the whole of the *peregrinatio puerorum* would require another paper.

[2]A brief selection of the secondary literature on the *peregrinatio puerorum* should include: G. De Janssens, "Etienne de Cloyes et les croisades d'enfants au xiiie siècle," *Bulletin de la Société Dunoise* 90 (1891): 109-33; P. Alphandéry and A. Dupront, *La chrétienté et l'idée de croisade*, vol. 2 (Paris, 1959), pp. 115-48; G. Miccoli, "La 'crociata dei fanciulli' del 1212," *Studi Medievali*, 3rd ser., 2/2 (1961): 407-43; N. P. Zacour, "The Children's Crusade," in *A History of the Crusades*, ed. K. M. Setton, 2: *The Later Crusades, 1189-1311*, ed. R. L. Wolff and H. W. Hazard (Philadelphia, 1962), pp. 325-42; P. Raedts, "The Children's Crusade of 1212," *Journal of Medieval History* 3 (1977): 279-323. The last-cited reference also includes a good, although not altogether complete, bibliography of the sources.

[3]See J. Riley-Smith, "The First Crusade and the Persecution of the Jews," in *Persecution and Toleration*, ed. W. J. Sheils, Studies in Church History, 21 (Oxford, 1984), pp. 51-72.

[4]E. O. Blake and C. Morris reopen the controversy over Peter's role in the First Crusade without by any means resolving it ("A Hermit Goes to War," in *Monks, Hermits and the Ascetic Tradition*, ed. W. J. Sheils, Studies in Church History, 22 [Oxford, 1985], pp. 79-107).

[5]Cf. *Chronicon Sancti-Medardi Suessionensis*, in *RHGF*, vol. 18, ed. M. J. J. Brial (Paris, 1822), p. 721, an admittedly later text, composed in the 1250s, which does both, calling the movement a wonder ("mirabile") and comparing it to mysterious animal migrations. An historical perspective begins when the chroniclers of the 1251 *pastores* looked backwards to the *pueri* of 1212, which resulted in a tendency to use collective designations for each movement, rather like sect names, which do not necessarily describe the actual status or condition of the enthusiasts.

[6]See Zacour's valiant effort, "The Children's Crusade," pp. 328-30.

[7]The best edition of the Laon chronicler unfortunately contains no critical introduction: A. Cartellieri and W. Stechele, eds., *Chronicon universale anonymi Laudunensis 1154-1219* (Leipzig, 1909), pp. 70-71 (hereafter, *Chron. anon. Laud.*).

[8]On Alpais of Cudot see J. F. Hinnebusch, ed., *The "Historia occidentalis" of Jacques de Vitry: A Critical Edition* (Fribourg, 1972), pp. 87, 257. The Laon

chronicler, *Chron. anon. Laud.*, p. 67, records her death under the last entry for 1210.

[9]See L. Tinsley, *The French Expressions for Spirituality and Devotion: A Semantic Study* (Washington, D.C., 1953), pp. 28-37. For the crusading context: F. W. Wentzlaff-Eggebert, "'Devotio' in der kreuzzugspredigt des mittelalters," in *Ritterliches tugendsystem*, ed. G. Eifler (Darmstadt, 1970), pp. 422-30. For a later medieval Italian revival, described as a *devotio*, see G. Dickson, "The Flagellants of 1260 and the Crusades" (SMR, 4), *Journal of Medieval History* 15 (1989): 227-67, at p. 246. But this is a subject that requires a thorough exploration.

[10]G. Dickson, "The Burning of the Amalricians" (SMR, 3), *Journal of Ecclesiastical History* 40 (1989): 347-69, here note pp. 350-51.

[11]Raedts, "The Children's Crusade of 1212," p. 284. For discussion of the Laon Anonymous chronicler see N. Backmund, *Die mittelalterlichen geschichtsschreiber der Prämontratenersordens* (Louvain, 1972), pp. 267-72.

[12]See P. Alphandéry, "Les croisades d'enfants," *Revue de l'Histoire des Religions* 73 (1916): 259-82, at p. 273; taken up again in Alphandéry and Dupront, *La chrétienté et l'idée*, pp. 117-18. Alphandéry argues that the Laon Anonymous was indebted to the story of St. Bénézet, the shepherd boy who reputedly built a bridge across the Rhône at Avignon in 1177, after Christ had ordered him to do so, and an angel had visited him in the guise of a poor pilgrim. Now, the Laon Anonymous does indeed recount the story of St. Bénézet *s.a.* 1177 (see *RHGF*, ed. M. Bouquet, vol. 13 [Paris, 1786], p. 682), but the version of the Anonymous differs markedly from Bénézet's *vita* (cf. *Acta Sanctorum*, Aprilis, vol. 2, ed. J. Bollandus [Paris, 1866], pp. 254-63). In the Laon chronicle (1) he is called *juvenis* and not *puer*; (2) no mention is made of sheep or shepherds; (3) there is no mention of the vision or voice of Christ; (4) there is no angel who wears pilgrim dress. Compared to the *vita*, the Laon chronicler's report is more sober in tone, and it is more plausible in many other respects. There is also a strong possibility that the hagiographic legend of St. Bénézet was composed many decades after 1212 (see F. Lefort, "La légende de saint Bénézet," *Revue des questions historiques* 23 [1878]: 555-70, at pp. 555-57). Also see H. Fros, ed., *Bibliotheca hagiographica latina*, n.s. (Brussels, 1986), pp. 130-31. Alphandéry's reservations are therefore groundless.

[13]The *Chron. anon. Laud.* does not mention Châteaudun but places Cloyes "iuxta castrum Vindocinum" (i.e., Vendôme), p. 70.

[14]*Chron. anon. Laud.*, pp. 70-71: ". . . Stephanus . . . dicebat, Dominum sibi in specie peregrini pauperis apparuisse, et ab eo panem accepisse. eique literas regi Francorum deferendas tradidisse."

[15]This is a point I failed to realize when I discussed Stephen in my paper (SMR, 7) "Charisma and Revivalism in the Thirteenth Century," given at the Ettore Majorana Centre for Scientific Culture, International Workshop on Medieval Societies, Erice, Sicily (24-30 September 1989), conference on "Les Pouvoirs informels dans l'église et la société du bas moyen âge." At that same conference, Prof. Colette Beaune raised a number of interesting, if somewhat debatable, points concerning the *pueri* of 1212 in her paper, "Messianisme royal et messianisme populaire en France au XIIIe siècle." These papers are awaiting publication in the Erice series of conference proceedings.

[16]Such fanciful figures are of course quite typical of thirteenth-century chroniclers; see the comments of A. Murray, *Reason and Society in the Middle Ages* (Oxford, 1985), pp. 179-80.

[17]*Chron. anon. Laud.*, pp. 70-71.

[18]G. Dickson, "The Advent of the *pastores* (1251)" (SMR, 1), *Revue Belge de Philologie et d'Histoire* 66 (1988): 249-67, at p. 250, passim.

[19]It is surprising, therefore, that among the valuable essays contained in R.-H. Bautier, ed., *La France de Philippe Auguste: Le temps des mutations* (Paris, 1982), several of which bear upon the king's royal image and mystique, none at all refers to Stephen's movement. One would have thought that an incident in which a multitude of French shepherds assembled in quest of their king would have been taken as something of a landmark in the charismatic history of the Capetians.

[20]See M. Markowski, "'Crucesignatus': Its Origins and Early Usage," *Journal of Medieval History* 10 (1984): 157-65.

[21]G. Z. Gray, *The Children's Crusade: An Episode of the Thirteenth Century* (London, 1871), p. 30.

[22]The fundamental study remains that of H. Delehaye, "Note sur la légende de la lettre du Christ tombée du Ciel," *Bulletins de l'Académie Royale de Belgique* (Classe des lettres . . .) no. 2 (Brussels, 1899), esp. pp. 172-212; further bibliography and fourteenth- and fifteenth-century additions in C. Brunel, "Versions espagnole, provençale et française de la lettre du Christ tombée du Ciel," *Analecta Bollandiana* 68 (1950): 383-96, and idem, "Nouvelle version proven-

çale de la lettre du Christ tombée du Ciel," ibid. 69 (1951): 55-56. For England there is additional discussion in *An English Miscellany Presented to Dr. F. J. Furnivall* (Oxford, 1901), pp. 355-62, 397-407.

[23]See J. L. Cate, "The English Mission of Eustace of Flay (1200-1201)," in *Etudes d'Histoire . . . Henri Pirenne*, ed. F. L. Ganshof et al. (Brussels, 1937), pp. 67-89.

[24]H. Hagenmeyer, *Peter der Eremite* (Leipzig, 1879), p. 117.

[25]*Gesta Friderici Imperatoris*, trans. C. C. Mierow as *The Deeds of Frederick I* (New York, 1966), p. 25.

[26]It must not be overlooked that because of such distinctive attributes popular charismatic leaders, such as Nicholas and Stephen, could assume independent spiritual identities.

[27]Alberic of Trois-Fontianes, *Chronicon* (*MGH SS* 23, ed. P. Scheffer-Boichorst [1874], p. 893) says that their route was from near Vendôme to Paris ("a partibus castri Vindocini Parisius"); the three near-identical texts are from the *Anonymi continuatio append. Roberti ad Monte* (*RHGF* 18, ed. Brial), p. 344; *Chronicon Savigniacensis*, ibid., p. 351 (this text exactly reproduces the previous one); *Annales Gemmeticenses* (*MGH SS* 26, ed. O. Holder-Egger [1882]), p. 510, deviates only very slightly from these. Naturally, all three of these texts raise problems of criticism. The tale told in Matthew Paris's *Chronica majora*, vol. 2, ed. H. R. Luard, Rolls Ser. (London, 1874), p. 558, is an imaginative reconstruction of primary texts.

[28]Walteri de Coventria, *Memoriale*, vol. 2, ed. W. Stubbs, Rolls Ser. (London, 1873), p. 205. On this chronicler, whose account of 1212 is not free from mythic elements, see A. Gransden, *Historical Writing in England c.550 to c.1307* (London, 1974), pp. 339-40.

[29]Raedts, "The Children's Crusade of 1212," p. 288: ". . . written long after the children's crusade. . . . He made ample use of the chronicle of William of Andres in his treatment of the children's crusade."

[30]In *MGH SS* 25, ed. O. Holder-Egger (1880), p. 828.

[31]See his "Jean d'Ypres ou de Saint-Bertin (+ 1383)," *Revue Belge de Philologie et d'Histoire* 2 (1922): 475-94, here note pp. 485, 494.

[32]Alphandéry, "Les croisades d'enfants," p. 261. Alphandéry and Dupront, *La chrétienté et l'idée*, omit this point.

[33]I am most grateful to Dr. Michael L. Ryder, author of *Sheep and Man* (London, 1983), for this information, and also to my colleague Prof. Angus MacKay for suggesting that I consult Dr. Ryder.

[34]See n. 2 above: Credit for stressing the Spanish crisis in the context of the 1212 enthusiasm belongs to De Janssens, "Etienne de Cloyes et les croisades d'enfants," pp. 112-13. Also see Miccoli, "La 'crociata dei fanciulli'," pp. 440-42; Zacour, "The Children's Crusade," pp. 326-28; and Raedts, "The Children's Crusade of 1212," pp. 304-05.

[35]G. LeBon, *The Crowd* (London, 1900), p. 134.

[36]For Innocent III's letter to the archbishop of Sens and his suffragans, of whom the bishop of Chartres was one: *PL* 216, col. 514, no. 155, and Innocent's *supplicatio generalis*, cols. 698-99. Cf. D. Mansilla, ed., *La Documentacion Pontifica hasta Innocencio III* (Rome, 1955), pp. 503-04, no. 473. For discussion of the problems, see Miccoli, "La 'crociata dei fanciulli'," pp. 440-41.

[37]P. Bétérous, "Quelques aspects de la piété populaire au xiiième siècle, à travers les miracles mariaux," in *La Piété populaire au moyen âge*, Actes du 99e Congrès National des Sociétes Savantes, 1 (Paris, 1977), pp. 283-91, here at p. 289. Also see E. F. Wilson, *The "Stella maris" of John of Garland*, Mediaeval Academy of America, pub. no. 45 (Cambridge, Mass., 1946), pp. 3-4, 186-87.

[38]See the new edition of Jean le Marchant's *Miracles*, ed. P. Kunstmann, *Bulletin de la Société Archéologique d'Eure-et-Loir. Mémoires* 26 (1973), here at pp. 124-26 (cap. 12, "Un miracle qui avint au gens de Boneval": note 1.15: "De Bonneval, vers Chetiaudun"); pp. 190-205 (cap. 25), which conveniently includes the Latin version.

[39]G. Henderson, *Chartres* (Harmondsworth, 1968), pp. 34-37 and passim. R. Branner, *Chartres Cathedral* (London, 1969), pp. 74-75.

[40]Branner, *Chartres Cathedral*, pp. 75, 78-79. Also note: A. Priest, "The Masters of the West Façade of Chartres," *Art Studies* 1 (1923): 28-44, esp. pp. 41-44.

[41]W. R. Cross, *The Burned-Over District* (Ithaca, 1950), remains a remarkable study in the regional geography of revivalism.

[42]See C. Métais, "Croisés chartrains et dunois," *Bulletins de la Société Dunoise* 8 (1894-96): 198-216.

[43]During the summer of 1210 (E. de Lépinois, *Histoire de Chartres*, vol. 1 [Chartres, 1854], p. 125).

[44]Y. Delaporte, ed., *L'Ordinaire chartrain de xiiième siècle, Société Archéologique d'Eure-et-Loir. Mémoires*, 19 (Chartres, 1953), pp. 51, 130.

[45]U. Berlière, "Les processions des croix banales," *Bulletins de la classe des lettres et des sciences morales et politiques*, Académie Royale de Belgique, 5th ser., 8 (Brussels, 1922), pp. 419-46, here at p. 419.

[46]M. Mollat, ed., *Histoire de l'Ile-de-France et de Paris* (Toulouse, 1971), p. 117.

[47]A. Chédeville, *Chartres et ses campagnes, xie-xiiie siècle* (Paris, 1973), p. 459.

[48]On the Lendit fairs see L. Levillain, "Essai sur les origines de Lendit," *Revue Historique* 155 (1927): 241-76, here at p. 265.

[49]Chédeville, *Chartres et ses campagnes*, pp. 454-55.

[50]A good introduction to the subject is provided by G. M. Spiegel, "The Cult of Saint Denis and the Capetian Kings," *Journal of Medieval History* 1 (1975): 43-70, and the same author's helpful study *The Chronicle Tradition of Saint-Denis: A Survey* (Brookline, Mass., 1978). See also C. Beaune, *Naissance de la nation France* (Mayenne, 1985), pp. 83-125, on the patronage of St. Denis.

[51]For what Saint-Denis received from the relic booty of 1204, see P. E. D. (Comte) de Riant, "Les Dépouilles religieuses enlevées à Constantinople . . . ," *Mémoires de la Société des Antiquaires de France*, 4th ser., 6 (1875): 1-214, here at pp. 180-81. For the *capillis Domini*: F. Duchesne, ed., "Gesta alia Philippi Augusti," *Historiae Francorum Scriptores*, vol. 5 (Paris, 1649), p. 259.

[52]E. A. R. Brown and M. W. Cothren, "The Twelfth-Century Crusading Window of the Abbey of Saint-Denis," *Journal of the Warburg and Courtauld Institutes* 49 (1986): 1-40 and plates 1-12.

[53]Odo of Deuil, *De profectione Ludovici vii in orientem*, ed. and trans. V. G. Berry as *The Journey of Louis VII to the East* (New York, 1948), pp. 16-19.

[54]J. W. Baldwin, *The Government of Philip Augustus* (Berkeley, 1986), p. 23.

[55]After his death there were reports of miracles: J. W. Baldwin, "Le sens de Bouvines," *Cahiers de Civilisation Médiévale* 30 (1987): 119-30, here at pp. 129-30.

[56]See Dickson, "Burning of the Amalricians," pp. 348, 355, 368.

[57]On Guillaume le Breton see Spiegel, *The Chronicle Tradition*, pp. 60-67.

[58]Note the remarks of Baldwin, *Government*, pp. 207-08, 397.

[59]Prof. John W. Baldwin of The Johns Hopkins University most kindly provided me with information concerning Philip Augustus's itinerary during June 1212. But he is definitely not responsible for any inferences I have drawn from this.

[60]Raedts, "The Children's Crusade of 1212," pp. 295-300; and esp. G. Duby, "Les pauvres des campagnes dans l'occident médiéval jusqu'au xiiie siècle," *Revue d'histoire de l'église de France* 52 (1966): 25-32, here pp. 30-32.

[61]See Dickson, "Flagellants," n. 9 above, pp. 233-34, citing Hermann of Altaich: "in primis sibi multi nobiles et mercatores, postea rustici et pueri assumpserunt," *MGH SS* 17, ed. P. Jaffé (1861), p. 402), where the *pueri* are clearly a social grouping.

[62]Cf. A. W. Wybrands, ed., *Gesta abbatum Orti Sancte Marie* (Leeuwarden, 1879), from the *Vita Fretherici* (abbot, 1163-75) written by Sibrand of Mariëngaarde, most likely in 1230 (p. xviii): The hero's conduct stands out from that of the other shepherds ("Verum aliis suis coëvis lasciventibus et levitate puerili . . . ," p. 3). This seems to be an age-occupational cohort, rather like Stephen's, with stereotyping similar to that of the Laon Anonymous, except that waywardness has replaced innocence as a defining characteristic.

[63]Personal communication (dated 3 May 1989) from Prof. André Chédeville of the University of Rennes 2, to whom I owe a debt of gratitude.

[64]*Chron. anon. Laud.*, pp. 70-71.

[65]Ed. A. E. Cobby; transl. and intro. G. S. Burgess (New York, 1988), pp. 141-44.

[66]*Chron. anon. Laud.*, p. 71: "huiusmodi innocentes."

[67]T. F. Crane, *The Exempla of Jacques de Vitry* (London, 1890), pp. 120-21; 259, no. 286.

[68]R. Hilton, *Bond Men Made Free: Medieval Peasant Movements and the English Rising of 1381* (London, 1973), p. 101.

[69]*Chron. anon. Laud.*, p. 71: ". . . Dominus facturus esset aliquid magnum et novum super terram . . ." (a sentence with clear biblical echoes, perhaps of Vulg. Jer 31.22, "Quia creavit Dominus novum super terram . . .").

[70]Vulgate Jer 31.22: the above sentence ends, "quod longe aliter provenit."

[71]M. Maccarrone, *Studi su Innocenzo III* (Pauda, 1972), pp. 99-100; H. E. Mayer, *The Crusades*, 2nd ed. (Oxford, 1988), p. 217.

[72]In general, see P. Rousset, *Histoire d'une idéologie: la croisade* (Lausanne, 1983), pp. 201-13.

MILITIA DEI: A CENTRAL CONCEPT FOR

THE RELIGIOUS IDEAS OF THE

EARLY CRUSADES AND THE

GERMAN *ROLANDSLIED*

Horst Richter

Miles Dei, miles Christi (soldier of God / Christ) are names for the new type of soldier, the crusader in contemporary reports of the first Crusades. His military service in a Holy War against the infidels for the liberation of the Holy Land can be called *militia Dei / Christi*. This article undertakes to demonstrate that these are more than mere names, and that the biblical traditions connected with *miles Christi* or *militia Christi* allow us to regard them as a conceptual center for the religious ideas of the early Crusades and the *Rolandslied*. The argumentation begins with the *Rolandslied* and its peculiar mixture of martial and religious spirit, which still awaits a better understanding.[1]

The *Rolandslied* was composed about 1172 in Regensburg, Bavaria, by the cleric Konrad.[2] His source, to which he himself makes reference, is the Old French *Chanson de Roland.* But although Konrad claims not to have added or omitted anything, he created a very different poem: not only more than twice as long (9094 vs. 4002 lines) but also imbued with an intense religious spirit foreign to the *Chanson de Roland.* The ideas expressed by Konrad in his original and substantial prologue refer to the Crusades and their ideology. There are indeed many parallels to the historical reports of the early Crusades, in details as well as in religious thought. Roland and the twelve peers are presented as heroes of a Holy War against the infidel. They mark themselves with the cross of the Crusades; they listen to, and later they themselves deliver, crusading sermons that contain all the ideas of actual sermons. They are ready to become martyrs in the service of God; and later on Konrad tells how each of them achieved martyrdom on the battlefield. For this they will receive the crown of martyrs in Heaven as their reward. While alive and fighting, they are motivated by the highest religious principles and, in turn, are depicted by Konrad as ideal representations of the Christian hero—the *miles Christi.*[3]

Indeed, Konrad uses the German equivalents of this name very frequently. He calls his heroes *gotes helden, gotes degene,* and is quite creative in inventing other names: *gotes herten, gotes strange, gotes herstrange, gotes wigande, gotes rechen, gotes chemphe.*[4] (It is to be noted here that *miles Christi* or *miles Dei* are names used to designate the crusader, particularly in the chronicles and reports of the first Crusades, at a time when the term *crusader* did not yet exist.[5])

Konrad's enthusiasm was not confined to the creation of these names. A spirit of religious zeal going beyond anything found in other poems or historical reports of the Crusades has puzzled and often dismayed German literary critics. The religious ideas and concepts expressed here are more in line with the monastic religiosity of the Early Middle-High German "Cluniac literature," which flourished in the hundred years preceding the *Rolandslied.* For example, Bishop Turpin demands of the Christian leaders that they observe the seven canonical hours (*Rol.* 261), and he gives detailed advice for a life in imitation of Christ (*Rol.* 256-58).

At the same time, these lofty ideas are combined with an extreme martial spirit; thousands upon thousands of infidels are dismembered, beheaded, piled up into mountains of corpses by individual Christian heroes. Battle scenes abound, and blood flows in rivers from the battlefield. Although he is a cleric, Konrad is a master of the battle scene, and in this respect the *Rolandslied* can be compared only with the heroic spirit of the *Nibelungenlied*. It is understandable that this particular combination has not succeeded in generating interest in the poem in modern times. In research, no serious attempt has as yet been made to get to the core of the ideology of the poem. An understanding of this religious core will necessarily have to precede a more coherent and meaningful evaluation of the text.

In this context I shall deal with the concept of *militia Dei*, which I hope to use to promote a better understanding of the structure of religious values motivating the crusaders of the historical records as well as Konrad's heroes in the idealized account of the German *Rolandslied*. In order to do that, I shall have to discuss the idea of *militia Dei*, the military service for God, and the related names for the soldier of Christ or God, the *miles Christi* or *miles Dei*, in the reports of the early Crusades, and to a large extent also in earlier Christian teachings.[6]

It must be remembered that *miles Christi* and *militia Dei* were not at all new terms.[7] As far as we know, it was St. Paul who was the first to use *miles Christi* to designate the soldier-like service that he and his fellow apostles gave to the Lord, as we shall see below. Endorsed by his authority, in the Middle Ages it had come to mean *militia spiritualis*, the spiritual soldiership of monk and priest, who fought arduous battles against sin, evil, and the devil himself, the one in his cell or monastery in a life of abstinence and daily prayers, the other by celebrating mass in church. But now that this name was also used by the crusading army, *militia Dei* had taken on a very real meaning: it designated a real war against enemies of flesh and blood, enemies in a literal sense.

It should further be noted that the terms *miles Dei, militia Dei* had not been unofficially appropriated by the crusading soldiers. Churchmen—and quite likely Pope Urban II himself—had extended their traditional meaning to include this new class of real warriors who had given up fighting among themselves, as Christians slaughtering fellow Christians, and who were now prepared to turn against the "pagan" enemies of the Christian religion under the leadership of the Church.

Pope Urban II is reported by Fulcher of Chartres, participant and chronicler of the First Crusade, to have said in his sermon to the assembly in Clermont (where a Crusade was preached for the first time):

> nunc fiant Christi milites, qui dudum exstiterunt raptores; nunc iure contra barbaros pugnent, qui olim adversus fratres et consanguineos dimicabant; nunc aeterna praemia nanciscantur, qui dudum pro solidis paucis mercennarii fuerunt. pro honore duplici laborent, qui ad detrimentum corporis et animae se fatigabant.[8]

> (Now let those become *milites Christi*, who once were brigands. Now let those fight legitimately against barbarians, who formerly fought brothers and relatives. Now let them receive eternal rewards who before were mercenaries for a few pennies; now let them fight for double honors [i.e., in Heaven and on earth] who before labored to the detriment of their body and soul.)

This shows that with the institution of the Holy War there was extended to the new class of warriors an invitation to be included in the ancient and until recently exclusive group of *milites Dei*. The offer was enthusiastically accepted, as many reports show. The soldiers had indeed been offered more than a mere name. *Militia Dei* characterized a concept and an acclaimed form of Christian life; it had developed a rich meaning and it was highly esteemed because it had been authorized by St. Paul himself. It will be necessary to outline this in more detail.

It is in the second letter to Timothy that St. Paul perceives the work of the apostles in the image of soldierly duties, when he admonishes his correspondent (2 Tm 2.3): "Labora sicut bonus miles Christi Jesu" (Work like a good soldier of Jesus Christ).

Although St. Paul uses only once the expression for which Jerome's Latin rendering is *miles Christi*, it became a term of great significance for the early Church, not the least so because certain guidelines and qualifications St. Paul added in the subsequent verses helped to clarify his perception of the work or service ("labora") of the soldiers of Christ, the *militia Dei*, as it was soon called by the Church Fathers; see 2 Timothy 2.4-5: "Nemo militans Deo implicat se negotiis saecularibus, ut ei placeat, cui se probavit. Nam, et qui certat in agone, non coronatur, nisi legitime certaverit" (No one doing battle for God is to involve himself in the affairs of this world, since his aim is to please his superior. An athlete is not crowned if he has not contended according to the rules).[9]

Thus St. Paul has qualified his first statement in three important points. First, verse 4 refers to the command not to love this world (as also in 1 Jn 2.15, 16). Christ's disciples had thus renounced the world to follow him (as, for example, St. James and St. John in Mt 4.20, 22). It was also understood in reference to Christ's famous command to those who wanted to be his disciples, Luke 14.26: "Si quis venit ad me, et non odit patrem suum et matrem, et uxorem et filios, et fratres et sorores, adhuc autem et animam suam, non potest meus esse discipulus" (If anyone comes to me, and hates not his father, and mother, and wife, and children, and brothers, and sisters, and also his own life, he cannot be my disciple) and to Christ's promise of hundredfold reward and eternal life to those who leave their possessions and family and follow him in an act of *imitatio Christi* (Mt 19.29).

Second, the reward will be the crown, signifying the athlete's wreath of triumph or victory. In the following centuries for a Christian this crown became the highest reward—namely eternal life as in the famous passage where the *corona vitae*, the "crown of life," is promised to him who succeeds in resisting temptation, an assurance given by the Lord "to them that love him" (Jas 1.12).

Third, this reward will be given only to those who fight *legitime*, according to the rules. The *lex* or *leges* referred to is the body of Christian law, the commandments to which the faithful have to submit their lives.

In another letter St. Paul named the opponents against which the Christians have to do battle. See Ephesians 6.11-12: "Induite vos armaturam Dei, ut possitis stare adversus insidias diaboli: quoniam non est nobis colluctatio adversus carnem et sanguinem: sed adversus principes et potestates, adversus mundi rectores tenebrarum harum, contra spiritualia nequitiae, in coelestibus" (Put on God's armor, that you may resist the devil's ambushes. For we do not have to do battle against [enemies of] flesh and blood, but against the princes and powers, against the leaders of the world of this darkness, against the evil spirits in the heavenly places). The battle is, therefore, by no means directed against exterior enemies of the Christian faith; it is a war against the devil and his demons and against sin. And, in a famous passage that has been quoted time and time again, St. Paul goes on to describe the various parts of the "armor of God" that the warrior has to put on, Ephesians 6.14-17:

> State ergo succincti lumbos vestros in veritate, et induti loricam justitiae, et calceati pedes in praeparatione Evangelii pacis: in omnibus sumentes scutum fidei, in quo possitis omnia tela nequissimi ignea extinguere: et galeam salutis assumite, et gladium spiritus (quod est verbum Dei).

> (So stand with truth buckled around your waist, and dressed with the breastplate of justice, and your feet shod with the preparation of the gospel of peace: in all things carrying the shield of faith, with which you can extinguish all the fiery arrows of the evil one: and take the helmet of salvation and the sword of the spirit, which is the word of God.)

Thus this war is a purely spiritual one, fought with the spiritual weapons of faith. Soon it will be subsumed under the term *militia spiritualis*, which will become one of the keywords and central concepts of the Christian religion.

Many more related expressions could be cited here. For instance, St. Paul refers to his fellow apostles and missionaries as "commilitones" (Phlm 2; 2 Phil 2.25); of himself he asserts, "Bonum certamen certavi" (I have fought a good fight) (2 Tm 4.7).

In the next centuries the idea of spiritual soldiership gained considerably in influence. To a great extent this was due to the serious conflicts of the early Church with the powerful sect of the Markionites, who wanted to eliminate the Old Testament from the canonical list of books. One of Markion's arguments was that he considered many of the books of the Old Testament too warlike. Opposing this, the Church Father Origen held that the Old Testament battles were not to be understood literally but rather, as he called it, "spiritually."[10] That is, he proposed an allegorical interpretation of certain writings, because in his view the apostles would never have given the historical books of the Jews to the Christians "nisi bella ista carnalia figuram bellorum spiritualium gererent" (if these real wars were not to be understood as a figure of spiritual war) (Origen, *in Jesu Nave*, hom. 15).[11]

Such an interpretation transferred St. Paul's idea of *militia spiritualis* back into the Old Testament. In his commentaries on the book of Joshua, for example, Origen depicted Joshua's battles as prefigurations of the spiritual struggles of Jesus Christ or the apostles against the powers of evil and sin. Consequently, an enormous growth of battle and war imagery can be observed in Church writings: Christ's soldiers, led by their greatest heroes, St. Peter and St. Paul, fight mighty battles, win great booty, and return to the camp of the Lord bathed in blood:

> . . . qui tantum pugnaverunt, tot gentes barbaras deleverunt, tot hostes prostraverunt, tanta spolia, tot triumphos ceperunt, qui cruentis manibus de caede hostium redeunt, quorum pes tinctus est in sanguine et manus suas laverunt in sanguine peccatorum. Interfecerunt quippe in matutinis omnes peccatores terrae, et imaginem eorum exterminaverunt de civitae Domini. Vicerunt quippe et peremerunt diversas daemonum gentes. . . .[12]

([Sts. Peter and Paul are our great war heroes] who fought so
many battles, destroyed so many barbaric nations, cut down
so many enemies, gained so much booty and so many tri-
umphs, who come back with hands bloody from the killing
of their enemies, whose feet are red from the blood and who
washed their hands in the blood of the sinners. For they
killed in the morning / at the morning prayer ["in matutinis"]
all sinners of this earth and exterminated their image from
the city of God, for they killed and vanquished various nations of demons.) (my translation)

This is extreme imagery and quite close to the descriptions of
the actual bloody events in Jerusalem after the conquest in 1099 by
the new soldiers of God, close also to Konrad's numerous bloody
battle scenes in the German *Rolandslied*. But the battles depicted
here by Origen were meant as being of a spiritual nature. The army
was an army of piety and their arms were the Christian virtues:

In populo Dei sunt quidem, sicut Apostolus dicit, qui militant Deo: illi sine dubio, qui se non obligant negotiis saecularibus: isti sunt qui procedunt ad bellum et pugnant adversus gentes inimicas et adversum spirituales nequitias pro reli-
quo populo . . . pugnant autem isti orationibus et ieiuniis,
iustitia et pietate, mansuetudine et castitate cunctisque con-
tinentiae virtutibus, tamquam armis bellicis communiti.
(Origen, *in Num. hom.* 25, pp. 310-11)

(Among God's people there are some, as the Apostle says,
who do battle for God, those without doubt, who do not involve themselves in worldly affairs [see 2 Tm 2, 4, above]: it
is they who proceed to war and fight against hostile peoples
and the evil spirits for the rest of the people [see Eph 6, 12,
above]. . . . But they fight by prayers and fasting, through justice and piety, through gentleness and purity, through all the
virtues of temperance and abstinence, fortified as though by
arms of war.) (my translation)

True heroes and officers of this *militia Dei* were those who
put their entire lives into the service of the Lord; and Origen
quoted St. Paul's stipulation, that they were never to involve
themselves in the affairs of this world (see above). These chiefs

of war would never be disunited; there would never be discord and division among them.[13] Unanimity, brotherly love, unity, and concord were also the virtues demanded and stressed in the historical records of the First Crusade; the *Rolandslied* emphasizes this idea again and again, depicting the poet's crusading heroes as a fraternity of twelve, never to be disunited.

In the Latin Church of the West, Tertullian and Cyprian passed on the ideas of *militia Dei* in their teaching, and they were so successful and the concept became so prevalent that its original figurative meaning was almost forgotten. The Christians of the West regarded themselves literally as *militia Dei*, and from them the Middle Ages would receive the concept.[14]

While the apostle, the missionary, and the ascetic constituted the *militia spiritualis* for St. Paul and Origen, for Tertullian and Cyprian it was almost exclusively the martyr,[15] and he was to become the most glorified representative of the *militia Dei*. In dying for Christ and his teachings the martyr left this world and its concerns, his possessions as well as his family, to follow Christ and to imitate literally his sufferings. Purged and purified, he was thought to ascend directly to Heaven after his death, there to receive the highest crown for his *militia* and to sit on a throne beside Christ as his brother with the rank of counsellor on the day of the Last Judgment. He represented the highest ideal of a *miles Dei*. "Vos primores et duces ad nostri temporis praelium facti caelestis militiae signa movistis" (You are the leaders and dukes in the battle of our time, you move/carry the standards of our heavenly *militia*), said Cyprian (*Ep.* 28, 1-2)[16] to them; and that they kept that status throughout the Middle Ages is demonstrated by Honorius of Autun's characterization of the martyr: "Qui enim boni milites hostes fortiter pugnando devicerunt, et causa imperatoris summi augustaeque Ecclesiae sanguinem suum fuderunt, ideo victoria potita jam coronati cohaeredes regni esse meruerunt" (*Spec. eccles.* 1031) (They defeated the enemy as good soldiers in a courageous fight; and for the causes of the highest emperor and the august Church they shed their blood, therefore they have

earned to be crowned co-inheritors of the kingdom of Heaven)
(my translation).[17]

Accordingly, the crusading *milites Dei* were also held to be
martyrs. The rewards, authority, and status of those earlier martyrs were transferred to them.

From the fourth century on it fell to the monk to carry on the
idea of *militia spiritualis*.[18] The monastic idea gained steadily in
influence after the Christian religion had become the officially acknowledged state religion and the old heroic struggle for the Christian faith had become largely obsolete. It had become convenient
and advantageous to be a Christian. In those times, the monk was
thought to continue the old fight for God, because he tried in his
turn to live strictly by St. Paul's commands: the Apostle's demand
of the *miles Christi*, 2 Timothy 2.4, not to be involved in the affairs
of this world and to leave everything behind, meant for monk or
hermit to lock himself away in his monastery or cell and to give
service to the Lord in a daily life of discipline, prayer, and
self-abnegation. *Militia* was now used also as a term for the monastic life. Benedict of Nursia's influential rules, composed in the
sixth century to provide norm and discipline to the monastic life,
were accordingly called by their author "lex, sub qua militare vis"
(regulations under which you will do military service) (*Reg. Ben.*
58.21).[19] Thus *lex* is to be understood as a reference to St. Paul's
other stipulation (2 Tm 2.5), that only those athletes will be
crowned who fight *legitime*, according to the rules. "Militans sub
regula vel abbate" (*Reg. Ben.* 1.3, 4) was Benedict's own definition
of cenobitic monastic life. There is no need to stress the importance of the Benedictine Order for the Christian West, as missionaries and as teachers. It was in the West that a close relationship with the nobility developed. For a long time it was common
practice to admit only a freeman to the monastic community, because, as St. Isidore clearly stated, the secular *militia* was carried
out also only by free men, the nobility. This led to mutual influence and, again, to a great increase in military imagery. In accor-
dance with the changing times *militia Dei* could later be called

equitatus Christi, that is, knighthood for Christ.[20]

Some conclusions can now be drawn. The new *miles Dei*, the soldier in a Holy War, had become a close relative of the earlier bearers of this title, the apostles, martyrs, and monks. He had thus inherited a name characterized by the rich semantic field of ideas and concepts that had evolved around these types of the Christian life. He participated in traditions that reached back to the very root of Christianity. And where the former *miles Dei* waged a spiritual battle against sin and the devil, the new *miles Dei* was fighting a real battle against the children of the devil, the pagan enemies of the Christian faith who would not acknowledge the Lord. Accordingly, the description of their new *militia* was filled with the ancient formulae and concepts of the older *militia*. A few examples will suffice as illustration. Where the apostles, martyrs, and monks had left the world in an act of *contemptus mundi*, as they believed St. Paul had demanded of them, the crusader left his family and possessions for the Holy Land. Thus the anonymous *Historia belli sacri* says the following about the crusaders of the First Crusade:

> Isti sunt qui contempserunt vitam mundi, et pervenerunt ad praemia regni. Isti reliquerunt regna et praedia et divitias et abnegaverant semetipsos, et secuti sunt Domini nostri vestigia. . . . isti vero non pro sua, neque pro aliquo suorum, sed solummodo pro regno coelorum abierunt, et viriliter pugnaverunt, et vicerunt, adjuvante Domino. (*Prol.*, p. 173)[21]

> (It is they who have despised the life in the world and have attained the reward of Paradise. They have left their countries, estates, and all their wealth behind and have denied themselves and followed the footsteps of our Lord. . . . really they did not leave for their own good, or for the good of others, but only for the kingdom of Heaven, and fought like men, and gained victory with the help of God.) (my translation)

Or as Fulcher of Chartres begins his report (*Prol.* 1, pp. 115-18):

> Placet equidem vivis, prodest etiam mortuis, cum gesta virorum fortium, praesertim Deo militantium, . . . inter fideles sobrie recitantur. . . . quomodo mundi flore spreto

Deo adhaeserunt et parentes uxoresque suas, possessiones
quoque quantaslibet relinquentes iuxta praeceptum evan-
gelicum Deum secuti sunt, ad diligendum eum ardentius com-
puncti, ipso inspirate, animantur.

(It pleases the living and benefits even the dead to hear the
deeds of the courageous men, namely the warriors of God, so-
berly reported among the faithful . . . how, having spurned the
flower of this world, they adhered to God, and leaving their
parents, wives, all their possessions behind according to the
evangelical commandments they followed God, driven to a
burning love for him who had inspired them.) (my translation)

They fulfilled again, as the martyrs had done before them, the
idea of *imitatio Dei* when they took the sign of the cross and af-
fixed it on one shoulder. It is called "crucem post Christum por-
tare" (or "ferre") (to carry the cross following Christ) in the chronicles, and it is done in reference to papal promises of heavenly reward to the crusaders: "si, renunciatis omnibus quae possidebant,
crucem post Christum unanimiter portantes, periclitantibus con-
christianis ferrent auxilium" (if they renounced all their possessions and carried the cross after Christ in the spirit of unanimity
and brought help to their struggling fellow Christians) (Ekkehard,
Hieros. 6.2).[22]

Others emphasized that this *imitatio Christi* had to be carried
out in the spirit of willingness or eagerness, and—as it is mentioned again and again—"puro corde et mente" (with a pure heart
and mind). This had been demanded of the earlier martyrs, whose
sacrifice was acceptable only when given in this spirit of purity
and willingness; unanimity or brotherly love, also demanded from
the crusading armies, were concepts taken from the *militia Dei* of
monks in the monasteries.

The *Rolandslied* contains these ideas as well, but on a distinctly
higher level of intensity. In numerous and often substantial additions to his source, the *Chanson de Roland*, Konrad emphasizes the
religious motivations of his *gotes degene* or *milites Dei* in their battle against the armies of the infidels of Spain; and he takes full ad-

vantage of the possibilities of a fictional account: his soldiers of Christ are presented as the most glorified examples of *militia Dei*, motivated by religious ideals, that make them into incarnations of the *militia spiritualis* of apostle, martyr, and monk as well.

It will be sufficient to demonstrate the intensity of that religious spirit with one typical passage standing for many others throughout Konrad's text. Directly before the two opposing armies clash in their first battle, Konrad takes the occasion to show the spiritual preparations of the Christian armies of Roland and his twelve peers and also to add his comments about the Christian ideals that govern them in a substantial paragraph of seventy-one verses (*Rol.*, lines 3393-3464).

Konrad begins with a report on how the soldiers ask their priests to prepare them with a divine service in which they receive the Holy Communion, call to Christ for the forgiveness of sins, fortify themselves with confession, and thus are ready for a death of martyrdom (3393-3411). Konrad then expounds on how these true warriors of God, "di waren gotes degene" (3412), will not give up on their goal to regain our ancient inheritance, "daz unser alt erbe" (3415), that is, Paradise. Then the heroes are presented as ennobled by their Christian life (3417-18) and Konrad enumerates the individual virtues of their *militia spiritualis*:

> ia waren di herren edele
> in cristenlichem lebene.
> si heten all ain muot.
> ir herce hin ze gote stunt.
> si heten zucht unt scam,
> chuske unt gehorsam,
> gedult unt minne.
> si prunnen warlichen inne
> nach der gotes suoze.
>
> (3417-25)

They show unanimity (3419), heartfelt desire to be with God (3420), discipline and chastity (3421), purity and obedience (3422), patience and love (3423), and a burning desire for God's

119

sweetness (3434-25); and Konrad concludes this section with the assurance that they will assist us (as intercessors) to forget our misery here, since they are now in God's kingdom:

> wegen si uns muozen
> daz wir dirre armuote uergezen,
> want si daz gotes riche habent besezzen.
>
> (3426-28)

But Konrad starts anew in a second paragraph: again he mentions the readiness of the *gotes degene* (3429) with psalms and blessings, absolution and confession of faith, with tearful eyes and the great humility with which they turn to God to comfort their souls with the Holy Bread and the Lord's Blood (3430-39).

They then take arms and praise the Lord with joy like that of people in a wedding celebration, and Konrad concludes this description with his own characterization of his heroes:

> si haizen alle gotes chint.
> di werlt si uersmaheten,
> daz raine opher si brachten,
> do si daz cruce an sich namen.
> ze dem tode begonden si harte gahen.
> si chovften daz gotes riche.
> sine wolten ain ander nicht geswiche:
> swaz ainen duchte guot,
> daz was ir aller muot.
>
> (3444-52)

> (They all are called children of God. They despised this world, they brought the pure sacrifice when they took the cross. They began to hurry towards death. They bought God's kingdom. They did not want to leave each other: whatever one of them thought to be good, that was shared by all of them.)

And finally a quotation from Psalm 132.1 (Vulgate) with a further comment:

> Dauid psalmista
> hat uon in gescriben da:

wi groze in lonet min trechtin,
di bruderlichen mit<ain> ander sin!
er biutet in selbe sinen segen,
si scuolen iemir urolichen leben.
ain zu uersicht unt ain minne,
ain geloube unt ain gedinge,
ain truowe was in allen;
ir nehain entwaich dem anderen.
in was allen ain warhait:
des frovt sich elliu di cristinhait.

(3453-64)

(David, the psalmist, has written about them: how greatly will
the Lord reward those who are united in brotherly love. He
himself offers them his blessing, they shall live joyfully forever: one trust in God, one love, one faith and one hope, one
loyalty united them all. None of them abandoned the other,
one truth was in all of them: all Christians rejoice in them.)

These examples could easily be multiplied. They will, however, suffice for the point I want to make: it was not simply that
an old name was given to this new breed of soldiers but rather
that the Church, at the time of the reforms, made a conscious effort to incorporate the crusaders into the old and venerable *militia
Dei*, with all the benefits and the esteem the earlier had held also
extended to the new—and thus to expand this ancient corporation
and to fill it with new and contemporary life.

Particularly appealing for the crusaders in history and fiction
was the reward of martyrdom that had been offered by Pope
Urban II to everyone who would die in this Crusade. Guibert of
Nogent, another chronicler of the events at Clermont, reports him
to have said, "Nunc vobis bella proponimus quae in se habent
gloriosum martyrii munus, quibus restat praesentis et aeternae
laudis titulus" (*Orat.* VI, p. 578) (Now we propose to you a war
that includes the glorious reward of martyrdom, giving title
henceforth to present and eternal praise).[23]

Martyrdom granted immediate ascension into Paradise after
death, and the highest crown as one of the elected twelve times

twelve thousand mentioned in the Apocalypse (Rv 7.4-8) and as brothers of Christ, who will sit with him as councillors and intercessors at the day of the Last Judgment. The warriors of the *Rolandslied*, the *gotes helede*, *gotes herstrange*, etc., make every effort to gain this highest reward as well. In his introduction, and with the authority of his own voice, Konrad thus presents Archbishop Turpin and the other twelve peers (whom later, as the narrative unfolds, he permits to act accordingly):

er was der zwelue einer,	he was one of the twelve
di sich niene wolten gescaidin;	who wanted never to separate;
si ne uorchtin uûr noch daz	they were not afraid of fire or
swert.	sword.
got hat si wol gewert	God granted them willingly
des si an in gerten,	what they wanted from him
di wile si hi lebeten.	while they lived here.
an der martir si beliben	They gained martyrdom;
ze himile sint si gestigin;	they have ascended to Heaven;
nu mugen si uroliche leben:	now they may joyfully live:
da sint si rat geben.	there they are councillors.
daz habent si umbe got irworuen,	They have earned from God
daz si lebent imir ane groze	that they are alive for ever
sorgen.	without great cares.
(*Rol.* 225-36)	

But also in the reports of the Crusades there are many stories about warriors encouraged to the greatest of deeds and often enough to sheer recklessness to gain this highest reward. They did not care what might happen to them, because they would be rewarded either way: by the remission of sins here on earth and praise for valiant deeds, or by the imperishable crown and the heavenly rewards of martyrdom: "o quot milia martyrum in hac expeditione beata morte finierunt!" (O how many thousands of martyrs have died a blessed death on this expedition!)—this exclamation of Fulcher (*Prol.* 4, p. 117) reflects adequately the fervent tone of the ever-recurring topic of martyrdom.

Martyrdom may have already been an issue and a reward for the earlier soldiers in the service of the reforming popes or as soldiers of St. Peter,[24] but it is obvious that only from the First Crusade onward was it to become a strongly motivating force, charged with emotion. *Militia Dei*, however, is the name under which all the elements of what we call crusading religiosity may be subsumed. It is thus to be regarded as an important concept for the early Crusades and their historical reports, while Konrad uses the possibilities of a fictional account to full advantage, to create a coherent set of religious ideas for his German version, the *Rolandslied*, with the concept of *militia Dei* at its center.[25]

I have omitted here one form of *militia Dei* that became so important later, that is, the Order of the Knights Templar, promoted and enthusiastically welcomed by St. Bernard of Clairvaux as *novum genus militiae Dei*. The Templars, indeed, truly conjoined the spiritual side of the *militia* of the monk with the *militia saecularis* of the soldier; they were monks and soldiers and fulfilled the concept of *militia Dei* most truly. Thus they were the logical end of the development of *militia Dei* as outlined here. Again, Roland and his twelve peers together with their army of Christian warriors may well be regarded as ideal images created after this model.[26]

NOTES

[1]This study presents the first results of a larger and as yet uncompleted project concerning the concept of *militia Dei* from early Christian times to the Crusades. The project arose from the study of the religious thought of the *Rolandslied* and the idea that *militia Dei* might be regarded as a central concept for the religious ideas of the Middle High German text, as well as for the historical reports of the early Crusades.

[2]*Das Rolandslied des Pfaffen Konrad*, ed. Carl Wesle, 2nd ed. Peter Wapnewski, Altdeutsche Textbibliothek, 69 (Tübingen, 1967). All subsequent citations are to this edition, and all translations are mine.

[3]Horst Richter, *Kommentar zum Rolandslied des Pfaffen Konrad. Teil 1.*, Kanadische Studien zur deutschen Sprache un Literatur, 6 (Bern and Frankfurt, 1972), pp. 17-19.

[4]Gabriele Glatz, "Die Eigenart des Pfaffen Konrad in der Gestaltung seines christlichen Weltbildes," unpub. diss. (Freiburg, 1949): 22. See also Jeffrey Ashcroft, "'Miles Dei—Gotes Ritter': Konrad's 'Rolandslied' and the Evolution of the Concept of Christian Chivalry," *Forum for Modern Language Studies* 17/2 (1981): 146-66.

[5]Carl Erdmann, *Die Entstehung des Kreuzzugsgedankens* (Stuttgart, 1935; rept. Darmstadt, 1965), pp. 310-25. See also Jonathan Riley-Smith, "The First Crusade and St. Peter," in *Outremer. Studies in the History of the Crusading Kingdom of Jerusalem. Presented to Joshua Prawer*, ed. B. Z. Kedar, H. E. Mayer, R. C. Smail (Jerusalem, 1982), pp. 41-63, esp. 55-63.

[6]It will become apparent from the following that it is not the purpose of this essay to deal with the evolution of knighthood and chivalry in general; for that aspect I wish to make brief references to, among others, Georges Duby, trans. Cynthia Postan, *The Chivalrous Society* (Berkeley and Los Angeles, 1977); idem, trans. Arthur Goldhammer, foreword by Thomas N. Bisson, *The Three Orders. Feudal Society Imagined* (Chicago and London, 1980); the collection of articles in *Das Rittertum im Mittelalter*, ed. Arno Borst, Wege der Forschung, 349 (Darmstadt, 1976); Maurice Keen, *Chivalry* (New Haven and London, 1984); and the collection of articles in *Forum for Modern Language Studies* 17/2 (April 1981), particularly the first, by Tony Hunt, "The Emergence of the Knight in France and England 1000-1200," pp. 93-114, and its exhaustive reference notes. See also *The Study of Chivalry: Resources and Approaches*, ed. Howell Chickering and Thomas H. Seiler (Kalamazoo, 1988), published for TEAMS (The Consortium for the Teaching of the Middle Ages, Inc.).

[7]Adolf von Harnack, *Militia Christi. Die christliche Religion und der Soldatenstand in den ersten drei Jahrhunderten* (Tübingen, 1905; rept. Darmstadt, 1963).

[8]My translation of *Fulcherius Carnotensis Historia Hierosolymitana*, ed. Heinrich Hagenmeyer (Heidelberg, 1913), Lib. I, cap. III, 7, pp. 136-37.

[9]While the Vulgate version of verse 4b is somewhat vague ("ut ei placeat, cui se probavit"), the Greek original is quite specific that the soldier of Christ has to please his military commander. All English translations of the Vulgate are mine.

[10]See Harnack, *Militia Christi*, pp. 25-31. Harnack presents a collection of texts of the early Church writers in support of his argument (pp. 98-111). The texts presented here are based on Harnack's collection; that is, they were checked against the original text, wherever possible, and sometimes other relevant materials were added from the source. The English translations are mine.

[11]Origines, *Homiliae in libros Jesu Nave. Opera omnia*, vol. 11, ed. C. H. E. Lommatzsch (Berlin, 1841), p. 130; see also Harnack, *Militia Christi*, pp. 27, 102.

[12]Origines, *Homiliae in Numeros. Opera omnia*, vol. 10 (Berlin, 1840), pp. 315-16.

[13]See Origines, *in Num. hom.* 26, vol. 10, pp. 318-19.

[14]Harnack, *Militia Christi*, pp. 32-40.

[15]See also Hans Freiherr von Campenhausen, *Die Idee des Martyriums in der alten Kirche* (Göttingen, 1936). For the concept of martyrdom in the Crusades see: H. E. J. Cowdrey, "Martyrdom and the First Crusade," in *Crusade and Settlement*, ed. Peter W. Edbury (Cardiff, 1985), pp. 46-56.

[16]Harnack, *Militia Christi*, p. 110; see also St. Cyprien, *Correspondance*, vol. 1, Texte etabli et traduit par Le Chanoine Bayard, 2nd ed. (Paris, 1962), p. 68.

[17]Honorius Augustodunensis, *Speculum ecclesiae*, in *PL* 172:807-1108.

[18]For the following see Ernst von Hippel, *Die Krieger Gottes. Die Regel Benedikts als Ausdruck frühchristlicher Gemeinschaftsbildung* (Halle, 1936); also Stephan Hilpisch, *Geschichte des benediktinischen Mönchtums* (Freiburg, 1929).

[19]*Sancti Benedicti Regula Monachorum.* Textus critico-practicus sec. cod. Sangall. 914 adiuncta verborum concordantia cura D. Philiberti Schmitz addita Christinae Mohrmann enarratione in linguam S. Benedicti. Editio altera emendata (Maredsous, 1955).

[20]See Friedrich Heer, *Der Aufgang Europas. Eine Studie zu den Zusammenhängen zwischen politischer Religiosität, Frömmigkeitsstil und dem Werden Europas im 12. Jahrhundert* (mit Kommentarband) (Zürich, 1949); see p. 152 and esp. 152.33 on p. 76 of the added volume of commentaries for his sources.

[21]Anon., *Tudebodus imitatus et continuatus. Historia peregrinorum euntium Jerusolymam ad liberandam sanctum sepulcrum de potestate ethnicorum*, in *Recueil des Historiens des croisades. Historiens occidentaux*, 5 vols. (Paris, 1844-95), 3:165-229. The English translation is mine.

[22]*Ekkehardi Uraugensis abbatis Hierosolymita seu Libellus de oppressione liberatione ac restauratione sanctae Hierosolymitanae Ecclesiae*, ed. H. Hagenmeyer (Tübingen, 1877). The English translation is mine.

[23]Guibert of Nogent, *Gesta Dei per Francos*, in *RHC Hist. occ.* 4:115-263. His version of Pope Urban's sermon is presented here from the collection: *Urbani II Papae sermones III: Orationes in concilio Claromontano habitae de expeditione Hierosolymitae I-VIII*, in *PL* 151:565-82. The English translation is mine.

[24]See Erdmann, ch. 7, "Militia sancti Petri," in *Die Entstehung des Kreuzzugsgedankens*, pp. 185-211; also, I. S. Robinson, "Gregory VII and the Soldiers of Christ," *History. The Journal of the Historical Association* 58 (1973): 169-92.

[25]A renewed interest in the religious ideas of the crusading movement is apparent in historical research; see, e.g., J. A. Brundage, *Medieval Canon Law and the Crusader* (Madison, 1969); idem, "The Army of the First Crusade and the Crusade Vow: Some Reflections on a Recent Book," *Mediaeval Studies* 33 (1971); H. E. J. Cowdrey, "Pope Urban II's Preaching of the First Crusade," *History* 55 (1970); idem, "Martyrdom and the First Crusade"; J. T. Gilchrist, "The Erdmann Thesis and Canon Law, 1083-1141," in *Crusade and Settlement*, ed. P. W. Edbury (Cardiff, 1985); E.-D. Hehl, *Kirche und Krieg im 12. Jahrhundert* (Stuttgart, 1980); particularly the research articles and books by J. Riley-Smith, e. g., *What Were the Crusades?* (London, 1977); idem, "An Approach to Crusading Ethics," *Reading Medieval Studies* 6 (1980); idem, "Crusading As an Act of Love," *History* 65 (1980); idem, *The First Crusade and the Idea of Crusading* (London, 1986); et al. I wish my essay to be regarded as a contribution to this aspect of research into crusades from the side of medieval literature.

[26]See Gotthard Fliegner, *Geistliches un weltliches Rittertum im Rolandslied des Pfaffen Konrad*, Deutschkundliche Arbeiten, A.9 (Breslau, 1937). For Bernard and the Templars see S. Bernardi *Opera*, 3. "Liber ad milites Templi de laude novae militiae," ed. J. Leclercq and H. M. Rochais (Rome, 1963), pp. 206-39; an English translation of the treatise is available: "In Praise of the New Knighthood," trans. Conrad Greenia, in *Bernard of Clairvaux: Treatises III* (Kalamazoo, 1971).

CHRISTIANS AND MOORS IN

¡AY JHERUSALEM!

Donna M. Rogers

¡Ay Jherusalem! is an anomaly in medieval Spanish literature: it is a crusade poem. Throughout the period of the European Crusades to the Holy Land, Spain was more concerned with the Muslims who occupied the Iberian Peninsula than with those who were troubling the Christians of far-off Jerusalem. Consequently, there was little attention to or interest in the Crusades on the part of Spain; and with all the resources of the Christian North dedicated to the Reconquest of the South, Spain had little time, money, or energy to spare for the Holy Land. For these reasons, then, it is not surprising to discover that the literature of medieval Spain includes very few references to those "foreign" Crusades; rather, it concerns itself to a very great extent with the heroes of the Christian Reconquista.

In 1960 María del Carmen Pescador del Hoyo, a Spanish historian, published her transcription of an unusual poem that had been discovered in the National Historical Archives in Madrid.[1] *¡Ay Jherusalem!* is a thirteenth-century poem of 110 lines, in

127

twenty-two stanzas; the version discovered in Madrid is a copy from the late fourteenth or early fifteenth century.

¡Ay Jherusalem! describes the events leading up to the fall of Jerusalem in 1244. The poet refers to a "Conçilio santo" (holy council), which is most likely the first Council of Lyons, held in 1245.[2] It was at this council that the news of the loss of the city, contained in a letter from Robert, patriarch of Jerusalem, brought the pope and all those present to tears. In stanza 11 of *¡Ay Jherusalem!* our poet tells us:

> Léese la carta en el Conçilio santo:
> papa e cardenales fazían grand llanto,
> ronpen sus vestidos,
> dan grandes gemidos
> por Jherusalem.

> (The letter is read at the Holy Council:
> the pope and the cardinals mourn greatly,
> they tear their garments,
> they sigh deeply
> for Jerusalem.)

The poem begins with an announcement of woeful news from Jerusalem; the poet cannot rest for weeping and sighing. He speaks of a seven-and-a-half-year siege of Jerusalem by the Moors, an alliance of "Babylonians," "Africans," "Ethiopians," and "Tartars." The Christians, starving and suffering greatly, await relief and succor. With the approval of the patriarch they write a letter to the pope, in blood, to seek his assistance. When the letter is read, the pope and the cardinals are grieved and call Christians to the aid of their brothers in Jerusalem. But the seas are stormy and the winds are against them, and the besieged Christian defenders of Jerusalem begin to lose faith that they will be rescued. The fateful day arrives; the city is attacked, the Christians vastly outnumbered by the Moors. The battle is joined and the Christians fight valiantly, slaying one hundred of the enemy for every one of their number who falls. But theirs is a lost cause: the Moors are victorious.

Christian clerics are put in chains, young women are chained and tortured. The children are burned alive and their mothers' breasts cut off; hands and feet are chopped off as well. The Moors sack the Holy Sepulchre; they use the priests' vestments for horse blankets, the Holy Sepulchre for a stable, and the crosses for hitching-posts. The poet concludes by claiming that anyone who hears his song and remains unmoved cannot be a true servant of God and will not be part of the rebuilding of Jerusalem.

To date there have been very few studies of *¡Ay Jherusalem!*: since its transcription in 1960 exactly four articles on it have appeared. Eugenio Asensio clarified its historical and literary context; Henk de Vries conducted a numerological study of the poem and the two others found with it; Alan Deyermond revised Asensio's estimate of its date of composition and pointed out its typological relationship to biblical passages; and Patricia Grieve extended Deyermond's typological analysis and examined what she called the "architectural" elements of the poem.[3] Some work remains to be done in this area; the typological analysis can probably be further expanded to account for some of the descriptive details, and no one has managed to hazard much of a guess as to who the anonymous poet might have been.

These points, however, I leave for another study. In this essay I shall examine the portrayal of the Christians and the Moors in *¡Ay Jherusalem!*, and how the structure of the poem relates them to one another. I shall then comment on the poet's use of his heroes and villains as symbols of the message he wished to convey.

De Vries described the structure of *¡Ay Jherusalem!* as symmetrical, and clearly it is; in an effort to link the three poems of the manuscript, however, de Vries devotes the greater part of his study to a numerological analysis. Grieve demonstrates clearly that the poem contains close parallels to the recounting of the fall of Jerusalem in Lamentations.[4] Lamentations has a concentric arrangement, and the structure of *¡Ay Jherusalem!* could also be conceived as a straight line drawn through concentric circles. The acrostic of the poem is probably also based on those of chapters

1, 2, 4, and 5 of Lamentations; in *¡Ay Jherusalem!* and in each of the aforementioned chapters of Lamentations the twenty-two verses correspond to the number of letters in the Hebrew alphabet.

I believe, however, that the structure of the poem is based on another image that is biblical in origin: the ladder in Jacob's dream of Genesis 28.12 ("And he dreamed, and behold a ladder set up on the earth, and the top of it reached to heaven: and behold the angels of God ascending and descending on it"). Deyermond comments in passing, at the end of his study, that

> la visión judeo-cristiana de la historia no [es] como un ave fénix, una interminable repetición cíclica, sino como una escala. Dentro de este esquema, cada relación tipológica es la relación entre dos peldaños de la escala y su comprensión ayuda al hombre a entender el plan divino.[5]

> (the Judeo-Christian vision of history is not like a phoenix, an interminable cyclical repetition, but rather like a ladder. Within this scheme, each typological relationship is the relationship between two rungs on the ladder and understanding it helps man to understand the divine plan.)

Deyermond is referring to a concept elaborated by C. A. Patrides, who states that "to Christians history is like Jacob's Ladder, 'ascending by degrees magnificent' towards the Eternal City."[6]

As the subject matter of *¡Ay Jherusalem!* is clearly historical, the ladder image is appropriate. Moreover, Jacob's ladder is a common medieval religious and literary image, from early Christian writers to roughly contemporary figures such and Dante and Llull (Lull).[7] Drawing on this analogy, the structure of *¡Ay Jherusalem!* can be seen as a ladder, with each stanza representing one of its rungs.

In order to explain the symmetrical typological relationship contained in the ladder structure of *¡Ay Jherusalem!*, one must look for its center. Stanzas 11 and 12 comprise the heart of the poem: they describe the reading of the letter of blood by the pope and the cardinals, and their reaction, the exhortation to all Christians to go to the aid of their brothers in Jerusalem. Stanzas 1 through 10, the first ten rungs of the ladder, set the stage and prepare the listener for this plea; stanzas 13 through 22, the upper and concluding rungs, are a graphic description of the horrors perpetrated by the Moors and the martyrdom of the Christians. The final stanza, the topmost rung, makes explicit reference to the building of the new Jerusalem, by placing a "canto" (stone) there. Both the image of the stone and that of the ladder were identified with Christ in the Middle Ages through biblical typology. In the Old Testament the stone in Jacob's dream is explicitly identified as God's house (Gn 28.22), as the foundation of the Church; in the New Testament Jesus identifies his sayings as a rock (Lk 6.46-49). Jacob's ladder is described in Genesis as the way to Heaven; in the New Testament Christ himself is the way to Heaven ("I am the way, the truth and the life; no man cometh unto the Father, but by me" [Jn 14.6]).

These two groups of ten stanzas (1-10, 13-22), the lower and upper rungs of the ladder, are in balance and in opposition to each other. At the center of the ladder (stanzas 11-12) are the pope and the "Conçilio santo." We can see thematic relationships between the symmetrically opposite rungs. For example, stanza 2 is opposite stanza 21: the "nueuas llorosas" or woeful tidings of stanza 2 are a foreshadowing and a warning of the most shocking news the poem contains, stanza 21's report of the desecration of the Holy Sepulchre. Stanza 3's "lloros e sospiros" (weeping and sighing) likewise prefigure the torture of women and children so graphically described in stanza 20. The infidel "moros perros" (Moorish dogs) of stanza 5 are contrasted with stanza 18's holy "sacerdotes," "frayres," and "abades" (priests, friars, and abbots). Stanza 6 warns of a tremendous alliance of Babylonians, Africans, Tartars, and others; its opposite, however, stanza 17, tells us that the Christians' valor is so great that one hundred of this great enemy horde die for every Christian slain. The lances of stanza 7 prefigure the "grand batalla" (great battle) of the "cavalleros" (knights) in stanza 16. Stanza 8 tells of the "pocas viandas" (few food supplies) and "mucho ferir" (much wounding) of the besieged Christians; in stanza 15, after the siege and the attack, there are "pocos cristianos" (few Christians) and "muchos moros" (many Moors). The "poco"/"mucho" contrast has been extended to the combatants themselves. As a final example of these correspondences, the "letras de sangre" (letters of blood) of stanza 9 are a vivid image of the color red; this color image is reflected in stanza 14, where the only adjective in the entire poem appears: "tan negro día" (such a black day). The parallels are obvious: the ladder image is a symmetrical symbol that provides a useful structure for the poem.

I have discussed the "opposing" rungs of the ladder and their relationship to each other. A series of binary oppositions is one of the devices most frequently used in medieval Spanish literature to explain both structures and themes. The most obvious thematic opposition of all in ¡Ay Jherusalem! is that of the Christians and the Moors. The Christians embody the positive moral values of piety, humanity, valor, fortitude; the Moors are referred to as "perros" (dogs); they try to starve out the Christians during the long siege. After they enter the city they maim and torture women and children; finally, the ultimate insult, they desecrate the Holy Sepulchre and turn it into a stable.

The references to Christians and Moors in ¡Ay Jherusalem! are, like the poem's structure, symmetrical: the word "moros" is used six times, as is the word "christianos." An enumeration of Babylonians, Africans, and Tartars is balanced by "sacerdotes," "frayres," and "abades." "Morería" (Moorishness) opposes "christiandad" (Christianity).

The two stanzas at the midpoint of the ladder, 11 and 12, contain the following references to Christians: "Conçilio santo," "papa" (pope), "cardenales" (cardinals), "christiandad," "Trinidad" (Trinity), and "christianos." Surrounding this concentrated cluster of words symbolizing Christian faith are "moros," in stanzas 10 and 14, just as the Moors themselves literally surrounded the city of Jerusalem. These two references very specifically reinforce the idea of surrounding: in stanza 10 the Moors with their siege have closed off the "altar de Syón"; in stanza 14 the Moors are literally "encima," or on top of, the heart of Christendom: they have entered the Holy City.

The typological aspects of these references to Christians and Moors are striking, as well: as Grieve has pointed out, *¡Ay Jherusalem!* alludes to the Old Testament fall of Jerusalem related in Lamentations by referring to the attacking Moors as Babylonians.[8] The final stanza of the poem urges all those Christians who hear it to come to the service of God and to help in the creation of another holy council, this time "el Conçilio santo de Jherusalem." The typological connection here is surely to the New Jerusalem, the heavenly Jerusalem of the Book of the Apocalypse, to be built by the Christians who join the Crusade.

To conclude, *¡Ay Jherusalem!* is an interesting anomaly in the corpus of medieval Spanish literature. Spain created its own version of crusade literature, with mighty Christian heroes battling Muslim invaders; the difference is that those battles took place on the Iberian Peninsula and not in the Holy Land. But in *¡Ay Jherusalem!* the anonymous poet made true crusading literature. By calling the attackers of Jerusalem "moros" he stated unequivocally to a Spanish audience that Christian Spain and Christian Jerusalem faced a common enemy.

NOTES

[1]María del Carmen Pescador del Hoyo, "Tres nuevos poemas medievales," *Nueva Revista de Filología Hispánica* 14 (1960): 242-50.

[2]Alan Deyermond, "'¡Ay Jherusalem!', estrofa 22: 'traductio' y tipología," in *Estudios ofrecidos a Emilio Alarcos Llorach*, vol. 1 (Oviedo, 1977), pp. 286-89.

[3]Eugenio Asensio, "*¡Ay Jherusalem!*: planto narrativo del siglo XIII," *Nueva Revista de Filología Hispánica* 14 (1960): 251-70; Henk de Vries, "Un conjunto estructural: el 'Poema tríptico del nombre de Dios en la ley'," *Boletín de la Real Academia Española* 51 (1971): 305-25; Deyermond, "'Traductio' y

tipología," pp. 283-90; Patricia S. Grieve, "Architectural and Structural Building Blocks: The Poetic Structure of *¡Ay Jherusalem!*," *Forum for Modern Language Studies* 22 (1986): 145-56.

[4]Grieve, "Architectural Building Blocks," p. 151.

[5]Deyermond, "'Traductio' y tipología," p. 290.

[6]C. A. Patrides, *The Grand Design of God: The Literary Form of the Christian View of History* (Toronto, 1972), p. 9.

[7]John Chrysostom mentions a ladder ascending from earth to Heaven (*PG* 59, cols. 454-55); John Climacus's *Scala Spiritualis* also envisioned the ladder as the means of ascent to Heaven (*PG* 88, cols. 596-608); Dante uses the image of the ladder in a dream in *Purgatorio* 9; and Llull's *Liber de ascensu et descensu intellectus* is based on three related ladders (see Lina L. Cofresí, "Hierarchical Thought in the Spanish Middle Ages: Ramon Lull and Don Juan Manuel," in *Jacob's Ladder and the Tree of Life: Concepts of Hierarchy and the Great Chain of Being*, ed. Marion L. Kuntz and Paul G. Kuntz [New York, 1987], pp. 153-59).

[8]Grieve, "Architectural Building Blocks," p. 147.

THE LETTER OF

JEAN SARRASIN, CRUSADER

Jeanette M. A. Beer

In 1249 Jean Sarrasin, one of the chamberlains of Louis IX, wrote a letter to his friend Nicolas Arrode of Paris. The letter was dated 23 June, just seventeen days after Louis and the crusaders had taken possession of Damietta. Its main purpose was the transmission of the latest news but, understandably enough, the letter was more than a mere "bulletin from the front."

After the announcement of the crusading victory Jean narrates in summary fashion the crusaders' movements before the capture of their first target. Encapsulated within this early part of the letter are some forty-seven lines describing the negotiations with the Mongols. Jean then outlines the main events of the recent victory at Damietta, the crusaders' installation in that city, and their first moves to (re)introduce Christian control. The letter ends with Jean's surmises about the probable course of action for the next few months.

This invaluable letter is extant only because its content was relevant to the purposes of a continuator of the *Livre d'Eracle*,[1]

JEANETTE M. A. BEER

the French translation of Guillaume de Tyr's *Historia Hierosoly-mitana*. This "Rothelin continuator" has incorporated Jean's letter, salutations and all, into his narrative with a preliminary explanation that the crusaders assembled on the island of Cyprus in 1248:

> Et en cele ille meismes s'assemblerent li croisié, et vindrent avec elx pour aler encontre les ennemis de la foi Jhesu Crist. Adonques estoient li an de l'Incarnacion Nostre Seigneur Jhesu Crist .M. et .CC. et .XL. et .VIII., le moiz de septembre.[2]

> (And in this same island the crusaders assembled, and came with them to go against the enemies of the faith of Jesus Christ. This was the year of the Incarnation of Our Lord Jesus Christ 1248, the month of September.)

The text of the letter is as follows:

> A seigneur Nicolas Arrode Jehans Sarrazins, chambrelens le roy de France, salus et bonne amour. Je vous fais a savoir que li roys et la royne, et li quens d'Artois, et li quens d'Anjou et sa femme, et je, sommes haitié dedens la cité de Damiete que Dieus, par son miracle, par sa misericorde et
> 5 par sa pitié, rendi a la crestienté le dimenche de la quinsainne de Pentecouste.
> Aprés ce, je vous fais a savoir en quele maniere ce fu. Il avint, quant li roys et li os de la crestienté furent entré es nez a Aiguemorte, que nous feismes voile le jour de feste saint Augustin qui est en la fin d'aoust ; et arrivames
> 10 en l'isle de Cipre quinze jours devant la feste saint Remi, c'est a savoir le jour de la feste saint Lambert. Li quens d'Angiers descendi a la cité de Lymeçon, et li roys et nous, qui avec lui estions en sa nef, que on apeloit la Monjoie, descendismes l'andemain bien main, et quens d'Artois entor tierce a ce port meismes. Nous fusmes en cele isle a mout pou de gent, et sejour-
> 15 nasmes iluec jusques a l'Ascencion pour atendre l'estoire qui n'estoit mie venue.
> Il avint que, au Noel devant, que li uns des grans princes des Tartarins que on apeloit Eltetay, et crestiens estoit, envoia au roy de France en Nycoisie, en Cypre, ses messages. Li roys envoia a ces messages frere
> 20 Andrieu de l'ordre saint Jaque. Et li message, qui rien ne savoient cui on y deusí envoier, le connurent ausi bien, et freres Andrieus eulz, con nous

136

connoistriens li uns l'autre. Li roys fist venir ces messages devant lui, et
parlerent assez en lor langages. Et freres Andrius disoit le françois au roy,
que li plus grans princes des Tartarins avoit esté crestiens le jour de la
25   Thiphaigne et grant plenté de Tartarins avecques lui, meismement des plus
grans seigneurs. Encore disoient il que Etheltay, a tout son ost des
Tartarins, seroit en l'aide au roy de France et de la crestienté encontre le
caliphe de Baudas et encontre les Sarrazins. Car il entendroit a vengier les
grans hontes et les grans damages que li Choramin et li autre Sarrazin
30   avoient faites a Nostre Seigneur Jhesucrist et a la crestienté. Il disoient que
leur sires mandoit encore au roy que il passast en Egypte au nouviau temps,
pour guerroier le soudant de Babiloine, et li Tartarin en ce point meisme
enterroient pour guerroier en la terre le caliphe de Baudas; car en tel maniere
ne porroient il aidier li un aus autres.
35   Li roys de France ot conseil d'envoier ses messages avecques ceulz a Eltheltay, leur seigneur, et au souverain seigneur des Tartarins, que on apeloit
Quioquan, pour savoir la verité de ces choses. Il disoient que, jusques la ou
Quioquan manoit, avoit bien demi an d'errure, mais Eltheltay lor sires et li
os des Tartarins n'estoit mie moult loins; car il estoient en Perse que il
40   avoient toute destruite et mise en la subjection des Tartarins. Bien disoient
encore que li Tartarin estoient mout a la volenté le roy et de la crestienté.
Quant ce vint a la quinsaine de la Chandeler, li messages les Tartarins et li
message le roy s'en alerent tout ensemble, ce est a savoir frere Andrieu de
saint Jacque, et uns siens freres, et maistres Jehans Goderiche, et uns autres
45   clers de Poissi, et Herbers li Sommeliers, et Gerbers de Sens. Et quant ce
vint a la mi quaresme, li roys oï nouveles d'eulz que il s'en aloient la baniere
desploïe au maistre des Tartarins, parmi la terre des mescreans, et que il
avoient ce que il voloient par la doutance des messages au maistre des Tartarins.
50   Aprés ces choses, li roys et toute s'estoire, que il esmoit bien a .ij.m. et .v.c.
chevaliers, et .v. mil arbalestriers et grant plenté d'autre gent a pié et a
cheval, entrerent es nez et monterent sus mer a Lymeçon et aus autres pors
de Cypre, le jour de l'Ascencion qui adonques fu le tresieme jour de may,
pour aler en la cité de Damiette, ou il n'avoit pas de Cypre plus de trois
55   journees. Nous fumes sus mer vint et deus jours, et moult eumes de contraires et de travaus en la mer.
    Le vendredi aprés la Trinité, entor tierce, venismes devant Damiete et grant
partie de nostre estoire avecques nous, mais ele n'i estoit mie toute assez. Et
bien avoit trois lieues jusques a terre. Li roys fist l'estoire aancrer et manda
60   tantost touz les barons qui la estoient. Il s'asamblerent tout dedens Monjoie,

la nef le roy, et s'acordererent que il iroient prendre terre l'endemain bien matin et malgré lor anemis, se il lor osoient deffendre. Commandé fu que on apareillast toutes les galies et touz les menuz vaissiaus de l'istoire et que l'endemain bien matin y entraissent tout cil qui entrer y porroient. Bien fu
65 dit que chascuns se confessast et appareillast et feist son testament, et atornast bien son affaire comme por morir, se il pleust a Nostre Seigneur Jhesucrist.

Quant ce vint l'endemain bien matin, li roys oy le service Nostre Seigneur et tele messe que on fait en mer, et s'arma et commanda que tout s'armaissent
70 et entraissent en petis vaissiaus. Li rois entra en une coche de Normendie, et nostre compaignon avec lui et li legas ausi, si que il tenoit la vraie crois et seignoit les gens armees qui estoient entré les menuz vaissiaus por aler prendre terre. Li roys fist entrer en la barge de cantier monseigneur Jehan de Biaumont, Maihieu de Marli et Gofroi de Sargines, et fist metre le confanon
75 monseigneur saint Denis avec euls. Cele barge aloit devant et tout li autre vaissel alerent aprés et suirent le confanon. La coche ou li roys estoit, et li legas delez lui, qui tenoit la sainte vraie crois, et nous, estions touzjours alans derrieres.

Quant nous aprochasmes de la rive a une arbalestree, mout grant plenté de
80 Turs a pié et a cheval et bien armé, qui estoient devant nous sus la rive, traissent a nous mout espessement, et nous a euls. Et quant nous aprochasmes de terre, bien ij. m. Turs, qui la estoient a cheval, se ferirent en la mer bien avant encontre nos gens, et assez de ceulz a pié. Quant nos gens qui estoient bien armé es vaissiaus, meismement li chevalier, virent ce,
85 n'entendirent pas a suir le gonfanon monseigneur saint Denis, ainz alerent en la mer a pié tout armé, li uns jusques as aisseles, li autres jusques as mameles, li uns plus en parfont et li autre mains, selonc ce que la mers estoit plus parfonde en un lieu que en un autre. Assez y ot de nos gens qui traisent leur chevaus par grant peril, par grans travaus et par granz prouesces hors
90 des vaissiaus ou il estoient. Adonques s'esforcierent nostre arbalestrier et traisent si durement et si espessement que c'estoit merveilles a veoir. Lors vinrent nos gens a terre et la gaaignierent.

Quant li Turc virent ce, si se ralierent ensamble et parlerent en leur langage, et vindrent sus nos gens si durement et si fierement que il
95 sambloit que il les deussent touz occirre et decouper. Mais nos gens ne se murent de sus le rivage, ainz se combatirent si viguereusement que il sambloit que il n'eussent onques souffert ne prisons ne travaus ne angoisses de la mer, par la vertu de Jhesucrist et de la sainte vraie crois que li legas tenoit en haut desus son chief encontre les mescreans.

100 Quant li roys vit les autres saillir et descendre en la mer, il voult descendre
avec euls. Mais on ne li vouloit laissier et toutevoies descendi il outre leur
gré, et entra en la mer jusqu'a la chainture, et nous touz avec lui. Et, puis
que li roys fu descendus en la mer, dura la bataille grant piece. Quant la
bataille ot duré par mer et par terre des la matinee jusques a midi, lors se
105 traisent li Turc arrieres et s'en alerent et entrerent dedenz la cité de Damiete.
Li roys demoura seur la rive a tout l'ost de la crestienté. Il ot en cele bataille
ou peu ou nul perdu des crestiens; des Turs y ot occis bien jusqu'a .v.c. et
moult de leur chevaus. Il y ot occis quatre amiraus. Li roys qui avoit esté
chevetains en la bataille ou li quens de Bar et de Montfort avoient esté
110 desconfit delez Gadres, fu occis en cele bataille. Ce estoit, ce disoit on, li
plus granz sires de toute la terre d'Egypte aprés le soudant, et bons
chevaliers et hardis et sages de guerre.
L'endemain, ce est a assavoir le dimenche aprés les octaves de la Pentecouste, au matin, vint uns Sarrazins au roy et dist que tout li Sarrazin s'en
115 estoient alé de la cité de Damiete, et que on le pendit, se ce n'estoit voirs. Li
roys le fist garder et envoia gens pour savoir la certaineté. Avant que il fust
nonne, certainnes nouveles vindrent au roy, que grant plenté de nos genz
estoient ja dedenz la cité de Damiete, et la baniere le roy seur une haute tour.
Quant nos gens oïrent ce, moult durement loerent Nostre Seigneur et
120 mercierent de la grant debonnaireté que il avoit faite aus crestiens; car la cité
de Damiete estoit si fors de murs et de fossez et de grant plenté de tours fors
et hautes, de hordeis et de barbacanes, et de grant plenté d'engins, d'armes
et de viandes, et de quanque mestier estoit pour vile deffendre, que a paines
peust nulz hons cuidier que ele peust etre prise, se par trop grant painne non
125 et par trop granz travaus, par force de gens. Moult le trouverent nos gens
bien garniee de quanque mestier estoit.
On trouva dedens en prison .liij. esclaves de crestiens qui avoient esté
laiens, ce disoient, vint et deus ans. Il furent delivré et amené au roy. Et
disoient que li Sarrasin s'en estoient fui des le samedi par nuit et que li
130 Sarrasin disoient li un a l'autre "que li pourcel estoient venu." On y trouva
ausi ne sai quans Suriens crestiens, qui manoient laiens en subjection des
Sarrazins. Quant cil virent les crestiens entrer en la vile, il prirent crois et les
portoient, et par ce n'orent garde. On leur laissa leur maisons et ce qu'il
avoient dedens, aprés ce que il orent parlé au roy et au legat.
135 Li roys et li os se desloga et s'en alerent logier devant la cité de Damiete.
L'endemain de la feste saint Barnabé l'apostre, li roys entra premiers dedens
Damiete, et fist despechier le maistre mahommerie de la vile et toutes les
autres, et en fist faire eglises dediees en l'onneur de Jhesucrist.

Nous cuidons bien que nous ne nous mouvons de la cité jusqu'a la feste
140 touz sains, pour la croissance dou flun de paradis qui la queurt, que on
apele le Nil; car on ne puet aler en Alixandre, ne en Babiloine, ne au
Chaaire, quant il s'est espanduz par la terre d'Egypte. Ne il ne doit des-
croistre, ce dist on, devant adonques.

Sachiez que nous ne savons mie du soudant de Babiloine, mais on fait en-
145 tendre au roy que autre soudant le guerroient. Et sachiez bien que, onques
puis que Diex nous ot rendue la cité, on ne vit pres de nostre ost fors
Beduins sarrazins qui viennent aucune fois a deus liues pres de l'ost. Et
quant nostre arbalestrier vont traire a euls, si s'enfuient. Cil meismes
viennent par nuit dehors l'ost por embler chevaus et testes de gens. Et dist
150 on que li soudans donne dis besanz por chascune teste de crestien que on
li aporte. Et coupoient en tele maniere li sarrazin Beduin les testes des
pendus, et deffouoient les cors qui estoient enfouy en terre pour avoir les
testes pour porter au soudant, si que on dist. Uns Beduins sarrazins qui y
venoit touz seulz y fu pris, pour ce le garde on encore. Ces larrecins
155 pooient il faire legierement, car ja soit ce que li rois ait dedens la cité de
Damiete la royne sa femme et une partie de son harnois dedenz le palais et
les fremetez le soudant de Babiloine, et li legas son harnois dedenz les
sales et les fremetez le roy qui fu occis en la bataille quant nous arrivasmes,
et chascuns des barons ait aussi son grant ostel et bel dedens la cité de
160 Damiete selonc ce que il convient, nequedent li os de la crestienté et li roys
et li legas sont logié dehors la vile. Pour ces larrecins, que li sarrazin Beduin
faisoient, ont li crestien commencié a faire entour l'ost bons fossez, parfons
et larges; mais il ne sont mie encore parfais.

Ainsi rendi Nostre Sires Jhesucris par sa misericorde la noble cité et la tres
165 fort de Damiete a la crestienté, [quant l'an de l'Incarnation estoit mil .ccxlix.
ans] le dimenche aprés les octaves de Pentecouste, c'est a savoir le sisime
jour du mois de jung qui adonques fu en dimenche.

Ce fu trente ans aprés ce que li crestien l'orent conquise par granz travaus
et par granz labours encontre les Sarrazins et la reperdirent dedens l'an
170 meismes, quant il alerent pour asseoir le Chaaire, et li fluns crut et s'espandi
entour eulz que il ne porrent avant ne arriere. Pour cele chose cuidons nous
que li os ne se doist mouvoir de Damiete devant que li fluns sera descrus et
revenuz arriere dedens ses chaneus. Faites savoir ces lettres a touz nos
amis.

175 Ces lettres furent faites en la cité de Damiete, la vegile de la nativité monseigneur saint Jehan Baptiste, qui fu ce mois meismes.

THE LETTER OF JEAN SARRASIN, CRUSADER

(To Sir Nicholas Arrode [from] Jean Sarrasin, chamberlain to the king of France: affectionate greetings.[3] I inform you that the king and queen, the count of Artois, and the count of Anjou and his wife, and I rejoice in being inside the city of Damietta which God by his miracle, mercy, and

5   grace restored to Christendom on the Sunday of the second week after Pentecost.

And now I tell you how this came about. It happened when the king and the Christian army had embarked at Aigues-Mortes that we set sail on the feast-day of St. Augustine, which is at the end of August; and we arrived

10   on the island of Cyprus fifteen days before the feast of St. Rémy, that is to say, on the feast of St. Lambert. The count of Anjou disembarked at the city of Limassol, and the king and those of us who were on his ship called the *Monjoie* disembarked very early the next day, then the count of Artois at the same port around terce. We were on this island with very few

15   men, and we stayed there until Ascension Day to await the fleet which had not yet arrived.

It happened that, the Christmas before, one of the great Mongol princes, called Aljighidai, who was a Christian, sent his envoys to the king of France at Nicosia in Cyprus. The king despatched Brother Andrew of the

20   order of St. Jacques to meet those envoys. And the envoys, not knowing at all who was to be sent there, knew him and he them as well as we would know each other. The king sent for these envoys and they spoke for a long time in their own language. And Brother Andrew interpreted in French to the king, reporting that the highest Mongol leader had become a Christian on the feast of Epiphany, together with a great

25   number of Mongols including some of the higher nobility. They further said that Aljighidai and his Mongol army would assist the king of France and Christendom against the caliph of Baghdad and against the Saracens. For he would like to avenge the great shame and great loss inflicted by

30   the Chorasmians and other Saracens upon Our Lord Jesus Christ and upon Christendom. They said their lord also told the king that he should cross into Egypt in the spring to wage war against the sultan of Babylon and that the Mongols would simultaneously launch an attack on the territory of the caliph of Baudas; in this way the two would not be able to give each other aid.

35   The king of France was advised to send his envoys along with the Mongol envoys to their lord Aljighidai and to the sovereign leader of the Mongols, the Great Khan, who was called Gaiouk, in order to confirm the truth of these things. They said it was a full six months' journey to the place where Gaiouk

lived, but that Aljighidai their lord and the Mongolian army were not far away;
40 for they were in Persia, which they had razed to the ground and made
subject to Mongolian rule. They said further that the Mongols were very
well disposed to the king and to Christendom.
When the fortnight of Candlemas came, the Mongol envoys and the king's
envoys, namely Brother Andrew from St. Jacques, and one of his fellow-
brothers, and Master John Goderiche, and another cleric from Poissy, and Herbert
45 le Sommelier, and Gerbert of Sens departed together. And at mid-Lent the
king received the news that they were headed for the Mongol leader,
travelling through pagan territory with banner unfurled, and that they had
what they needed through the fear inspired by the Mongol leader's
envoys.
50 After this the king and his whole fleet, which he estimated at a good 2500
knights, 5000 archers, with a full complement of other foot- and horse-
soldiers, embarked in their ships and sailed up to Limassol and to the other
Cyprus ports on Ascension Day which was on 13 May, en route for the city
of Damietta, which was less than three days away. We were on the sea for
55 twenty-two days and experienced many storms and travails on the water.
The Friday after Trinity around terce we reached Damietta together with a
great part of our fleet, but it was nowhere near full strength. And it was a
good three leagues to the land. The king ordered the fleet to weigh anchor
and immediately summoned all the barons who were there. They all
60 assembled in *Monjoie*, the king's ship, and agreed that they would set out to
capture the territory very early the next morning, their enemies
notwithstanding if they dared to stand in their way. It was ordered that all
the galleys and small vessels of the fleet be made ready and that all who
could embark should do so very early the next morning. It was duly announced that
65 each man should be shriven, should prepare himself, and should make his
will, readying his affairs for death if such was the will of Our Lord Jesus
Christ.
Early the next morning the king heard the service of Our Lord and
the kind of mass that is celebrated at sea, and he armed himself and ordered
all to arm themselves and get into the small vessels. The king got into
70 a Normandy barge and we, our companions, and the legate got in with
him; and he held the True Cross and blessed the armed men who
had got into the little vessels to take possession of the land. The king got
Sir John of Beaumont, Matthew of Marly, and Geoffroy of Sargines to enter
75 the longboat, and he had the gonfalon of St. Denis placed with them. That
barge was in front and all the other vessels fell in after it, following the

gonfalon. The barge containing the king and the legate beside him, holding
the True Cross, and us, stayed at the back.

When we came within crossbow range of the shore, a large number of Turks
80 on foot, on horseback, and fully armed faced us on the shore and
shot rains of arrows at us as did we at them. When we came close to
land, a good two thousand Turks who were there on horseback and many
foot-soldiers plunged forward into the sea to attack our men. When our
men, fully armed in their ships, even the horsemen, saw this, they paid no
85 attention to following the gonfalon of St. Denis, but, armed as they were,
went into the sea, one up to his armpits, another up to his chest, some
deeper, some shallower, depending whether the sea was deeper in one place
than in another. There were a lot of our men who, with great danger,
suffering, and acts of bravery, dragged their horses out of the vessels
90 where they were. Then our archers got into the fray, shooting so hard and
fast that it was marvelous to see. Then our troops came to the land and
seized it.

When the Turks saw this, they rallied and parleyed in their language, and
95 came at our men so hard and so fiercely that it seemed they would kill and
cut down all of them. But our men did not budge from the shore, instead
they fought so energetically that it seemed they had not gone through
confinements or travails or sea-sickness, by the power of Jesus Christ
and of the holy True Cross, which the legate held up high above his head against
the pagans.
100 When the king saw the others leaping down into the sea, he wanted to go
down with them. But they tried to stop him; nevertheless he descended
against their will, and went into the sea waist-deep, and all of us went with
him. And after the king had gone down into the water, the battle lasted a
long while. When the battle had gone on by sea and by land from early
105 morning until midday, the Turks retreated and went into the city of
Damietta. The king stayed on the shore with the Christian army. In this
battle there were few if any Christians lost; on the Turkish side there were
up to five hundred lost plus many of their horses. Four emirs were killed there.
The king who had led the battle in which the counts of Bar and of Montfort
110 were defeated near Gaza was killed in this battle. He was reputedly the
most important lord of all Egypt after the sultan, a good soldier, brave, and
expert in war.

The next day, which was the Sunday after the octaves of Pentecost, in the
morning, a Saracen came to the king and said that all the Saracens had left
115 the city of Damietta, they could hang him if this was untrue. The king put

him under guard and sent to ascertain the truth. Before none, the certain
news came to the king that very many of our men were already in Damietta
and the king's gonfalon was atop a high tower. When our men heard this,
they energetically gave praise to Our Lord, thanking him for
120 the great bounty he had shown to the Christians; for the city of Damietta
was so fortified with walls, ditches, an abundance of strong, high
towers, hoardings, and barbicans, an abundance of machines, arms, and
provisions, and whatever was necessary to fortify a town that it would be
difficult to imagine it could be captured without exceedingly great effort,
125 travail, and manpower. Our men found it well supplied with all necessities.
In prison they found fifty-three Christian slaves who had been inside there, it
was said, twenty-two years. They were delivered and brought to the king.
And they said that the Saracens had fled that Saturday before, during the
130 night, and that the Saracens were saying to one another that "the pigs had
come." They found there also I do not know how many Syrian Christians
who were living in there in subjection to the Saracens. When they saw
the Christians entering the town, they took up crosses and wore them
and in this way had no fear. They were allowed to keep their houses
and what they had inside them, after they had spoken to the king and to the
legate.
135 The king and the army left their quarters and moved in front of the city of
Damietta. The day after the feast of St. Barnabas the apostle, the king
entered first into Damietta and dismantled the main mosque of the town as
well as all the others, turning them into churches dedicated to the glory of
Jesus Christ.
We think we shan't be moving from this city until All Saints' Day on
140 account of the swelling of the river of Paradise that flows there, called the
Nile; for one cannot go to Alexandria, Babylon, or Cairo when it has spread
over the land of Egypt. And it is not likely to subside before then, they say.
Realize that we know nothing of the sultan of Babylon, but the king has
145 been given to understand that other sultans are waging war against him.
And rest assured that since God delivered over the city to us, only Bedouin
Saracens, who sometimes come within two leagues of the army, have been
seen near the camp. And when our archers go to shoot at them, they flee.
These same people come outside the camp at night to steal horses and
150 human heads. And it is said that the sultan gives ten bezants for every
Christian head brought to him. And the Bedouin Saracens were said to cut
off in this manner the heads of hangèd men, and to dig up bodies that had

been buried in the ground to have their heads to carry to the sultan. A
Bedouin Saracen who came all alone was captured there, and is still being
155 held for it. These thefts were easily carried out, for although the king has
within Damietta city his wife the queen and some of his arms and equipment
in the palace and the sultan of Babylon's strongholds; and the legate has his
equipment in the halls and the strongholds of the king who was killed in
the battle when we came to shore; and each of the barons also has in the city
160 of Damietta a great, fine lodging appropriate to his needs, nevertheless
the Christian army and the king and the legate are quartered outside the town.
Because of those thefts that the Bedouin Saracens were committing, the
Christians have begun to make good, deep, wide ditches around the army;
but they are not yet finished.
So Our Lord Jesus Christ in his mercy delivered the noble, the very
165 powerful city of Damietta over to Christendom in 1249, the Sunday after
the octaves of Pentecost, that is the sixth day of the month of June, which that
year was on Sunday.
This was thirty years after the Christians had won it with great labors and
efforts against the Saracens and lost it again within that very year when
170 they went to besiege Cairo, and the river became swollen and flooded
around them so that they could not go forward or back. On this account we
think that the army must not move from Damietta until the river has fallen
and returned within its banks. Make this letter known to all our friends.
175 This letter was drawn up in the city of Damietta on the vigil of the feast of
St. John the Baptist, this very month.)

The letter begins with the briefest and simplest of formalities:
the name of addressee ("seigneur Nicolas Arrode"), addressor
plus rank ("Jehans Sarrazins, chambrelens le roy de France"),
then the conventional salutation "salus et bonne amour." Nicolas
was not, in fact, the only person for whom the letter was intended. He is directed by Jean (lines 173-74) to share the letter
with their friends, a valuable confirmation of what one might log-
ically have surmised: that the composition and despatch of a vernacular communication from a newly captured city in Egypt was
no small undertaking. It deserved to be shared among several
recipients, and for them a thoughtful selection of details would be
made to supplement the immediately urgent news.

In 1249 the most urgent news item for the *seigneurs de Paris*

145

was undoubtedly the safe arrival of the royal party inside Damietta, and that news is therefore conveyed (2-6) with telegraphic conciseness:

> I inform you that the king and queen, the count of Artois, and the count of Anjou and his wife, and I rejoice in being inside the city of Damietta which God by his miracle, mercy, and grace restored to Christendom on the Sunday of the second week after Pentecost.

The phrases "par son miracle, par sa misericorde et par sa pitié" should not be dismissed as mere formulae. Through them Jean's friends would understand the astonished relief of the crusading army at their easy capture of Damietta. Meaningful within their context, they are made poignant now by the faith and expectation they reveal.

Jean's dating of the momentous event by "le dimenche de la quinsainne de Pentecouste," while abbreviated, is appropriate in a letter addressed to friends. Jean assumes that certain information, including the year of his departure, will already be known. He therefore makes no formal mention of it even in the place where it would be customary, at the letter's end: "Ces lettres furent faites en la cité de Damiete, la vegile de la nativité monseigneur saint Jehan Baptiste, qui fu ce mois meismes." One has only to compare the carefully situated opening of Villehardouin's *La Conquête de Constantinople*[4] to perceive that Jean's intentions are less than cosmic. Chronicler and letter-writer may have shared subject-matter and style, but the immediate public was different.

Jean now explains unpretentiously how his letter will proceed: "And now I tell you how this came about" (7). For the narration he employs the simplest and most common of all introductions: "il avint que" (it happened that). For Jean the happenings of the Crusade began with his own departure.[5] He reports that he left with the royal party from Aigues-Mortes on the feast of St. Augustine (23 August). They arrived at the island of Cyprus fifteen days before the feast of St. Lambert (17 September). His dating may be by feast-days, but hagiographic considerations play no part in the selection and reporting of the facts. The matter-of-fact royal chamberlain provides a valuable corrective, both substantively and psychologically, to Joinville's biography/hagiography. He notes without fanfare that it was the count of Anjou who was first to disembark at Limassol (11-12). The king and the rest of the royal party disembarked early the next morning, and the count of Artois around the hour of terce.

At this point a subject emerges that is outside Jean's personal experience but is nevertheless reported at unusual length (17-49). The digression, if one is to call it that, is triggered by the statement "Nous fusmes en cele isle a mout pou de gent, et sejournasmes iluec jusques a l'Ascension pour atendre l'estoire qui n'estoit mie venue." The waiting time was actually a very long one for a fleet wintering over: 17 September 1248 to 30 May 1249. Is it possible that the chamberlain wished to provide some explanation for the long "winter" in Cyprus by the king's negotiations with the Mongols? Alfred Foulet even suggests that the whole letter may have served as an information bulletin from the king, who wished to keep his subjects informed on overseas events: "Il est possible que le roi ait voulu tenir au courant des affaires d'Outremer tous ceux qui avaient part à l'administration de son royaume."[6] For whatever reason, the second occurrence of that innocuous phrase "il avint que" (17) launches the letter into a sequence of events that is outside Jean's original chronology.

"It happened that"[7] the Christmas before emissaries were sent to Louis at Nicosia by the Mongol general Aljighidai (Jean's rendering of his name is "Eltetay," "Etheltay," or "Eltheltay"). These Mongol emissaries spoke first with the king's representative, the Dominican friar Andrew of Longjumeau. They then spoke through an interpreter to the king at Limassol, expressed sympathy with his crusading ideals, and promised support in the spring when he sailed against the sultan Ayub.

Their support never came, of course. Any sympathy that the Mongols may have had for Louis's cause evaporated with the death of their influential general Aljighidai. Perhaps our knowledge that the negotiations would prove abortive makes this section of Jean's letter seem disproportionately long. It is important not to assess it merely as royal propaganda for that reason, however. The subject of the Mongols had an intrinsic fascination, and decades later Joinville would remember details of it. For Jean's friends in Paris the report of those optimistic envoy-interpreters on their way to the Great Khan himself must have generated almost as much excitement as Damietta's capture! And if Louis had needed justification for the Cyprus wintering, there were more convincing arguments, which Jean does not think to mention. The Grand Masters of the Hospitallers and the Templars, as well as the Syrian barons, had perhaps been responsible for Louis's decision, since they had strongly urged him not to hazard his fleet against the winter storms. As the Templar of Tyr records,

> Le roy Henry de Chipre et les autres seignors de Yblin la
> refurent à mout grant henour et à mout grant joie, et demoura
> en Chipre tout sel yver, et vindrent d'Acre au leur ostel les
> maistres dou Tempel et de l'Ospitau, et chevaliers et autres
> gens, et en Chipre conseillierent et ordenerent de passer au
> primtens en Egipte.[8]

> (King Henry of Cyprus and the other lords of Ibelin were there
> in full honor and rejoicing, and he remained in Cyprus all that
> winter; and the Masters of the Temple and the Hospital,
> knights and others, came from Acre to their place of lodging,
> and in Cyprus advised and ordered a spring crossing to Egypt.)

Disappointingly for the army, the envoys were still travelling by the middle of Lent and had no definitive news to report. Louis therefore decided to move the whole fleet from Limassol at last.

The end of the Mongol explanation is signalled by the vaguely chronological phrase "aprés ces choses" (50). From this point onward the letter narrates salient events in strict sequence. Jean dates the departure from Limassol both by feast-day ("le jour de l'Ascension") and by day of the month ("le tresieme jour de may"), perhaps seeing symbolism in the former and historical importance in the latter.

He is tersely reticent about the journey, although twenty-two days of storms and travails suggest that it was eventful. He merely says, "Nous fumes sus mer vint et deus jours, et moult eumes de contraires et de travaus en la mer" (55-56). Such brief mention of an established topos, the storm at sea, proved an irresistible temptation to one of the scribes of the Rothelin continuation. Seven of its thirteen manuscripts supplement Jean's letter with a long interpolation at this point.[9] The borrowed material is repeatedly labelled as extraneous with the phrases "es autrez livrez ancienz"[10] (in the other ancient books), "aucunz dient"[11] (some say), "l'en treuve en escripture"[12] (we find in writing), and, more specifically, "en un livre que l'en apele Cesar, treuve l'en des perilz"[13] (in a book called *Caesar*, we find an account of the perils). The interpolation must be judged unfortunate. Legendary ocean hazards like Charybdis, Mt. Aetna, and the sirens may conceivably have contributed to the fears of the crusaders but had no other possible relevance.

They are not unimportant in their implications, however. They demonstrate, for example, that there was such affinity between the styles of a vernacular letter and a vernacular translation of classical *auctores* that the two could be juxtaposed. The compiler's courteous invitation to his readers that they skip the interpolation at will is informative:

> Mes pour ce que les genz des terrez qui sont loingtaingnes
> de la mer se merveillent quant il oient parler des tempestes et
> des perilz qui sont en mer, et des manierez diversez de serpenz
> et de bestes, et de monstres des deserz qui la repairent, et de la
> nature dou flun de Nil, qui chiet en mer par .III. mestrez channiex
> desouz Egypte, nous laironz .I. pou a conter et a dire nostre estoire,
> et dironz de ces choses, tout ausint comme nous avonz trouvé es
> autrez livrez ancienz.
> Cil qui de ce oir n'auront cure porront trespasser cestui leu et
> retorner a l'estoire que nous conterons ci aprez ces choses.[14]
>
> (But because people who live in lands far
> from the sea marvel when they hear about storms and
> perils of the sea, and about the different kinds of serpents,

beasts, and monsters dwelling in the desert, and about
the nature of the river Nile, which goes down to the sea by three main channels
below Egypt, we shall suspend the telling of our narration for a while
and shall tell of these matters, just as we have found them
in the other ancient books.
Those who have no desire to hear this will be able to skip this part and
return to the history we shall be telling after these matters.)

For the compiler the concept of authority, a necessary validation for "estoire," has shifted from the traditional "li livre"[15] to a single vernacular document: Jean's letter. Sources that would have had precedence as authoritative previously ("l'escripture," "livrez ancienz," "un livre que l'en apele Cesar") are three times presented as dispensable, subservient both in interest and in importance to "l'estoire" of Jean's 1249 newsletter to his friends in Paris. Thus, with the instruction "Mes or retornons a conter de nostre estoire que nous avionz devant lessié,"[16] the seven aberrant manuscripts of the Rothelin continuation return to Jean's text.

Jean reports that "le vendredi aprés la Trinité" (i.e., 4 June) "entor tierce, venismes devant Damiete" (57). His information is a useful corrective to Joinville's account, which misrepresents the day of the crusaders' arrival as Thursday, 27 May.[17] Joinville has some advantages through hindsight, however. He knows the reasons for the non-arrival of many ships:

> Un vent grief et fort qui venoit devers Egypte, leva en tel maniere que de deux mille et huit cens chevaliers que le roy mena en Egypte, ne l'en demoura que sept cens que le vent ne les eust dessevrés de la compaignie le roy, et menez en Acre et en autres terres estranges, qui puis ne revindrent au roy de grant piece.[18]

> (There arose, coming from the direction of Egypt, a wind so violent that out of 2800 knights whom the king took to Egypt there remained only 700 whom the wind did not separate from the king's company and take to Acre and other foreign lands; and they returned to the king only long afterward.)

Jean was too close to the events to know the whereabouts of the non-arrivals. His statement about them is therefore vague, yet it is non-alarmist (presumably out of consideration for the friends and relatives to whom his letter would be circulated): "venismes devant Damiete et grant partie de nostre estoire avecques nous, mais ele n'i estoit mie toute assez" (57-58).

His narration of the crusaders' dawn landing is, however, admirably specific. A full three leagues separated the boats from the land: "bien avoit trois lieues jusques a terre." (As usual in Jean's economical style, the adverb is weighted with significance.) This simple piece of information defines the physical and psychological barrier confronting the Christians and gives clarity and structure to the narrative. Since Joinville nowhere supplies this rudimentary fact, *his* description is impressionistically chaotic[19] by comparison with the chamberlain's.

The next sixty-one lines of the letter (57-118) summarize the events leading up to the capture of the city. Jean combines overview with an appreciation for individual detail. Adverbs are again used with significance, conveying the rain of Turkish arrows ("traissent a nous mout *espessement*" [81]) and the crusaders' returning fire ("Adonques s'esforcierent nostre arbalestrier et traisent si *durement* et si *espessement* que c'estoit merveilles a veoir" [90-92]).

The varying depth of the water is graphically conveyed to those at home by noting the degree of submersion of the wading crusaders: "alerent en la mer a pié tout armé, li uns jusques as aisseles, li autres jusques as mameles, li uns plus en parfont et li autre mains, selonc ce que la mers estoit plus parfonde en un lieu que en un autre" (85-88). Jean also registers from his view aboard the *Monjoie* the hasty consultation of the Turks as they concoct an emergency plan of action. He is obviously close enough to hear their incomprehensible words: "Quant li Turc virent ce, si se ralierent ensamble et parlerent en leur langage" (93-94).

As a member of the royal household, and one who was close to Louis much of the time, Jean monitors the king's actions with particular concern—but without hagiographic intent. While Join-ville saw Louis's landing at Damietta as the first demonstration of his saintly will to sacrifice his person,[20] Jean reports only that the king followed the others into the water against all advice (100-02). This efficient royal chamberlain, who would soon be a financial controller in Paris, supplies an admirable account of all salient details, exemplifying the best aspects of administrative prose. Even the marshal Geoffrey de Villehardouin, his closest counterpart in temperament and occupation, resorted to heroic stylistic devices in moments of high drama.[21] Jean does not swerve from the consistency of past-tense usage for past events.

His news becomes more summary after the Turks' surrender—there has been little time as yet to achieve much beyond giving thanks (119-20), entering the city to deliver prisoners (129-32), and reconsecrating the churches (136-38). Obviously the city's plunder had not been distributed yet or our good administrator would have mentioned it to his friends.[22] But he notes for their benefit that the crusaders were happy to find the city well fortified and well supplied (121-26). The sentence "Moult le trouverent nos gens bien garniee de quanque mestier estoit" would be particularly reassuring when *another* winter abroad might be pending.

And now with easy naturalness the letter returns (139) to present time and to surmise about the future. Anticipating questions his friends may be asking, Jean says, "We think we shan't be moving from this city until All Saints' Day." Concerning the army's present safety in an unknown city, he is understandably anxious but cautiously reassuring. The crusaders are uncertain of the neighboring territories but have so far experienced only a few Bedouin raids. Happily, the Bedouins' purpose was not attack but rather the collection of severed heads for bounty. The army has begun to construct good, deep, wide trenches for protection—the occurrence of three consecutive adjectives in "*bons* fossez, *parfons* et *larges*" is unusual in Jean's style! "Mais il ne sont mie encore parfais" (163). Those seven simple words reflect better than any elaborate explanation the underlying fears of an untried army camping in unknown territory.

Jean immediately recalls the letter to a more positive note. A simple recapitulatory summary of their achievement (164-67) is followed by an explanation of the hazards that might threaten it (168-71). The decision to heed past experience and to wait until the Nile's floodwaters should recede was certain to meet with the approval of the prudent *seigneurs de Paris*. And if the final sentence of the letter, "Faites savoir ces lettres a touz nos amis" (173-74) *could* be interpreted as Louis's command, it could just as readily be the expression of Jean's own thoughts. Letter-writers of any age sign off with just such farewells.

It is fortunate that the Rothelin continuator chose to retain Jean's notation of the place and date of writing below the letter. The formulaic phrases underline the unique contribution of this unusual document, frozen in time at that ephemeral moment when the Seventh Crusade was surprised by victory and looked forward cautiously to the ultimate triumph of Christendom.[23]

NOTES

[1]*Continuation de Guillaume de Tyr de 1229 à 1261, dite du manuscrit de Rothelin*, in *Recueil des historiens de croisades, Historiens occidentaux*, vol. 2 (Paris, 1859), pp. 484-639.

[2]*RHC Hist. occ.* 2:568. It should be noted that for the text of the letter itself I have preferred Alfred L. Foulet's edited version, *Lettres françaises du XIIIe siècle* (Paris, 1924), pp. 1-8 (hereafter, *Lettres*), with one change: I have eliminated Foulet's numbered paragraphs, which he justified as follows: "Pour plus de commodité, nous avons réparti notre texte en paragraphes" (p. 10). They are less convenient for our purposes, and, more important, they obscure the epistolary nature of the original.

[3]All translations in this essay are my own.

[4]"Sachiez que .M. et .C. et quatre vinz et .XVII. anz aprés l'incarnation Nostre Sengnor Jesu Crist, al tens Innocent, apostoille de Rome, et Phelippe, roy de France, et Ricchart, roy d'Engleterre, ot un saint home en France, qui ot

nom Folques de Nuilli (cil Nuillis si est entre Ligni sor Marne e Paris) et il ere prestres et tenoit la parroiche de la ville," p. 2.

[5]Fulk of Neuilly's inspirational preaching was the beginning point of Ville-hardouin's narrative of the Fourth Crusade (see n. 4 above).

[6]*Lettres*, p. vii.

[7]Similar usage of "il avint que" is seen in the unpretentious chronicling of Robert de Clari, where narrative interest often dominated chronology. See Jeanette Beer, "The Notion of Temporality in Early Vernacular History," *New Zealand Journal of French Studies* 1 (1987): 5-15.

[8]*Chronique du Templier de Tyr*, in *Les Gestes des Chiprois*, ed. Gaston Raynaud (Geneva, 1887), p. 147.

[9]For further details of the interpolation's sources see Louis-Ferdinand Flutre, *Li Fait des Romains dans les littératures française et italienne du XIII*[e] *au XVI*[e] *siècle* (Paris, 1932), pp. 3-5.

[10]*RHC Hist. occ.* 2:571.

[11]*RHC Hist. occ.* 2:572.

[12]*RHC Hist. occ.* 2:572.

[13]*RHC Hist. occ.* 2:573.

[14]*RHC Hist. occ.* 2:571.

[15]For formulaic appeals to "li livre" in the surprising context of Ville-hardouin's eyewitness chronicling of a crusade see Jeanette Beer, "Villehardouin and the Oral Narrative," *Studies in Philology* 67/3 (July 1970): 276-77.

[16]*RHC Hist. occ.* 2:589.

[17]"Le jeudi aprés Penthecouste ariva le roy devant Damiete," *Vie de saint Louis*, ed. Noel L. Corbett (Quebec, 1977), para. 148.

[18]*Vie de saint Louis*, para. 147.

[19]See *Vie de saint Louis*, paras. 150-65.

[20]"Le premier fait la ou il mist son cors en avanture de mort, ce fu a l'ariver que nous feimes devant Damiete," *Vie de saint Louis*, para. 7.

[21]See Jeanette Beer, *Villehardouin–Epic Historian* (Geneva, 1968), pp. 31-56.

[22]Cf. Villehardouin, *La Conquête de Constantinople*, ed. Edmond Faral (Paris, 1938), paras. 254-55; Robert de Clari, *La Conquête de Constantinople*, ed. Philippe Lauer (Paris, 1924), para. 81.

[23]This essay is part of a chapter entitled "Letters in the Vernacular" in my book *Early Prose in France* (forthcoming from Medieval Institute Publications).

CRUSADE PROPAGANDA IN THE

EPIC CYCLES OF THE CRUSADE

Robert Francis Cook

Two lengthy and complex series of medieval French *chansons de geste* have the First and Third Crusades as their subject. Not all of the poems in these cycles actually claim to show events in the Holy Land, but among them the late-twelfth-century *Chanson d'Antioche*, the later *Chanson de Jérusalem*, and their continuations and revivals of the thirteenth and fourteenth centuries all purport to tell the tale of the armed pilgrimage from the time of Peter the Hermit to that of Saladin. In their most developed forms the Crusade Cycles run to over sixty thousand lines of rhymed formulaic verse, a number that may equally well either intrigue or horrify the curious medievalist.[1]

Like all literary cycles, these cycles tell a story, that of the early Crusades, with numerous additions and subtractions; but that is not their only purpose, and not necessarily their primary one. The story told, even in the latest and putatively most bastardized forms, is exemplary. The audience is called upon to admire the great personages whose tale it is hearing, and perhaps to emulate them. The form of the appeal is both direct and indirect, as I shall demonstrate.

The two Cycles of the Crusade offer an unusual combination of elements both to historians of ideas and to literary historians. On the one hand, they describe some of the most important events in the history of Christendom. On the other hand, they are indeed epics (at least in the form we have), and not chronicles, memoirs, or battlefield despatches. They apply the literary techniques of the *chanson de geste* to events for which we have information from other sources. Such information is usually not available for the epic, or is so scanty it cannot be used for many of the purposes we should like. Furthermore, it is rare for cycles of popular literature to take actual events as their subjects. The crusade epics give us a sense of what the European public counted as worthy of emphasis in the crusading story. Often something more than emphasis is involved, for this is essentially the story of a mighty and un-blemished past.

In an earlier study on the *Chanson d'Antioche*, I have treated the phenomena of epic exaggeration and simplification—the ap-pearance in literature of events and characters known to be in some sense historical, yet transformed by the myth-making machinery of topos and motif.[2] As the waffling of the preceding sentence shows, the subject inspires profound thoughts about the relationship be-tween the *chanson de geste* and history. That topic is, of course, too broad to treat here. I should like to concentrate instead on one of its aspects: my subject is the epic treatment of the Crusade—with its larger-than-life participants—as a myth of unity and success.

The style and spirit of the medieval French epic are ideally suited to the recounting of ancient deeds that are thought to be, first of all, heroic, and also essential to the definition of a religious or social community. The *chanson de geste*, whatever its subject matter, is in large part a song of combat and struggle; it presents a world of contrasts, between the honorable and the dishonorable, the followers of the True Faith and the infidels, the proper leader and the weak or inadequate one, that has long been recognized among literary scholars as mirroring the ideological world of the crusader. The rhetoric of formula and enumeration, the motifs of council, battle, and strategy, are well suited to the task of conveying the ideals of the holy warrior. Epic singlemindedness is not an attitude we associate with proper historiography, but the twelfth century had other ideas of what is proper, and a great deal of epic style and substance is in fact shared by the chroniclers, as Louis Bréhier has noted for the *Gesta francorum*, for example, or as Cola Minis has shown in some detail for Albert of Aachen.[3] It is all the more surprising, then, to discover that such recent studies of the crusading mentality as Paul Rousset's *Histoire d'une idéologie: La croisade* or Lothar Struss's *Epische Idealität und Historische Realität* contain no discussion of popular crusade narratives.[4]

Hence a few words of background may be in order. First, the crusade epics had an unusually long life, of over two hundred years. The oldest element in the oldest, or First Crusade Cycle is, as usual, the central part of the narrative, the section describing the preparations for the expedition of 1096 and the crusaders' first great victory, the taking of Antioch. The composition of this "branch," the *Chanson d'Antioche* as we know it, dates from the latter part of the twelfth century. The time lag implies ideological connections between the Third Crusade and the epic poems about the First. Let me note at once that we do not have to have a precise date for any of the works under discussion if we grant (with Rousset and others) that the crusading movement was a phenomenon of long duration, not a punctual phenomenon or series of them. We are not required to place the *Chanson d'Antioche* precisely in 1187 or 1190 in order to consider that it probably served a propaganda effort that was nearly continuous, despite obvious ebbs and flows of interest.

This relationship is borne out by study of the last poems of the last (or Second) Crusade Cycle, which is in large part a reworking of the First, and also contains many thousands of lines of new material on such imaginary characters as Baudouin de Sebourc (third king of Jerusalem in the epic succession) and the Bâtard de

Bouillon (an imaginary child of Baldwin I). These works apparently date from the period 1330-50, were probably still being revised in the 1360s and 70s, and were copied and read as late as the sixteenth century. Thus they are contemporary with the great age of crusading propaganda, and they are also among the last poems written in *chanson de geste* form.

We commonly say that the Crusades were over by the time the Hundred Years' War began, but that was not, of course, the opinion of contemporaries.[5] Crusade propaganda in the fourteenth century began with Philip the Fair's campaign of pamphlets, partly orchestrated from Avignon by Clement V. Philip VI of France took the cross in 1332, John the Good in 1363; Philippe de Mézières urged Richard II of England to join Charles VI in doing so as late as 1390. There was a much-heralded attack on Alexandria in 1365 (though few Northern Europeans took part, apparently), and even the disaster of Nicopolis in 1396 could not have taken place without a fairly large number of people who had once intended their expedition to be a success. Hence the impulse to argue that the motivation for making and remaking crusade epics was from first to last bound up with the need to stir crusading fervor in the West.

Between the date of composition of the oldest poems of the Cycles and that of the most recent there stretches a series of some thirteen different texts, created in fits and starts throughout the late twelfth, the thirteenth, and the early fourteenth centuries, and thematically concentric around the Antioch poem. The Cycles include in particular an interesting retelling of the Swan Knight legend that makes the Swan Knight a progenitor of the house of Bouillon. Lohengrin indeed takes his name from Lotharingia, that Lorraine that was once in part Godfrey of Bouillon's fief, and the legend supports the notion that the great crusader was a man of extraordinary lineage.

In order to understand the place of these texts in the history of the crusade movement it is important to keep in mind two points about them. First, they were not made by or for crusaders, and they show no signs of any links with the Holy Land, despite the persistence of scholarly references to that will-o'-the-wisp Richard the Pilgrim.[6] The preserved crusade epics were written in France and Flanders to communicate with a European audience a century or more after the fact. None of them shows any sign of reflecting any direct experience of the authors'.

Second, it follows that these works are genuinely epic in nature. Their style, their narrative procedures, and the attitudes they reveal make it impossible to confuse them with chronicles, in the last analysis. Rather, they are literary works, offering material drawn from chronicles, from local traditions, and just possibly from lost earlier poems, with epic convention as the usual vehicle of that material. The crusade epics exploit widely used, generically specific themes and techniques to exalt crusader activity, in precisely the way the epic usually exalts the heroic past for the sake of a later audience. Further, they carry on the *chanson de geste* tradition of the narrator's commentary, the only explicitly hortatory element in their rhetoric.

In poems with historical pretensions, the most striking among epic characteristics surely are the tendency to exaggeration and the concomitant simplification and ideological purification of events. These are texts that place a value on action—indeed a notable proportion of the *Antioche* text is combat for its own sake, even when the eyewitness chroniclers mention no combat. Every battle—and there is an astounding quantity of them—is hard fought; most involve great numbers, and all lead to victory for the cause of Christianity. Epic crusaders are invariably devout pilgrims as well as superb fighters, except when their transgressions are temporarily referred to (as they are in the chronicles also) as being God's reason for delaying their ultimate successes.[7] It is not surprising, then, that the historically ambiguous circumstances of the discovery of the Holy Lance at Antioch, for example, are presented in the Crusade Cycles as clear and unequivocal, as a sign of approval from God.

The atmosphere of pious violence thus created is familiar to anyone who has read, for instance, the *Song of Roland*. It is supported and strengthened by motifs found elsewhere in literature, such as the conversion of Saracen worthies or the love of a Saracen maiden for a hardy crusader (a regular occurrence in the later texts), not to mention topics of divine intervention, such as the presence of combatant saints on the field of battle (the latter being one of numerous traits shared with the early crusade chronicles).

The process of exaggeration, with its concomitant simplification, is applied to crusaders and future crusaders of various degrees of social prominence—not only Godfrey of Bouillon and Stephen of Blois, Bohemond and Tancred but also Thomas of Marle, Renaud Porchet, and Enguerrand of Saint-Pol. Numerous imaginary or untraceable characters soon appear—Richard of Chaumont, Raimbaut Creton, Baldwin of Beauvais—and they are treated in the same way as are the well-known leaders, as single-minded and exalted heroes of incredible prowess. There are occasional human-interest vignettes even in the oldest texts. For example, during the siege of Antioch the friends of a certain Evervin of Creil (not otherwise known) decide in his absence to roast his faithful donkey, this emergency measure being dictated by a general famine on the eve of the great battle against Kerbogha. When the stout-hearted Evervin discovers this, he sits down to enjoy supper with the rest, stating in good soldierly fashion that whether the morrow's battle be won or lost he will not be needing the donkey any more.

Finally, in a classic case of epic wish-fulfillment and aggrandizement, the greatest warriors of Islam, Kerbogha, Toghtekin of Damascus, Saladin, the imaginary Abilant, and their sisters and fiancées are converted to the Christian cause, take up western ways, and share their conquerors' adventures. Their relationships with the crusaders tend both to magnify the power of the Christian faith and (thanks to the women) to suggest the potential for secular forms of conquest.

The career lent Godfrey of Bouillon in the epic tales gives what is no doubt the clearest illustration of these mechanisms at work. The powerful image of Godfrey is the most striking of all mythical exaggerations in the Cycles. The historical *advocatus sancti Sepulcri* played a vital role in the capture and government of Jerusalem in 1096-97, of that there is no doubt. But the epic Godfrey has instead of a crusader's career the career of a literary Charlemagne, wound about with presages and portents. Long before the First Crusade, in an episode called *The Return of Cornumarant*, he meets the Saracen king of Jerusalem, his future enemy, whose city he is, of course, destined to capture. Cornumarant has come to the West in disguise, hoping to assassinate Godfrey, at the urging of a soothsayer who has predicted the Crusades to him. Later, at Constantinople, when the First Crusade takes on formal shape, Godfrey is immediately elected by his fellow pilgrims to be their supreme leader. His battlefield adventures are numerous, including a courageous stand made alone at Antioch against a horde of enemies. Godfrey becomes the first crusader king of Jerusalem when that city is taken, and he marries the sister of his enemy Kerbogha, who has been converted to Christianity. He dies the victim of poison given him by the jealous patriarch Heraclius. His standard is taken up by his brother Baldwin as a matter of right.

None of this (and there is much more) corresponds to what we know about Godfrey's career. In every case it crystallizes the crusading idea around his person by exaggerating his singularity and importance. He was never king of Jerusalem, any more than he was the grandson of the Swan Knight. He never married, and Kerbogha never converted; and although there is no way of proving that Godfrey was not poisoned, the overwhelming presumption among historians is that he died of natural causes. In the thirteenth-century continuations of the *Chanson de Jérusalem*, however, his romanticized death, besides rationalizing his loss through the application of a motif, comes to fit a scheme of explanation that accounts in entirely unhistorical fashion for the collapse of the crusader kingdoms. Like Camelot, Outremer succumbs to internal strife and not to the enemy, for Godfrey's unfortunate queen, Florie, and Tancred, the queen's lover, are accused of murdering him; Tancred is eventually put to death by Godfrey's family; and the men of his lineage enter into civil war with the Bouillonnais in the East, thus weakening the crusaders and allowing the victory of Saladin over the forces of the Cross.

These elements of magnification, here applied to the figure of a single man, have parallels both in the presentation of other individuals and where the entire expedition is concerned. The Antioch material is preceded in the manuscripts by a prologue (paralleled in the chronicle of Albert of Aachen) in which Peter the Hermit visits Jerusalem and in a vision receives direct instructions from Jesus himself concerning the need for an attack on the infidels who are desecrating the Holy Sepulchre (lines 300-20). Thus, in a sense, the entire core of the Crusade Cycle is placed under the sign of God's eternal plan and is presented as expressing divine will.

Among individuals, Saladin himself is subjected to another procedure with similar effects. In the later texts of the Cycle he is presented as being not a full-blooded Kurd or Arab but the half-Arab son of a French Christian woman with cousins in the ranks of the crusaders. In this way the unhappy notion of a victory of the locals over the western invaders of the Holy Land is partly erased from the late forms of the Cycle. This version of history presents narrative challenges that are met in the usual manner: through the application of motifs taken from folklore, romances, or earlier epics. Saladin too visits the West, learns its customs, is made a knight, seduces a queen of France (at least in the Saladin continuation, now known only in prose), and dies a secret Christian.[8] Saladin's secret conversion illustrates the literary procedure of the anonymous epic authors particularly well, for it combines the not-uncommon motif of the debate of Christian, Moslem, and Jew with a disguised self-baptism. Saladin, offered water on his deathbed, shows that the Christian has won the debate he has just heard, for he surreptitiously makes the sign of the cross over the water before using it to wash himself. The theology may be shaky, but the intent to express the inevitable conquest of Islam by Christianity is obvious.

My title thus implies, in a way, a foregone conclusion. The epic transformation of history can always be read as an argument for an ideology, and the crusading mentality has long been associated with the *Chanson de geste*. I do not, nevertheless, mean to claim the status of propaganda for this general atmosphere and set of procedures alone. Of particular interest, in the case of the Crusade Cycles, is the interplay between the action—which epic technique presents as ideal—and the commentary on that action in narratorial interventions. The action and the characters of the participants serve as a setting that predisposes the hearers to give assent to the recitant's propositions about crusading and its rewards. In these overt claims (some of which I have reproduced in the Appendix below), the exemplary nature of the literary crusade serves to support an explicit invitation to imitate the early crusaders.

Again, these narratorial interventions do not occur frequently, and they seem to be absent from certain texts or branches of the Cycle. For example, I have found none in those prologues concerning the founding of the house of Bouillon (*Chevalier au Cygne, Enfances Godefroi*) and none in those continuations where the influence of the chroniclers is strongly felt. There seem to be no exhortations to speak of in either the romantic tale of the *Chétifs* or in the *Chrétienté Corbaran*. Precise information on the *Chanson de Jérusalem* will have to await the appearance of Thorp's edition. There remains a sporadic but fairly traditional form of direct address to the audience that is remarkable for occurring in both the oldest text of the two Cycles, the *Antioche*, and in two of the newest, *Baudouin de Sebourc* and the *Bâtard de Bouillon*. The texts I have reproduced will give an idea of how the narrator in these texts refers to the ideal he is promoting.

The first six come from *Antioche*, the next two from the *Bâtard*, and the last two from *Baudouin de Sebourc*. They state as fact (I.24-27) that the efforts of the historical crusaders bought them places in Heaven (see also examples III.118-20, VII, and X).

They describe the Crusade as being every Christian's duty (text II). The third excerpt presents the fanciful notion that harmony and fair dealing prevailed among the crusaders—a literary purification of an often sordid reality. The fourth claims that God himself orders the violent destruction of the Arabs of Palestine. The fifth occurs as the Frankish army suffers famine during a countersiege before Antioch. It puts into the mouth of Godfrey of Bouillon a harangue that not only promises God's protection to those who are his warriors on earth but incorporates for good measure a reference to the legendary floating tomb of Mohammed at Mecca, which Godfrey promises to capture (a promise made good by his brother in the later Cycle).

The effect of any direct address, one taking of a rhetorical stance different from that of the narration itself, was certainly strong. After all, the epic recitant made his living by exhorting the audience to close attention and adequate payment. The sixth example from *Antioche* plays on this convention: don't pay me if you don't want to, says the recitant, but whatever you do, don't forget the inimitable valor of the crusaders!

The fourteenth-century examples are remarkably similar. Text VIII compares the travails of the crusaders with the soft and thoughtless life led by the many who stay behind, and again (as did I, III, and VII) offers Paradise as a reward to the steadfast. A curious example from *Baudouin de Sebourc* (IX) specifies terms for God's bargain with the crusader: Arnold of Nijmegen expects to save precisely three souls by undertaking the armed pilgrimage, and he may choose which ones. When he is about to die (X) the same man explicitly states the martyr's credo that is part and parcel of the Christian warrior's death in battle from the *Song of Roland* and the William Cycle onward; here it echoes the general rule given in examples I, III, and VII.

We are clearly dealing with a popularized and rather unrefined concept of Holy War. The mechanisms of literature, specifically the pre-existing and entirely apposite techniques of epic, here work to tell a story that exalts the values and interests of western culture at the expense of a complicated crusading reality. It is easy to see, for example, why the somewhat embarrassing Second Crusade is passed over almost entirely in the epics, while the glorious First Crusade is recounted with enthusiasm even in the age of the Seventh and Eighth. To conclude, I repeat briefly that although historians of the Crusades very rarely mention popular literature, these themes and events, and the atmosphere that gives them their force, are just as important for understanding the history of the crusade idea as are the better-known formal treatises studied with such acuity by Aziz Atiya—those of Raymond Lull (Llull), Philippe de Mézières, Marino Sanudo, and a minor host of others. The poems of the Cycles of the Crusade were copied, sung, and constantly modified over at least three centuries. As long as the crusading idea stayed alive in northern France they constituted an energetic, if unofficial, parallel crusading propaganda, available in a form easily digested by a broad audience.

ROBERT FRANCIS COOK

APPENDIX

(*La Chanson d'Antioche*, ed. Suzanne Duparc-Quioc, vol. 1 [Paris, 1977]; translations are my own.)

I.

Huimais porés oïr de Jhursalem parler	16
Et de cels ki alerent le Sepucre honorer	
Com il firent les os de partout assambler:	
De France et de Berriu et d'Auvergne se per,	
De Pulle et de Calabre jusqu'a Barlet sor mer	20
Et deça jusqu'en Gales fisent la gent mander	
Et de tant maintes terres que jo ne puis nomer:	
De tel pelerinage n'oï nus hom parler.	
Por Deu lor convint tos mainte paine endurer,	24
Sois et faims et froidures et veller et juner;	
Bien lor dut Damedeus a tous gueredoner	
Et les armes a cels en sa glorie mener.	27

(Now you shall hear about Jerusalem	16
and how those who went forth to do honor to the Holy Sepulchre	
gathered armies from everywhere:	
From France, from Berry, from Auvergne,	
from Apulia and Calabria, as far as Barletta,	20
and in the other direction, from as far as Wales, they	
called people together,	
and from many other lands I cannot name.	
No one ever heard tell of such a pilgrimage.	
For the sake of God they suffered greatly,	24
from thirst and hunger, cold, sleeplessness and fasting.	
So did God necessarily reward them all,	
and bring their souls into his glory.)	27

II.

Crestiien avons non et nos l'apelons Crist,	95
Et quant nos çou creonmes	
que por nos le soufrist [i.e., the Crucifixion],	
Dont seroit ce bien drois qu'il nos en sovenist,	

Que Chrestiien por lui la sainte crois presist
Et qu'il alast vengier del linage Andecrist.   99

(We are called Christians and we call him Christ,   95
and because we believe he suffered on the Cross for us,
it is right that we should not forget,
that a Christian should take the cross for his sake
and go seek vengeance for him upon the descendants of the
    Antichrist.)   99

III.

Des bons barons de France drois est que je vos die   106
Ki par force conquisent la celestiel vie.
Il n'orent cure entr'els de mal ne de boisdie,   108
Onques li uns vers l'autre ne pensa felonie,
N'ot traïson entr'els ne engien ne envie,
Mauvaise covoitise fu entr'els molt haïe,
Mais bontés et proece fu amee et sivie. . . .   112
Ki moru par boin cuer Diex ne l'oblia mie,
Les armes en a mis en molt grant segnorie[,]
La u tos jors sera lor pensee acomplie.   120

(I should tell you about the good French knights   106
who won heavenly life by force or arms.
They had no thought for evil or trickery,   108
never did any of them think to harm another,
there was neither treachery nor scheming nor envy
    among them.
They shunned covetousness, but loved and upheld
    goodness and fairness. . . .   112
God did not forget any man who died with good heart,
but rather gave his soul great dominion,
so that his desires should be fulfilled.)   120

IV.

Nostre Sire vos rueve en Jhersalem aler,   128
La deffaee gent ocire et afoler,
Ki Deu ne volent croire ne ses fais aorer
Ne ses commandemens volentiers escouter,
Se crois ne son Sepucre aidier ne delivrer,   132
Mahom et Tervagan destruire et craventer

169

Et fondre lor ymages et a Deu presenter,
Sainte eglise refaire et mostiers restorer,
Ensi de tot en tot le treü aquiter,   136
Que il n'i ait paien qui ja l'ost demander.

(Our Lord calls on you to go to Jerusalem;   128
you are to kill and harm the infidel people,
who refuse to believe in God and adore his deeds
or follow his commandments heartily;
[You must] deliver his Cross and his Sepulchre;   132
you are to destroy Mahomet and Tervagan
and melt their idols and present the metal to God,
rebuild holy churches and restore monasteries,
and so you shall pay such a tribute   136
that no pagan will ever again dare to ask for one.)

V.

Or parla Godefrois de Buillon li hardis: 3451
"Signor, bon crestïen, por Deu de paradis,
Ne vos esmaiés mie del tans qui'st encieris,
Car Dex nos secorra par ses saintes mercis;   3454
Por l'amistié de lui sonmes en cest païs,
Il ne souferra ja ses pules soit peris.
Ja par nul destroit n'ert cis siege departis,
S'arons pris Anthioce et le palais vautis;   3458
Puis prandrons le Sepucre u Dex fu surrexis,
Si le delivrerons de tos ses anemis;
De Mieque briserons les murs et les palis,
S'en trairons Mahomet qui est en l'air assis   3462
Et les .ij. candelabres qui devant lui sont mis,
Ki ja furent en Rome por les treüs conquis,
Mais il n'estaindront ja, ançois ardront toudis. . . .   3465

(Then spoke brave Godfrey of Bouillon: 3451
"Good Christian lords, for God's sake,
do not be dismayed by this time of scarcity,
for God will help us through his holy mercy.   3454
We are in this land for love of him,
he will never allow his people to perish.
This siege will not be lifted on account of any distress,
    however great,
until we have taken Antioch and its vaulted palace.   3458

Then we will capture the Holy Sepulchre where God
   rose from the dead,
and will free it of all enemies.
We will smash the walls and palisades of Mecca
and drag out the floating statue of Mahomet   3462
and the two candelabras that stand before it
and that were taken as tribute from Rome;
they will never go out, they will burn forever. . . .)   3465

VI.

Hui mais orés cançon de bien enluiminee   7678
Issi com les escieles istront fors en la pree.
Jo nel di pas por çou, bone gens honoree,
Que jo ruisse del vo vaillant une denree,
Se iceste cancons molt bien ne vos agree,   7682
Mais iceste proece doit estre ramembree,
Car tels cevalerie n'ert jamais recovree.

(Now you will hear a song full of good,   7678
it will tell how the squadrons came out onto the prairie.
Good people, I am not saying this
because I want any penny of yours
if this song is not to your liking,   7682
yet this noble deed should be recalled,
for such knighthood shall never again be matched.)

*   *   *

(*Le Bâtard de Bouillon*, ed. R. F. Cook [Geneva, 1972]; translations
are my own; the edition contains only the Old French text.)

VII.

Or chevauchent li prinche qui servent Jhesucris: 54
Pour aquiter le regne ou Diex fu mors et vis,
Souffrirent moult de maus, de fain et de durs lis;
Mais chil qui loyamment s'i estoient commis
En ont aquis le regne qui est en Paradis.   58
Diex le dist de sa bouche, qui est Sains Esperis,
S'est chieux bien eüreus qui [en] tel lieu est mis,
Car tant con Diex durra, ara tout ses delis.   61

(Now the princes in Jesus Christ's service ride forth.   54
To free the land where God lived and died,
they suffered greatly, from hunger and hard beds;
but those who committed themselves to this loyally
thus won life in Paradise.   58
God said it with his own mouth, which is the Holy Spirit,
and so a man who is put in such a situation is very fortunate,
for as long as God exists, he will have every pleasure.)   61

VIII.

Bien doit estre, seignour, sifaite gent prisie   469
Qui pour l'amour de Dieu souffroient tel haschie.
Il sont tout adoubé demouré la nuitie,
Onques tente n'i fu la vespree drechie;   472
La gisent si lassét, n'est nuls qui le vous die.
Mal ressamblent aucun qui mainent autre vie,
De gesir sus blans dras et sus coute delie,
Si tienent toute nuit femmes en ribaudie,   476
Et boivent les bons vins, mengieuent char rostie;
Ne lor souvient de Dieu ne de Sainte Marie. . . .
Pour Dieu, entendés chi, s'amendés vostre vie,
Et s'entendés comment, et par quelle maistrie,   484
On akiert Paradis, chelle joie essauchie.
Tout adés qui bien fait il en a sa partie. . . .   486

(Such people, my lords, should be highly praised,   469
who suffered such pains for the love of God.
They spent the night in full armor;
no tent was raised that evening.   472
They lay down more tired than anyone could tell.
They have nothing in common with others who live differently,
lying in white sheets under fine covers,
with the pleasure of women's company at night,   476
drinking good wines, eating roast meat;
they never think of God or of Saint Mary. . . .
For God's sake, listen to this, and mend your lives,
and hear how, by what technique,   484
one wins Paradise, that supreme joy.
Anyone who does good always has his share. . . .)   486

CRUSADE PROPAGANDA IN THE EPIC CYCLES

*   *   *

(*Baudouin de Sebourc*, ed. L. S. Crist and R. F. Cook, in preparation.)

IX.

"Dame," che dist li roys [Ernoul de Nimaie],	277
tout chou laissiés ester;	
car j'ai par maintes fois oÿ dire et conter	
que qui va outre mer pour Sarrasins grever,	
s'il i va loyalment, .iij. armes puet sauver:	280
g'i voi pour le vostre ame envers Diu acquiter;	
pour l'ame de mon pere i voeil aussi aler,	
et l'ame de ma mere: ches trois voeil impetrer	
en cest[i] saint voiage qui tant fait a löer."	284

("My lady," said King Arnold of Nijmegen,	277
"forget all this,	
for I have many times heard tell	
that whoever goes east to attack the Saracens,	
if he goes with honest intent, can save three souls.	280
I am going to pay your soul's debt to God,	
I will go to save my father's soul as well,	
and my mother's: these are the three I wish to request	
through this holy voyage, so praiseworthy.")	284

X.

"Veschi gent sarrasine qui croient Tervogant.	410
Que feriens nous a Romme, nobile combatant,	
quant nous avons trouvé saint Piere chi devant?	412
Or se poeent sauver li petit et li grant;	
car chil qui chi morront, je vous jur et creant,	
les ames en iront ou Trosne reluisant,	
la ou il verra Diu en son propre samblant.	416
Il vaut miex a morir en Jesu Crist vengant	
que vivre faussement en che siecle mescant:	
en Paradis seront porté li trespassant."	419

("These are Saracens who believe in Tervogant.	410
Why should we go to Rome, worthy fighters,	
since we have found Saint Peter here before us?	412
Now the least of us and the mightiest can be saved,	

for those who die here, I swear to you,
their souls will go before the shining Throne,
they will see God face to face.　　　　　　　　416
It is better to die for Christ's revenge
than to live falsely in this pitiful world.
The dead will be carried to Paradise.")　　　419

NOTES

[1]The older, or First, epic Cycle of the Crusade is given detailed treatment, with full bibliography, in Karl-Heinz Bender and Hermann Kleber, *Le Premier cycle de la croisade. De Godefroi à Saladin: entre la chronique et le conte de fées*, pt. 1/2, fasc. 5 of *Les Epopées romanes*, vol. 3 of *Grundriß der romanischen Literaturen des Mittelalters* (Heidelberg, 1986). For the Second Cycle see Suzanne Duparc-Quioc, *Le Cycle de la croisade* (Paris, 1955), and Robert F. Cook and Larry S. Crist, *Le Deuxième Cycle de la croisade: Deux études sur son développement* (Geneva, 1972), with bibliography to date.

[2]Robert Francis Cook, *Chanson d'Antioche, chanson de geste: Le cycle de la croisade est-il épique?* (Amsterdam, 1980), including a bibliography and a summary of the poem's contents. A new edition has appeared since the writing of the study just mentioned: Suzanne Duparc-Quioc, ed., *La Chanson d'Antioche*, 2 vols. (Paris, 1977-78).

[3]L. Bréhier, ed., *Histoire anonyme de la première croisade* (Paris, 1964), pp. vi-vii; C. Minis, "Stilelemente in der Kreuzzugschronik des Albert von Aachen und in der volkssprachigen Epik, besonders in der 'Chanson de Roland'," in *Literatur und Sprache im Europäischen Mittelalter: Festschrift für Karl Langosch*, ed. Alf Onnerfors, Johannes Rathofer, and Fritz Wagner (Darmstadt, 1973), pp. 356-63.

[4]P. Rousset, *Histoire d'une idéologie: La croisade* (Lausanne, 1983); L. Struss, *Epische Idealität und Historische Realität* (Munich, 1980).

[5]For the official propaganda efforts undertaken during the fourteenth century see Steven Runciman, *A History of the Crusades*, 3 vols. (Cambridge, 1951-54), esp. "The Last Crusades," 3:427-62; Aziz S. Atiya, *The Crusade in the Later Middle Ages*, 2nd ed. (New York, 1965); and "The Crusade in the Fourteenth Century," in *The Fourteenth and Fifteenth Centuries*, vol. 3 of *A History of the Crusades*, ed. Harry W. Hazard (Madison, 1975), pp. 3-26.

[6]Sometimes described as an eyewitness participant, but see Cook, *Chanson d'Antioche*, pp. 15-30, and H. Kleber, "Wer ist der Verfasser der *Chanson d'An-*

tioche? Revision einer Streitfrage," *Zeitschrift für französische Sprache und Literatur* 94 (1984): 115-42.

[7]The notable exception to this rule is Stephen of Blois, whose historically attested flight from Antioch, deemed cowardly, becomes a mini-motif subject to epic logic. Stephen is made to desert the expedition *twice*, in defiance of all probability. The surrender of the Christian knights at Civetot (see Bender and Kleber, *Le Premier cycle*, p. 40) is not part of the story of the First Crusade proper; it may reflect the actual behavior of the survivors of the siege of Xerigordon (see Runciman, *History of the Crusades* 1:130).

[8]For Saladin's epic career see Peter R. Grillo, ed., *La Prise d'Acre, La Mort Godefroi, and La Chanson des rois Baudouin*, pt. 2 of *The Jérusalem Continuations*, vol. 7 of *The Old French Crusade Cycle* (Tuscaloosa, 1987); and Larry S. Crist, *Saladin: Suite et fin du deuxième cycle de la croisade* (Paris and Geneva, 1972).

THE SIEGE OF JERUSALEM

AS A CRUSADING POEM

Mary Hamel

There are a small number of poems about crusades in Middle English—poems, that is, in which a Christian military power, because it is Christian, is called upon to confront and overcome in battle a non-Christian invader or usurper in another country—because it is not Christian. This pattern derives from history, in the sense that the Third Crusade did take place, that Charlemagne did campaign in Spain, that Arabs and Berbers did desecrate St. Peter's in 846. Thus, in spite of their divagations from historical fact, the Middle English poems of *Richard Coer de Lyon* (on the Third Crusade), *Sir Ferumbras* and *The Sowdone of Babylone* (on the sack of Rome), and others of the Charlemagne cycle both have some warrant in history and serve to define the genre in terms of the model I have just described. But in strictly historical terms this model should not be relevant to a poem about the siege and conquest of Jerusalem in A.D. 70, for this was, according to the contemporary witness of Josephus's *Jewish War*, a campaign concerned with the subjugation of rebellious subjects by the imperial power without regard to religion.[1]

Yet in the fourteenth-century English alliterative poem *The Siege of Jerusalem* this political motive is explicitly rejected: "Hit nediþ noȝt at þis note : of Nero to mynde, / Ne to trete of no trewe : for tribute þat he askeþ" (lines 501-02).[2]

Instead, the crusading theme of vengeance for the wrongs done to Christ and his Cross is the primary motivation for the campaign:

> Her nys king noþer knyȝt : comen to þis place,
> Baroun, ne burges, : ne burne, þat me folweþ,
> Pat þe cause of his come : nys Crist forto venge
> Vpon þe faiþles folke : þat hym fayntly slowen.[3]
>
> (489-92)

The motive is comparable to the angel's charge to Charlemagne in the contemporary *Sege off Melayne*, "'þat þou venge alle [Christ's] dispyte'" (line 122) against the sultan, or the repeated theme of the earlier romance of *Richard Coer de Lyon*, that the crusaders were "To venge God off hys enemyes" (line 3346; see also 1328, 1676).[4]

It is a very old legend that turned the destruction of Jerusalem and the Temple by pagan Romans in A.D. 70 into God's vengeance on the Jews for the death of Christ. The story of the conversion of Titus to Christianity as the result of a cure at the hands of St. Veronica is supposed to date from the sixth century, and the *Vindicta Salvatoris*, which attributes his and Vespasian's campaign against the rebellious Jews in Jerusalem to such a conversion, from perhaps a century or two later. The story was then given wider currency by its inclusion in the legend of St. James the Less in the *Golden Legend*, and in England especially by a version appearing in Higden's *Polychronicon*.[5] The English poem *The Siege of Jerusalem* adapts and retells this legend of Christian vengeance on the Jews in a particularly effective style, the originality and vigor of its verse at times able to claim comparison with the best of the Alliterative Revival. Yet it also shares with its sources and other precursors a peculiarly repugnant brand of anti-Semitism that has made the poem difficult for modern readers to praise or enjoy. As A. C. Spearing has recently put it, *The Siege of Jerusalem* expresses "a horrible delight in the suffering of the Jews" that is "only a part of a morbid fascination with cruelty" in the poem as a whole.[6] My purpose in this essay is not to defend the poem from such charges but rather to try to put its cruelty and bigotry into perspective by looking at its context. That context, it seems to me, includes two very important features: the poem's identity as a crusading poem and its point in historical time. I shall argue, first, that although most of *The Siege of Jerusalem*'s morbid details can be traced all the way back to Josephus's *Bellum Judaicum*, where they may represent something close to historical fact, the poem nevertheless shares both its cruelty and its bigotry with narratives of the Crusades, both chronicle and fiction. I shall propose, second, that this poem, which has been firmly dated to the last decade of the fourteenth century,[7] is symptomatic of a peculiar fervor on the subject of crusading that can be identified in this decade—a fervor quenched by the failure of the Nicopolis Crusade in late 1396, which as J. J. N. Palmer has noted "appeared likely to put an end to all crusading activity for some time to come,"[8] and which therefore defines a probable *terminus ad quem* for the poem.

I

The morbid cruelty of a number of images in the *Siege* is extreme. Here we see, for example, famine so severe that denizens of the besieged city are reduced to cannibalism, including a woman of noble birth who roasts and eats her own child, saying:

> "Sone, vpon eche side : our sorow is a-lofte,
> Batail a-boute þe borwe, : our bodies to quelle,
> Withyn hunger so hote, : þat neȝ our herte brestyþ;
> Þerfor ȝeld þat I þe ȝaf : & aȝen tourne,
> & entr[e] þer þou cam out!" : & etyþ a schoulder.[9]

(1080-84)

This is one of the most horrendous images of the poem; yet it is one of those derived from Josephus's account of the actual first-century siege, where the lady killed and roasted her child partly to assuage her own hunger, partly to shame thieves who had stolen all her other food, partly to provide "the world a tale, the only thing left to fill up the measure of Jewish misery."[10] Nor is the *Siege*-poet's purpose in this episode to stir up hatred of the Jews; rather, he echoes Josephus's appalled pity, calling the woman "þat worþi wif," from whom bystanders go away "for wo, wepyng echone" (1089, 1093), and omitting the horrified—and explicitly anti-Semitic—condemnation by Titus and the Romans of this infanticide and cannibalism.[11]

Because famine was a frequent accompaniment of siege warfare, cannibalism could be said to be a minor theme of crusade narratives, though here there is no pity. Fulcher of Chartres, for example, tells us that the Christians besieged at Marra in 1098 were forced by hunger to cut up the bodies of slain Saracens, roast them, and eat them before they were fully cooked, and similar stories are told of this siege by other chroniclers of the First Crusade.[12] In the romance of *Richard Coer de Lyon* this theme is treated with a peculiar hideousness, for here the eating of Saracens comes about not because of famine but because of Richard's longing while he is gravely ill for some pork. When he learns after he has recovered that his cook has served him boiled Saracen—pigs being scarce in the region—Richard thinks it an excellent idea:

> "What deuyl is þis?" þe kyng cryde,
> And gan to lauȝe as he were wood.
> "What, is Sarezynys flesch þus good?
> And neuere erst j nouȝt wyste?
> By Goddys deþ and hys vpryste,
> Schole we neuere dye for defawte,
> Whyl we may in any assawte
> Slee Sarezynys. . . ."[13]

(3214-21)

But this is not the worst. When an embassy of Saracens comes to try to ransom prisoners, Richard shows his contempt for their offer by inviting them to a dinner where he has the heads of those same prisoners—boiled—served to their friends, while he ostentatiously dines off one himself. It is hardly surprising that the Saracens call him "þe deuelys broþir" after this meal (3484); but Richard himself asserts—only partly ironically—as he sends the envoys home that

> "Þer is no fflesch so norysschaunt
> Vnto an Ynglyssche Cristen-man
> . . . .
> As is þe flesshe of a Sarezyn."[14]

(3548-52)

Another horrid image from *The Siege of Jerusalem* is that of the dead left unburied and piled around the walls of the besieged city so that the stench might add to the torment of the inhabitants:

> Suþ dommyn þe diches : with þe ded corses,
> Crammen hit myd karayn : þe kirnels vnder,
> Þat þe stynk of þe steem : myȝt strike ouer þe walles.[15]

(681-83)

Again, the ultimate source of this image is Josephus: when the Jews were no longer able to bury their dead "they threw them from the walls into the valleys" beneath, so that ultimately "the innumerable corpses piled up all over the city . . . were a revolting sight, and emitted a pestilential stench," while those who went out to battle "were forced to trample on the bodies" as they marched along.[16] And again there is a parallel in crusade narrative, for Fulcher says that after the capture of Jerusalem the massacred inhabitants were left unburied for several days:

> Oh what stench there was around the walls of the city, both
> within and without, from the rotting bodies of the Saracens
> slain by our comrades at the time of the capture of the city,
> lying wherever they had been hunted down![17]

181

One reason for such appalling conditions is made explicit in the romance of *Richard*: having slaughtered the defeated Saracens in one battle, "No man wolde þo [those] dogges berye" (4585). That being so, it is a relief to learn from the *Gesta Francorum* that the victorious crusaders at Jerusalem at last arranged to have the Saracen corpses at Jerusalem burned in huge funeral pyres.[18]

Other images in *Siege* demonstrate a terrible violence. In this poem we see missiles from siege engines knocking heads off bodies and fetuses from the womb:

> Þer wer selcouþes sen, : as segges mowe here:
> A burne with a balwe-ston : was þe brayn cloue,
> Þe gretter pese of þe panne : þe pyble forþ strikeþ,
> Þat hit flow in-to þe feld, : a forlong or more.
> A womman, bounden with a barn, : was on þe body hytte
> With þe ston o[f] a staf[-slyng], : as þe storyj telleþ,
> Þat þe barn out brayde : fram þe body clene
> & was born vp as a bal : ouer þe burwe walles.[19]
>
> (821-28)

These remarkable if implausible images are also derived from Josephus's *Bellum Judaicum*, from the siege of Jotapata, to which Josephus was eyewitness:

> The effectiveness of "the engine" can be gathered from the incidents of that night: one of the men standing near Josephus on the rampart got into the line of fire and had his head knocked off by a stone, his skull being flung like a pebble from a sling more than six hundred yards; and when a pregnant woman was struck in the belly on leaving her house at daybreak, the unborn child was carried away a hundred yards; so tremendous was the power of that stone-thrower.[20]

No images quite so vivid are to be found in crusade narrative, though the *Itinerarium* tells us that one of Richard the Lionheart's mangonels at the siege of Acre hurled a stone that killed twelve men at once.[21] Other crusade narratives offer worse images associated with engines. Fulcher, for example, speaks of Turks using engines to hurl the heads of Christians of Antioch over the walls at the siege of that city in 1097 (p. 94); the author of the *Gesta Francorum*, however, tells us that the Christians had done the same thing to Turkish heads, hurling them into the city at the siege of Nicaea earlier in the same year.[22]

Another image of horror in *The Siege of Jerusalem* shows escapees from the siege being cut open to find the treasures, gold and jewels, that they have swallowed:

> [Wiþou]ten leue of þat lord, : ledes hem slowen,
> [G]oren euereche a gome, : & þe gold taken;
> Ffayn[ere] of þe floreyns : [þan of] þe frekes alle.[23]
>
> (1166-68)

Again, this is from Josephus:

> . . . the rumour ran round the camps that the deserters were arriving stuffed with gold. The Arab unit and the Syrians cut open the refugees and ransacked their bellies. To me this seems the most terrible calamity that happened to the Jews; in a single night nearly two thousand were ripped up.[24]

And again there is a precise parallel in crusade narrative, for Fulcher exclaims after the fall of Jerusalem in 1099,

> How astonishing it would have seemed to you to see our squires and footmen . . . split open the bellies of those they had just slain in order to extract from the intestines the bezants which the Saracens had gulped down their loathsome throats while alive! For the same reason a few days later our men made a great heap of corpses and burned them to ashes in order to find more easily the above-mentioned gold.[25]

The cruelty of such images and ideas is made the worse by the religious bigotry that is used to justify them: the Jews in *The Siege of Jerusalem* are called "deueles" (184), "fals of byleue" (513), "þe heþen syde" (609), "folke . . . þat þe fende serued" (834), "þe fals men" (551), "þe feyþles folke" (593), while the Roman army—not just Titus and Vespasian—are characterized as "þe Cristen" (424, 835) and "knyȝtes of Crist" (357); before battle

Roman warriors cross themselves (524), and their victory over the Jews is directly attributed to Christ's intervention (608).[26] It is in such language that the poem most clearly associates itself with actual crusading texts; yet it is, oddly, less violent than some of the language used of the Saracens in the crusade texts. As an example, Urban II's exhortation to the First Crusade as Fulcher reports it speaks of them as a "vile race" and cries out, "Oh what a disgrace if a race so despicable, degenerate, and enslaved by demons should thus overcome a people endowed with faith in Almighty God . . . !"[27]

Fictional treatments are more imaginative in their abuse: as the title character gathers his troops in *The Sowdone of Babylone*,

> Alle these people was gadred to Agremore,
> Thre hundred thousand of Sarsyns felle,
> Some bloo, some yolowe, some blake as more,
> Some horible and stronge as devel of helle.[28]

(lines 1003-06)

Fiercest in its hatred and contempt of Saracens is the romance of *Richard Coer de Lyon*, which as we have seen contemplates the eating of Saracen heads with complacency, if not with glee. Later in the narrative Richard splits his army into sections, each with a mission to capture Saracen cities and to kill all the inhabitants; Joshua-like, Richard commands that neither rich nor poor, husband nor wife, maid nor groom should be allowed to live "'But ȝiff [unless] he wole take Crystyndome!'" (3828). The campaign over, the leaders report: says one,

> "And j wan þe cyte off Ebedy,
> Gaynyd hem no mercy to crye;
> What scholde dogges doo but dye?
> Al þe fflok hoppyd hedeless;
> In þis manere j made pes,
> Destroyyd alle þe heþene blood.
> To Crystene-men al þe good
> I gaff þat j þerjnne ffond."[29]

(4670-77)

When Philip of France admits having granted mercy to those who begged for it, Richard is aggrieved: "'Ffor to graunte hem lyff ffor mede / Þou dost God a gret ffalshede'"[30] (4693-94). This point of view is stressed earlier in the story, when Richard kills the Saracen hostages at Acre.[31] Sixty thousand are led forth with their hands tied behind their backs and beheaded, and as this is going on,

> Pere þey herden an aungele off heuene
> Þat seyde: "Seynyours, tuez, tuese,
> Spares hem nouȝt, behediþ þese!"
> Kyng Richard herde þe aungelys voys,
> And þankyd God and þe holy croys.[32]
>
> (3748-52)

From this perspective, *The Siege of Jerusalem* is a work of moderation; at least the author still understands that his heroes' opponents, however false their belief appears to him, remain human. And he seems to understand and express the inherent pitifulness of the events; as remarked earlier, the story of the mother who ate her own child stirs up horror and pity rather than hatred. Moreover, he follows Josephus in showing the conqueror Titus's own pity for his victims: late in the siege he "profreþ pes : for pyte þat he hadde, / Whan he wist of her wo : þat wer withyn stoken"[33] (1131-32) but is refused by the leaders John and Simon—identified by Josephus as the real villains of the war. When Titus is told later that the Jews are throwing the bodies of their dead over the wall because they cannot bury them, he is anguished: "To trewe god he vouched / Þat [he] hadde profred hem pes : and grete pite hadde"[34] (1151-52), and he asks Josephus to urge them to yield. Though Titus later hardens his heart, judging and selling the unhappy survivors of the siege thirty for a penny,[35] the poet offers an unforgettable picture of their wretchedness:

> Þe peple in þe pauyment : was pite to byholde,
> Þat wer enfamy[n]ed for defaute : whan hem fode wanted.
> Was noȝt on ladies lafte : bot þe lene bones,
> Þat wer fleschy byfor : & fayr on to loke;

Burges with balies : as barels of þat tyme,
No gretter þan a grehounde : to grype on þe medil.[36]

(1243-48)

Yet in spite of the poet's occasional empathy, the overriding theme of vengeance for Christ's death is allowed to stifle humane impulses. The nastiest passage in the poem is the punishment meted out—anachronistically—to the high priest Caiaphas and his clerks, a complicated and messy torture involving flaying, drawing by horses, hanging upside down, and clawing by curs, cats, and apes (693-704). The poet concludes,

Þus ended coursed Cayphas : & his clerkes alle,
Al to-brused myd bestes, : brent at þe laste,
In tokne of tresoun : & trey þat he wroȝt,
Whan Crist þrow his conseil : was cacched to deþ.[37]

(721-24)

Nothing I have found in crusading narrative, chronicle or fiction, quite matches this gloating and sadistic passage,[38] though Richard the Lionheart savoring boiled Saracen's head before a Saracen audience comes close. But the long and hateful tradition that names all Jews as Christ-killers taints *The Siege of Jerusalem*, just as a different kind of religious hatred taints more conventional crusade literature. The poem's only redeeming feature in this regard is that it is not quite as bad as the somewhat later (ca. 1400) metrical poem about the siege called *Titus and Vespasian*. In this version Titus commands not only that the Jews be sold thirty for a penny but also that their new masters should cut them open for their swallowed treasure and then torture them to death:

"Hange hem, brenne hem, doo hem drawe,
Flee hem, bore hem, and doo hem sawe,
Roost hem, scalde hem, bete hem, and put,
And all to peces her limes kut,
And þus forddon hem lif and lyme;
Soo shull we qwenchen her venym.

And Goddes blessyng þey have ay,
Þat serveth hem [so], til domesday."

(lines 4229-36)[39]

Here, rather than in *The Siege of Jerusalem*, is the equivalent of the angel of *Richard Coer de Lyon* crying "'Tuez! Tuese!'"

II

This discussion has laid what may seem excessive emphasis on the negative side of crusade literature; but it is hard for a modern reader to disentangle the ideals of courage and service to Christ in such works from their values of vengeance and hatred and their tendency to gloat over horrors. In its own time a work such as *The Siege of Jerusalem* had a more immediate and unqualified appeal, to judge by the number of surviving manuscripts (more than of any other alliterative poem except *Piers Plowman*). Nor is it simply fortuitous that *The Siege of Jerusalem* was composed in the last years of the fourteenth century—or that the destruction of the Jews and Jerusalem in A.D. 70 figures in Philippe de Mézières's *Letter to King Richard II* of 1395. Speaking of war between Christians, the Anglo-French war especially, he exhorts his audience to

> remember Titus, son of Vespasian, Emperor of Rome, and himself later Emperor, at the siege of Jerusalem, in which eleven times one hundred thousand souls died by starvation and the sword, except for eighty and seven thousand who were sold at the rate of thirty for one denier, in quittance and remembrance of the thirty pieces of silver for which they sold the blessed Son of God.[40]

Reflecting on Titus's pity for his defeated enemies (whom he calls damnable), Philippe rebukes the Christian kings who are responsible for the slaying of fellow-Christians. But more to the point in the present context, the letter ties this ancient episode to

187

Philippe's own plan as set forth in his letter: the end of the war between England and France and the two realms' support for the end of the Great Schism of the Church, to be followed by the joint venture of the kings of England and France to "undertake the holy voyage" (p. 30) and reconquer the Holy Land—and thus rescue western Europe from the encroaching Turks under Sultan Bayezid I, who had already made significant advances in the Balkans and seemed certain to overwhelm Constantinople in a short time. Indeed, he is supposed to have threatened, like a character in a Charlemagne romance, to stable his horse in St. Peter's on his way to the conquest of the West.[41]

J. J. N. Palmer has shown that the Old Pilgrim Philippe's letter concerned more than a visionary's dream; it was, indeed, partial evidence of a serious plan being negotiated between the two nations. At the time of the letter the first phase of the plan was already being carried out: this was the joint expedition that was to lead to disaster at Nicopolis in 1396. As Palmer contends,

> The Nicopolis force was intended to be only the first of two great Christian armies whose ultimate destination was to have been Jerusalem itself. In accordance with contemporary crusading theory, the Nicopolis army was to have cleared the ground and established a forward base from which the second and greater of the two armies could set out for the Holy Land under the leadership of Charles VI and Richard II themselves. This was the strategy advocated by Philip de Mézières. . . . Other contemporaries testified to Charles VI's determination to lead a crusade in person; and Richard II gave vivid and enduring expression to his own readiness to participate in a joint royal expedition when he commissioned the Wilton Diptych.[42]

The allure of the crusading idea in the last decade of the fourteenth century had been shown by other, earlier activity such as Henry of Derby's journeys to Prussia and Jerusalem and the Barbary expedition led by the duke of Orléans in 1390. Taken as a crusading poem, *The Siege of Jerusalem* could be read both as a reflection of this activity and as a piece of propaganda favoring the longer-range English-French project against Jerusalem. For Philippe's plan was indeed to "remind [the two kings] continually of the wrongs which . . . the Sultan of Babylon and his prede[-ce]ssors [had] inflicted and [were] still inflicting on the blessed Son of God" and to persuade the two kings to take "upon themselves the task of avenging the wrongs done to the Crucified One, and the ancient shame born[e] by all Christian kings":[43] in the words of the poem, their cause must be "Cryst forto venge / Vpon þe faiþles folke" (*Siege* 491-92). Though indeed the poem describes a crusade against the Jews rather than the Saracens or Turks, it is still a work that pictures a divinely inspired conquest of the Holy City as well as God's vengeance on its occupants. Whether these were Saracen or Jew perhaps does not matter: it was possible in this age not only to picture Muslims as idolaters but also to call the shrine where their idols were kept a "Synagoge."[44]

Nicopolis brought hopes of such a conquest to an end. Of the perhaps three thousand Europeans who survived the battle, aside from the few of sufficient rank, wealth, or connections to promise high ransom, and those under the age of twenty sent as slaves to Turkish leaders elsewhere, the majority were beheaded in a scene reminiscent of Richard the Lionheart's earlier disposal of hostages.[45] When the news came to the West in December of 1396, an era came to an end; not even the personal visit of the eastern emperor to France and England in 1399-1400 was able to gain significant help for his desperate situation. Thus, as Aziz Atiya has said, Nicopolis was "the last of the great crusades."[46] Its epochal nature is evident in the poetry that was written afterwards, such as the *Sege of Melayne* and the Alliterative *Morte Arthure*—but that is matter for another time.

MARY HAMEL

NOTES

[1]Josephus, *The Jewish War*, rev. ed., trans. G. A. Williamson and ed. E. Mary Smallwood (New York, 1981), pp. 364-65 (VI, 328-50).

[2]E. Kölbing and Mabel Day, eds., *The Siege of Jerusalem*, EETS, o.s. 188 (London, 1932; rept. New York, 1971). My quotations and my translations (all from this edition) ignore the editors' italics.
(There is no need on this occasion to think about Nero, nor to speak of any truce for tribute he is asking for.)

[3](Here is neither king nor knight come to this place, baron nor burgess nor fighter who follows me, the cause of whose coming is not to avenge Christ upon the infidels that treacherously slew him.)
Cf. the *Itinerarium Peregrinorum et Gesta Regis Ricardi*, ed. William Stubbs, Rolls Ser., 38 (London, 1864), p. 32, I.xvii: "Fama rerum . . . quosdam concitat ad lacrymas alios accendit ad vindictam. . . . Pictaviae comes Ricardus ob ulciscendam crucis injuriam cruce insignitur." (The report of these things stirred some to tears, kindled others to vengeance. . . . Count Richard of Poitou took the cross to avenge the insult to the Cross.) Even Urban II in preaching the First Crusade incited his hearers to revenge, according to Robert the Monk; see James Brundage, *The Crusades: A Documentary Survey* (Milwaukee, 1962), p. 18, and August C. Krey, ed., *The First Crusade: The Accounts of Eyewitnesses and Participants* (Princeton, 1921; rept. Gloucester, Mass., 1958), p. 31.

[4]Sidney J. Herrtage, ed., *The Sege off Melayne*, EETS, e.s. 35 (London, 1880; rept. Millwood, N.Y., 1973); Karl Brunner, ed., *Der mittelenglische Versroman über Richard Löwenherz*, Wiener Beiträge zur Englischen Philologie, 42 (Vienna and Leipzig, 1913); all quotations from the *Richard* are from this edition. Translations of quotations from both works are mine.

[5]See Kölbing and Day, eds., *Siege*, pp. xv-xxiv. A more recently discovered source for *The Siege of Jerusalem* is the *Bible en françois* of Roger d'Argenteuil; see Phyllis Moe, "The French Source of the Alliterative *Siege of Jerusalem*," *Medium Ævum* 38 (1969): 147-54.

[6]A. C. Spearing, *Readings in Medieval Poetry* (Cambridge, 1987), p. 167.

[7]*Siege*, ed. Kölbing and Day, p. xxix; Mary Hamel, ed., *Morte Arthure: A Critical Edition*, Garland Medieval Texts, 9 (New York, 1984), pp. 54-56.

[8]J. J. N. Palmer, *England, France and Christendom, 1377-99* (Chapel Hill and London, 1972), p. 205.

[9]("Son, on every side our sorrow is present—battle around the town to kill our bodies, within hunger so keen that our heart nearly bursts; therefore give back what I gave thee, and turn back and enter where thou came out!"—and [she] eats a shoulder.)

[10]Josephus, *Jewish War* VI, 207, p. 354 (see n. 1. above).

[11]Cf. Josephus, *Jewish War* VI, 214-19, p. 354.

[12]Fulcher of Chartres, *A History of the Expedition to Jerusalem, 1095-1127*, trans. Frances R. Ryan (New York, 1973), p. 112. For an evaluation of stories of crusading cannibalism see Jill Tattersall, "Anthropophagi and Eaters of Raw Flesh in French Literature of the Crusade Period: Myth, Tradition and Reality," *Medium Ævum* 57 (1988): 240-53, esp. pp. 247-49; as she notes, evidence offering "incontrovertible proof" that cannibalism occurred (p. 253) is presented by Jonathan Riley-Smith, *The First Crusade and the Idea of Crusading* (Philadelphia, 1986), pp. 66, 818 n. 45.

[13]("What the devil is this?" the king cried, and began to laugh as if he were mad. "What, is Saracens' flesh thus good? And I never knew of it before? By God's death and his Resurrection, we shall never have to die for lack [of food], while we may slay Saracens in any assault.")

[14]("There is no flesh so nourishing to an English Christian . . . as that of a Saracen.") As Tattersall notes, "there is no trace of this story" in contemporary chronicle ("Anthropophogi and Eaters," p. 250); one may include the *Itinerarium* (n. 3 above).

[15](Then they fill up the ditches with the dead corpses, cram it with carrion under the battlements, so that the stink of the exhalation might strike over the walls.)

[16]Josephus, *Jewish War* V, 518, and VI, 2-3, p. 337.

[17]Fulcher of Chartres, *History of the Expedition*, p. 337.

[18]*First Crusade: Accounts* (see n. 3 above), p. 262.

[19](There were wonders seen, as men may hear: a soldier had his brain cloven by a round-stone—the missile strikes forth the larger piece of the skull,

that it flew into the field a furlong or farther. A woman, burdened with a child, was hit on the body with a stone from a staff-sling, as the story tells, so that the baby burst out clean from the body and was borne up like a ball over the town walls.)

[20]Josephus, *Jewish War* III, 245-46, p. 209.

[21]"Petrariæ itaque regis Ricardi die noctuque jugiter jaciebant, de quarum una certissime constat, quod unius lapidus jactu rostraverit in mortem duodecim homines" (*Itinerarium* III.vii, p. 219). (And so the catapults of King Richard shot continually, day and night, about one of which it is firmly established that the stone from one cast threw twelve men dead to the ground.)

[22]Brundage, *Crusades*, p. 47. The romance of *Richard Coer de Lyon* is for once milder: Richard has only hives of bees hurled over the walls into Acre during the siege that "dede þe Sarezynes ful gret schame, / Ffor þey hem stungge in þe vysage, / Þat alle þey gunne [began] ffor to rage" (2914-16). The bees were not original with the romance, however: defenders at the siege of Marra in 1098 are supposed to have hurled "stones . . . javelins, fire, wood, beehives with bees, and slack lime" with their engines at the Christian besiegers (*First Crusade: Accounts*, p. 211). Severed heads, nevertheless, are central images of crusading narrative: according to the *Itinerarium*, for example, the actual Richard liked to collect Turkish heads on raids and would return to camp with twelve or twenty or thirty at a time (V.xxix, p. 343). This theme is also literary: Charlemagne's knights behead a group of Saracen messengers in *Sir Ferumbras* and *The Sowdone of Babylone* and carry them on their own embassy to the sultan as an offensive gift; see Sidney J. Herrtage, ed., *Sir Ferumbras*, EETS, e.s. 34 (London, 1879; rept. 1966), lines 1662-67, and Emil Hausknecht, ed., *The Romaunce of the Sowdone of Babylone*, EETS, e.s. 38 (London, 1881; rept. 1969), lines 1799-1802 (translations from these editions are mine).

[23](Without [Titus's] leave men slew them, disemboweled each man and took the gold, gladder for the money than for any of the prisoners.)

[24]Josephus, *Jewish War* V, 551-52, p. 334.

[25]Fulcher of Chartres, *History of the Expedition*, p. 122; cf. also p. 154.

[26]There is actually a sort of warrant for this in Josephus: time and again he puts speeches into Vespasian's or Titus's mouth claiming that "God is on our side" (e.g., VI, 39-41, p. 340) and attributing the Roman victory to God's rejection of the Jewish people (see IV, 370-71, p. 264, and VI, 41, p. 370).

[27]Fulcher of Chartres, *History of the Expedition*, p. 66.

[28](All these people were gathered to Agremore, three hundred thousand deadly Saracens, some blue, some yellow, some black as mulberry, some horrible and strong as devils from hell.)

[29]("And I won the city of Ebedy—their cries gained them no mercy; what should dogs do but die? All the flock hopped headless. In this manner I made peace: destroyed all the heathen blood. I gave all the possessions that I found therein to Christian men.")

[30]("For to grant them life for a reward, thou dost great disloyalty to God.")

[31]This episode reflects in exaggerated form an historical event: after the fall of Acre a number of Turks remained in the crusaders' hands as surety for Saladin's promise to exchange European prisoners and deliver the supposed True Cross; when after a considerable time Saladin failed to keep his promise, Richard had 2700 of the hostages hanged (*Itinerarium* IV.iv, p. 243).

[32](There they heard an angel from heaven that said, "Lords, kill, kill, spare them not, behead these!" King Richard heard the angel's voice and thanked God and the Holy Cross.)

[33](. . . offers peace because of the pity he felt when he knew of the suffering of those who were stuck inside.)

[34](To true God he swore that he had offered them peace and had great pity.)

[35]Only the rationale for the enslavement, that Jesus was sold for thirty pence (1314-16), is original with later tradition, for Josephus notes that in spite of Titus's orders to kill deserters from the city the Roman soldiers spared them for the sake of money: "all the rest [of the deserters] were sold along with the women and children, the retail price being very low, as supply was far in excess of demand. . . . The number sold was enormous" (*Jewish War* VI, 384-86, p. 368). Although in the Crusades enslavement was primarily a weapon of the Saracens against the Christians, the reverse was not unknown; for example, survivors of the crusaders' siege of Caesarea in 1101, according to Fulcher, were bought and sold among the Franks as domestic slaves (*History of the Expedition*, p. 154).

[36](The people on the street were piteous to see, who had starved from want when they lacked food. There was nothing left on ladies but the lean bones, who

had been fleshy before and fair to look at; burgesses, with bellies like barrels before, [were] no larger than a greyhound to grip in the middle.)

[37](Thus ended cursed Caiaphas and all his clerks, all mangled by beasts, burnt at the last, in token of the treason and trouble that he had wrought when Christ by his scheme was driven to death.)

[38]It should be noted, however, that the episode is translated directly and in detail from the *Bible en françois*; see Moe, "French Source" (n. 5 above), p. 152.

[39]J. A. Herbert, ed., *Titus & Vespasian, or The Destruction of Jerusalem* (London, 1905). ("Hang them, burn them, disembowel them, flay them, pierce them, saw them up, roast them, scald them, beat them, and stab, and cut their limbs all to pieces, and thus destroy them life and limb; so shall we quench their venom. And those who serve them so have God's blessing forever, till Doomsday.")

[40]Philippe de Mézières, *Letter to King Richard II*, ed. and trans. G. W. Coopland (Liverpool, 1975), pp. 16-17 (English) and 89-90 (French). Hereafter only English-translation pages will be cited.

[41]Palmer, *England, France and Christendom*, p. 183.

[42]Palmer, *England, France and Christendom*, p. 205; on the significance of the Wilton Diptych see pp. 242-44. See also Christopher Tyerman, *England and the Crusades 1095-1588* (Chicago, 1988), pp. 294-301.

[43]Philippe de Mézières, *Letter*, p. 28.

[44]*Sir Ferumbras*, line 2535 (n. 22 above).

[45]Aziz S. Atiya, *The Crusade of Nicopolis* (London, 1934; rept. New York, 1978), pp. 95-97.

[46]Atiya, *Crusade of Nicopolis*, p. 113.

STRUCTURAL CONVERGENCE OF

PILGRIMAGE AND DREAM-VISION IN

CHRISTINE DE PIZAN

Susan Stakel

When Christine de Pizan began *Le Livre du chemin de long estude* in 1402 she was still entangled in the Quarrel of the Rose, the literary debate on the merits of Jean de Meun's portion of the *Roman de la rose*. It is clear she knew the *Rose* well, and it is one of the wonderful ironies of literary history that she was able to mine and renew so successfully a work that she had roundly condemned. In the *Rose* she found an interesting but almost incidental combination of dream-vision and (ultimately burlesque) pilgrimage. She borrows this framework for both *Le Chemin* and *L'Avision-Christine* but makes the two structures function in tandem. Pilgrimage literature and dream visions have long been studied as separate, unrelated genres. Their superimposition, as in Christine's allegories, reveals the surprising but very basic similarity of the two forms. Christine's structural choices must be seen as anything but incidental or serendipitous. From the melding of dream-vision and pilgrimage in her work there emerges a dynamic vehicle for the transmission of Christine's ideas that is much more effective in refuting Jean de Meun than was her exchange of letters with Jean de Montreuil and Pierre and Gontier Col.

That we still today refer to questers of many sorts as pilgrims (witness the titles of recent popular books such as *Pilgrim at Tinker Creek*, *Pilgrim in the Microworld*, *The Untidy Pilgrim: A Novel*, *The Pilgrim Hawk: A Love Story*) proves how easy it is to "metaphorize" the idea of pilgrimage and suggests the universality of the concept as an ideal that appeals to something very deep in the human psyche. St. Paul articulates this sentiment for Christians in the eleventh chapter of his *Letters to the Hebrews* when he defines them as aliens and sojourners seeking a heavenly homeland from which they have been exiled. Jerome's move to the Holy Land in the fourth century and the *peregrinatio* of the Irish monks in the sixth and seventh centuries actualized Paul's implied paradox that to return from exile one must undertake exile. Only by severing those ties that bind one to place is it possible to separate oneself from earthliness and worldly corruption. Away from the familiarity of everyday life, absorbed by the rigors of the journey, and immersed in the rituals of penance and purification, the pilgrim experiences the double movement described by Gregory the Great of quest beyond self and transformation within self.[1] The desired transformation in turn yields truth and wisdom tantamount to direct knowledge of God and, at its most extreme, mystical union with God.

There are many variations on the theme of pilgrimage, and as we move away from pilgrimage's Golden Age in the eleventh century, many corruptions of it. But all have a recognizable deep structure, whether we phrase it semantically (with F. C. Gardiner) as exile, journey, hardship, desire for the homeland, or sequentially (following the suggestion of Leonard Bowman) as departure, adventure, transformation, and return.[2]

While the earliest medieval use of pilgrimage in imaginative literature occurs in twelfth-century pilgrim plays, dreams are already an important element of early epics and saints' lives, where, emerging from the biblical tradition, they serve as a sort of mediation between God and the people of God, and thus invariably are meant to convey immutable truth. According to Herman Braet, when courtly literature drifts away from this tight alignment of the divine and the quotidian, when individuals and their feelings assume prime importance, dreams also come to center on the merely human, thereby losing their direct connection with eternal truth.[3] The romance reader is enjoined to reflect on the oft-posed question: *songe* (vision) or *mensonge* (lie)? The ambiguity is there to be exploited or explained away. When Guillaume de Lorris argues in the opening lines of the *Roman de la rose* that despite what many people say, dreams can indeed convey truth, it is the rhyming pair, not any assertion of veracity, that echoes through our heads:

> Aucunes genz dient qu'en songes
> n'a se fables non et mençonges;
> mes l'en puet tex songes songier
> qui ne sont mie mençongier;
> ainz sont aprés bien aparant. . . .[4]

> (Some say that in dreams
> there are nothing but fables and lies;
> but one can dream such dreams
> as are not deceptive
> but turn out later to be true. . . .)

Christine obviously considered the dream in the *Roman de la rose* to be of the deceptive kind and so was surely aware that her own fiction could be open to similar accusations. Like Guillaume de Lorris she insists in *Le Chemin* on the veracity of the dream:

> Ce ne fu pas illusion,
> Ains fu demonstrance certaine
> De chose tres vraie et certaine.[5]

(It was not illusion.
It was an accurate demonstration
of things absolutely true and certain.)

From the very beginning of her "estrange vision" Christine sets
herself cleanly apart from Guillaume's dreamer, who dresses in
haste using silk thread to sew up fancy sleeves, anxious to follow
a flock of birds he knows not where. The dreamer Christine follows not flighty birds but the Cumean Sibyl, "la deesse de Savoir"
(line 479), Aeneas's guide to the Underworld, Virgil's inspiration. Christine, like the lover in the *Roman de la rose*, is eager to
be off, but her clothing expresses the seriousness of her purpose
and gives us the first suggestion of pilgrimage:

> Si m'atornay d'un atour simple,
> Touret de nes je mis et guimple,
> Pour le vent qui plus grieve a l'ueil
> En octobre que grand souleil
> Et ma robe tout a esture
> J'escourciay d'une cainture,
> Afin qu'el ne me nuisist pas
> A marchier de plus legier pas.
>
> (701-08)

> (Simple garb did I don,
> A muffler and a wimple,
> For in October
> The wind grieves more the eyes
> Than does the sun.
> In haste I bound up my skirts
> With a belt lest they
> Hinder my passage.)

In *L'Avision* the first two lines make explicit Christine's conception of life as pilgrimage: "Ja passe avoye la moitie du chemin
de mon pelerinage, comme un iour sus lavesprir me trouvasse pour
la longue voye lassee et desireuse de heberge" (I had already
passed the midpoint on the path of my pilgrimage when one day
towards vespers I found myself tired out by the long journey and

desirous of lodging.)[6] We see her say her prayers, fall asleep, and divide into resting body and floating dream-spirit. Both dreams, then, have the traditional prologue that carefully delineates the border between waking state and dream state, a frontier that translates here as the marker of the pilgrim's departure or separation from the familiar world. In both dreams Christine feels not apprehension but an airiness derived from the freedom implicit in cutting the ties to material place. The dream, then, with its total eclipsing of the body, is the ideal vehicle of expression for pilgrimage.

The worlds that Christine explores provide comment on her everyday life but, as is typical of dreams, are fantastic in every way. Where the real pilgrim of the Middle Ages was separated from home and daily existence and engaged in the adventure of self-discovery via new roads, sights, and companions, Christine's pilgrims are dislocated through the poet's use of the marvelous, "le merveilleux." In *L'Avision* Christine witnesses her own birth from the mouth of Chaos, a figure who inhabits a "tenebreuse," watery country. He is so tall that his height cannot be determined. His head pierces the clouds, while his feet tread in deep valleys and his belly nearly drags on the earth. His clothing is dappled by all the colors of the rainbow. He inhales unformed matter and exhales "singulieres pieces." Dame Opinion, the second of Christine's guides, leads her charge to the familiar University of Paris, but there she finds whirlwinds of all possible colors swirling around the heads of the debating clerks and whispering ideas in their ears. In search of her third mentor, Dame Philosophie, Christine must go ever higher through rooms of indescribable beauty and richness to a "plus hault sommeton," where she gains access through an ivory gate to the blinding light of philosophy. The French countryside of *Le Chemin* metamorphosizes from October to the month of May, from a tension-fraught kingdom to a "terrestre paradis" (762) full of every good thing. The dreamer Christine travels with the Cumean Sibyl from Eden to the Holy Land to the ends of the earth, all in the blink of an eye. Christine admires the beautiful marbles of Constantinople, grieves over the ruins of ancient civilizations, and recites a list of the holy places she has visited in the same breath in which she describes the crocodiles, dragons, unicorns, giants, pygmies, and other curiosities she has seen along the way. When their path takes them to the edge of the world, Christine and the Sibyl leave by means of miraculously-appearing ladders that transport them to their final stopover, the firmament.

A recurring motif of criss-crossing paths in *Le Chemin* recalls the "progress" type of pilgrimage, in which life's voyager is asked to choose the correct way. Christine is not called upon to make a decision since the Sibyl is leading; but, as with most of Christine's apparitions, the Sibyl should be understood to be a part of herself, and the path they follow, that of Long Study, they follow because it is the one Christine has taken in her waking life. She had already passed up the "noire and tenebreuse" road that leads to Hell. Clearly then, Christine equates the search for truth through learning with salvation, and its opposite, self-satisfied ignorance, with damnation.

Up to this point in *Le Chemin* Christine's pilgrimage is orthodox. She leaves material existence behind (departure) and embraces the adventure of *long estude* on what we believe to be a quest for spiritual growth. Her road of study is unique in pilgrimage literature, but a constant in her own work, where the spiritual and the intellectual journeys merge. Bowman, in his survey of the voyage motif in medieval literature, indicates that "within or alongside this spiritual journey [to the New Jerusalem] was an intellectual journey as well, a quest against error and folly for truth and wisdom, which ultimately amounted to the knowledge of God" (p. 8). But there is in *Le Chemin* a high, straight path, pointed out by the Sibyl, which leads to face-to-face knowledge of God. Oddly enough, Christine is not permitted to try this road. She is not ready, the Sibyl says. It is at the moment when we expect Christine to seek the Heavenly Jerusalem that the path leads abruptly to the earthly Jerusalem, and her literal pilgrimage to sites in the Holy Land. As an allegorical pilgrimage the poem breaks down at this point, for there seems to be no desire to use knowledge for transformation. Even after gaining access to the firmament, Christine listens passively to discourses by Chivalry, Nobility, Wealth, and Wisdom. We find out later that she has written everything down and agreed to transmit what she has heard to the French court, in order that they might decide which of the four powers has the most accurate ideas. We of course know that all of these ideas flow from the pen of the fifteenth-century writer Christine de Pizan, but within the text she does not take credit for them, preferring instead to present herself as the scribe of others.

Le Chemin was only the second of Christine's longer works. Before the publication of *L'Avision* she produced *La Mutacion de fortune*, *Le Livre des faits et bonnes moeurs du sage roy Charles V*, *La Cité des dames*, and the *Livre des trois vertus*. So although only three years separate the two dream-visions, I think it fair to consider one a work of youth and the other a work of maturity. In many ways *L'Avision* completes *Le Chemin*. The pilgrimage motif carries through from departure, adventure, and struggle to self-realization, transformation, and affirmation. Dame Opinion has reviewed for Christine the history of human knowledge and reassured the young woman that (1) she has not erred in her own work and (2) future generations will appreciate her more than does her own. When the dreaming Christine comes face to face with Philosophy, the "merveille" of it all makes her faint dead away. There has been a definite progression, from understanding first the material, then the intellectual, and finally the divine sphere. After fainting, Christine is reborn to a new understanding of the principles of life. She begins to speak and recounts to Dame Philosophie the disappointments of her life and her hope of receiving Boethian comfort. Thanks to Philosophie, she realizes that it is her difficulties that have made her who and what she is. She emerges instilled with a new feeling of confidence in herself as woman and author.

Pilgrimage involves, last of all, return. The dreamer wakes up. In *Le Chemin* Christine returns to France as scribe and as messenger, but it is the Sibyl figure, so old that her body has faded away and left pure voice, that retains the key auctorial role. In *L'Avision* Christine surpasses the scribal function, to become truly an author. Her studies have led her from history to sciences to poetry, and in that final art she feels transformed. She has been the scribe of the Dame Courronnee, she listens to Dame Opinion, but after her encounter with Dame Philosophie she assumes the voice that, after all, has been hers all along. She will bridge the gap between individual and community by offering her own journey as an exemplum for all those who would ameliorate self and society. She has successfully made her own pilgrimage; now she will be a guide for others.

Pilgrimage and dream end simultaneously. Departure has meshed with dream-prologue, adventure with exposition, and transformation with awakening. Pilgrimages culminate in return, dreams in interpretation. In both cases we are dealing with the integration of truth into the original waking/left-behind life. Neither dream nor pilgrimage is, strictly speaking, a literary phenomenon, yet both surface repeatedly as thematic and schematic devices of imaginative writing. Once their shared structure is laid bare we can see its congruence with the "beginning—middle—end—integration of meaning" sequence that describes the traditional functioning of literary texts. Christine is responding to what she sees as a burlesque pairing of dream and pilgrimage in the *Roman de la rose* that leads to a clear case of *mensonge*. I believe that at least unconsciously she was also reacting to what Daniel Poirion calls the thirteenth-century decline in trust in the ability of literary language to signify, which he explores as a new phenomenon in the *Roman de la rose*.[7] Christine sometimes seems quite modern to us, but in many ways she was very much a traditionalist and thus presumably believed in the power of the Word. When she awakens in *L'Avision* she compares the three stages of her dream to jewels. The last, the encounter with Philosophie, reminds her of a cloudless ruby, a stone that pleases more, the more one looks at it. For Christine, then, the text is transparent; it reveals its truth and this truth is eternal, like the truth of all good literature, like the truth to be found at the end of pilgrimage.

NOTES

[1]For a succinct history of pilgrimage see Jonathan Sumption, *Pilgrimage: An Image of Medieval Religion* (London, 1979).

[2]See Gardiner, *The Pilgrimage of Desire: A Study of Theme and Genre in Medieval Literature* (Leiden, 1971), p. 12. Gardiner credits the influence of G. V. Smithers, "The Meaning of *The Seafarer* and *The Wanderer*," *Medium Aevum* 26 (1957): 137-53 and 28 (1959): 1-22. Bowman ("*Itinerarium*: The Shape of the Metaphor," in Itinerarium: *The Idea of Journey* [Salzburg, 1983], p. 5) derives his structure from the work of Joseph Campbell, *The Hero with a Thousand Faces* (Princeton, 1968).

[3]"Rêve, réalité, écriture: Du référentiel à la sui-référence," in *I Sogni nel medioevo*, ed. Tullio Gregory (Rome, 1985), p. 20.

[4]Ed. Félix Lecoy (Paris, 1965), vol. 1, lines 1-5. Translation mine.

[5]*Le Livre du chemin de long estude*, ed. Robert Püschel (Berlin, 1887; rept. Geneva, 1974), lines 454-56. All subsequent references are to this edition. All translations are my own.

[6]*Lavision Christine*, ed. Sr. Mary Louis Towner (Washington, D.C., 1932). All subsequent references are to this edition (which omits diacritical marks). Translations are mine.

[7]"Les Mots et les choses selon Jean de Meun," *L'Information littéraire* 26 (1974): 9-10, and idem, *Le Roman de la rose* (Paris, 1973), p. 43.

ISABEL OF PORTUGAL AND THE

FIFTEENTH-CENTURY BURGUNDIAN

CRUSADE

Charity Cannon Willard

Some years ago, Professor Aziz Atiya insisted that the defeat of the European knights at Nicopolis in 1396 marked the end of the crusade as an organized movement of Christendom against Islam for the deliverance of the Holy Land.[1] It is true that concern shifted to the rescue of Constantinople from the encroaching Turks, but, nevertheless, the dream of another crusade continued to stir the imagination of certain European rulers. Henry V of England, for instance, until his last days dreamed of leading a new crusade. In composing the first poem about the exploits of Joan of Arc, Christine de Pizan expressed the hope that the heroine of Orléans and the recently crowned Charles VII would jointly lead a new crusade, but nowhere was the idea more persistently nourished than at the court of Burgundy during the era of Philip the Good, son of the leader of the unfortunate European army at Nicopolis. The reasons for his interest are disputed; was it primarily a desire to avenge his father's defeat, or did concerns for a prosperous trade in the Middle East predominate? Whatever the motive, the crusade remained an uppermost preoccupation and would seem to have been a deciding factor in the duke's third marriage, to Isabel of Portugal, sister of Henry the Navigator, and also an inspiration for a whole generation of enthusiastic Portuguese crusaders, who were encouraged by their conquest of Ceuta in 1415.

Henry the Navigator's interests are well enough known, but those of his mother, Blanche of Lancaster, and his sister, Isabel, considerably less so. Blanche, John of Gaunt's daughter, was an energetic woman who did not hesitate to institute a reform of court morals shortly after her arrival in Portugal. She also introduced the English concept of chivalry there, strongly influencing her four sons and, very possibly, her only daughter. She was no self-effacing queen but had a strong sense of her role in society.[2] Although Isabel's activities in her native land were limited, her marriage in 1430 to Philip of Burgundy established her in a region where women had long played a significant role in government, from Johanna and Margaret of Constantinople in the early thirteenth century to Philip's grandmother Margaret of Flanders, who maintained her title and position even after the death of her husband, Philip the Bold. Although Isabel's activities must sometimes be surmised from entries in the ducal accounts, there is no doubt that she played an active part in diplomacy, and also in the education of her son, Charles, as well as in that of numerous nieces and nephews and even several of the duke's bastards, who were raised at court. She was an intelligent and very religious woman who readily adapted herself to Burgundian crusading ambitions.

From the earliest days of Philip the Good's reign, travelers had been dispatched to the Near East to gather information and make reports on conditions there; Guillebert de Lannoy, who travelled there from 1420 to 1423, and Bertrandon de la Broquière, whose embassy lasted from 1432 to 1439, are the best known of these.[3] Towards the end of the duke's life the crusade took on the proportions of a veritable obsession. The Feast of the Pheasant was merely one episode in this story.

Some reasons for the failure of this dream were already to be observed by looking at the Congress of Arras in 1435, where Isabel made her first appearance on the political scene. This gathering was arranged to justify Philip's switch of allegiance from England to France. Perhaps Isabel's chief contribution there derived from her relationship to Cardinal Henry Beaufort, her mother's half-brother, who was the leader of the English delegation. Isabel's presence helped to smooth over English humiliation and displeasure at Philip's desertion, but her pro-English sympathies were supported by a group of Burgundian knights, of whom the most important were undoubtedly the Lannoys, Guillebert and his brother, Hue; it also included the future chronicler Jean de Wavrin. At the same time there comes to light a pro-French faction, some of whom rather shamelessly accepted bribes from the French king. Notable in this group were the Croys, Antoine and Jean, and the Burgundian chancellor, Nicolas Rolin.[4] The relationship between the pro-English group and crusading interest is perhaps incidental, but the anti-crusading influence of the pro-French courtiers is of considerable significance. Not only did they further the views of both Charles VII and Louis XI in the ducal councils but also they were the cause of a serious quarrel between Philip and his son, which was a major factor in Isabel's retirement from the court in 1457. Even the historical record of the period was affected by this quarrel, for the chronicler Chastellain represents a pro-French point of view, whereas Jean de Wavrin is pro-English and pro-crusade.

It is through Wavrin's *Anciennes Chroniques d'Angleterre* that we learn of a contingent of Burgundian ships dispatched in 1444 to the aid of the Hungarian patriot John Hunyadi. There is also an account of their presence at the Christian defeat at Varna, on the Black Sea, after a voyage through the Dardanelles and a visit to Constantinople. The vividness of Wavrin's account suggests that he may have accompanied his nephew Walerand de

Wavrin, one of the leaders of the expedition.

It should be particularly noted that on the ships commanded by Geoffroy de Thoisy, the other leader of the fleet, more than a third of the sailors were Portuguese. Thoisy, a former companion of the voyager Bertrandon de la Broquière, had earlier been called upon for help by the Hospitallers of Rhodes. In 1441 he had already sailed to Rhodes by way of Lisbon, Ceuta, and the port of Villefranche, near Nice. At Villefranche in 1444 several ships were put under the command of Martin Afonso de Oliveira, a Portuguese member of the duchess Isabel's household. Although Rhodes was saved for the time being, little else was accomplished by these efforts. The presence of the Burgundians was felt in the Mediterranean for several years. Their adventures have sometimes been described as piratical, but these activities involved the duke in closer diplomatic relations not only with Constantinople but also with Venice and Naples. In 1445 there was even discussion of his taking possession of Genoa for use as a naval and crusading base. The duchess was further tempted by the idea of acquiring the city as an apanage for their son, Charles.[5]

All of this serves as an explanation of why the duke of Burgundy should have been expected to lend strong support to Pope Nicolas V's call for a crusade after the fall of Constantinople to the Turks in 1453. This, of course, was the inspiration for the Banquet of the Pheasant, celebrated at Lille in February of 1454. This is undoubtedly one of the best-known episodes in Burgundian history, for Olivier de la Marche's account of the festivities has been endlessly repeated, suggesting all too frequently that decadence and frivolity characterized the times—an idea fostered by Johan Huizinga's ever-popular *Waning of the Middle Ages*.[6] The plight of Constantinople also brought about a great flowering of crusade literature.

The year before, in 1453, Philip had sent the bishop Jean Germain to the French king, Charles VII, to exhort him to join a crusade, an expedition marked by the composition of Germain's *Discours du voyage d'Outremer (Discourse on the Voyage Over-*

seas),[7] which did not meet with any notable success in gaining the king's support, although in 1455 he did agree to let Philip recruit crusaders in France.[8] Although the duke's concept of the crusade may, in general, have been more old-fashioned than that of certain members of his court, he had commissioned the construction of three ships in Nice, referred to in Burgundian archives as a *nave*, a *caravelle*, and a *balenier*. The duchess interested herself in the construction of a *grand nave*, of which part of the crew was Portuguese. One rarely mentioned aspect of the problem was the difference between French and Burgundian views as to how such an expedition should be organized. The French view seems to have been characterized by the traditional chivalric idea that it was unknightly to fight anywhere but on dry land. (It is quite true that transporting horses any distance by ship posed problems.) The pro-English faction, however, including the duchess Isabel, was interested in the development of sea power and thought that a crusading venture should be carried out with naval power. It is unlikely that Isabel and other Burgundians involved in negotiating a new commercial treaty with England in 1449 would have been unaware of the serious Turkish threat to European commercial interests or, indeed, have failed to suspect the treachery of Genoese or even Venetian shipping interests in the Mediterranean. It is quite possible that the differing French views were merely a cover for the fact that neither Charles VII nor Louis XI had any intention of supporting a crusade. At the time when Charles VII might have been most willing to consider such a venture, relations between him and Philip the Good were strained by the unforeseen appearance at the Burgundian court of the dauphin Louis, seeking refuge from his father's displeasure.

It was also at about this time that Alfonso V of Aragon wrote to the seneschal of Italy concerning an embassy he had sent to the Burgundian court, praising Isabel's crusading fervor and urging her to reinforce the duke's crusading intentions.[9] In the long run, however, it was the pro-French element that gained the upper hand, partly because of the duke's pressing problems at home but primarily through the machinations of the Croys. Their ever-increasing influence over the duke as he grew older brought about the crisis of 1457, when Philip quarreled so bitterly with his son that Charles was virtually banished from court. The Croys also engineered the disgrace of Chancellor Rolin and encouraged the duchess to retire from court to a residence at La-Motte-aux-Bois, near Lille. But even from this retreat, she continued to exercise an influence on crusading projects.

By 1461 the flight to Rome of Thomas Paleologus, the last member of the Byzantine ruling family, who brought with him the head of St. Andrew the Apostle, fomented the crusading enthusiasm of Pope Pius II. The pope went so far as to write a curious epistle to Mohammed II, urging him to adopt Christianity not only for his soul's salvation but also because it would enable him to become a second Constantine. Not surprisingly, this missive fell on unreceptive ground. The pope also promulgated a new crusading effort. In the fall of 1463 a coalition was finally formed among the pope, Philip the Good, the Republic of Venice, and Matthias Corvinus, the king of Hungary. This was in fact the nearest the elderly duke of Burgundy came to setting out on a crusade.

Early in 1464, when there were signs of a reconciliation between the duke and Charles, Louis XI of France lost no time in taking advantage of his influence over the Croys and certain other Burgundian courtiers. It was his fear that Charles might be appointed regent during his father's absence, a development that would surely interfere with some of his own plans. He therefore sought an interview with Philip at Lille in February 1464 in which, pleading fear of an English attack on France, he persuaded the duke to postpone his departure until peace with England had been assured. He would then provide Philip with a contingent of ten thousand men for his crusade. On the basis of this promise Philip decided to send his natural son Anthony, with a sort of advance guard, to present his explanations and apologies to Pius II.

It would appear that the pope understood the situation more clearly than did the elderly duke, for although he did not question

Philip's good intentions he expressed his displeasure with those who had dissuaded him from carrying out his original plan. In an anathema pronounced on Holy Thursday of 1464 he referred to "kings who had dared to put any obstacle in the way of the crusade against the Turks," later adding in his *Commentaries* that this was intended to apply to "those who had diverted Philip, duke of Burgundy, from his holy purpose."[10] He was not alone in his misgivings. In an *Epître à la Maison de Bourgogne* dating from more or less the same period, certain Burgundian courtiers tried to insist that the duke's vows should be honored.[11] The influence of the Croys was far from uncontested. This document appears to date from the weeks between 8 March, when Philip announced his change of plans, and 21 May, when a reduced army departed under Anthony of Burgundy's command. A particular passage suggests foot-dragging on the part of some knights:

> O Burgundians, when your prince departs to the sound of the trump, who would not join him? Who would fail to carry out his given vow? What heart would be so cowardly as to fail to risk itself in the company of such a good prince? (p. 49)

As the ships commanded by Anthony of Burgundy sailed from Bruges, Pius II, although he was seriously ill, was determined to offer European princes an example of devotion to the crusading ideal. He himself took the cross in St. Peter's on 18 July, and in spite of his infirmities set out for Ancona, only to die there a month later, on 14 August.

The Burgundians, for their part, did not sail directly to Ancona but rather towards Ceuta in Northern Africa, where the king of Portugal, one of Isabel's nephews, was under siege by the Moors. The Burgundians helped to rescue the city before heading for Marseille, where they learned of the pope's death. Demoralized by the news and by an epidemic that caused considerable havoc, they nevertheless lingered in the Mediterranean until autumn. Isabel's influence over Anthony of Burgundy undoubtedly accounts for an unexpected turn of events. One contingent of Burgundians undertook the rescue of another of Isabel's nephews, Pedro of Portugal, who was contesting his claim to the throne of Catalonia with Juan II of Aragon. As early as May, Pedro had sent messengers to Burgundy to appeal for help. Negotiations were still in progress in August, including letters directed to Anthony of Burgundy and others of the expedition in the Mediterranean. On 19 September there was a direct appeal to the fleet for help; on 3 October one of Isabel's secretaries, Jacotin de Ramecourt, was in Barcelona.[12] The ultimate result was that a part of the Burgundian contingent participated in the Battle of Calaf in February 1465, where despite their efforts Pedro was defeated and his fate sealed. Isabel's attempt to achieve some practical results from the crusading mission was thwarted.

Thereafter, the Burgundians were obliged to make their way home as best they could, impeded by the open hostility of Louis XI, whose ambitions included the domination of Cataluña. Wavrin's *Chronicle* recounts Anthony's return. Before he left Marseille he was entertained by the duke of Calabria, René d'Anjou's son, who revealed that he had been charged by the French king to take Anthony prisoner. He had been unwilling to do this in view of the kind reception given at the Burgundian court to his unfortunate sister, Marguerite d'Anjou, the English queen, when Yorkist forces had obliged her to flee from England. Anthony returned home on horseback, leaving the ships to return to Sluys as best they could. Upon their arrival their artillery was inventoried, their crews paid off, and a sale of two of the ships (to Giovanni Portinari of the Medici Bank in Bruges) was arranged by Antoine de Croy.

It has generally been assumed that Burgundian crusading ambitions ended with Philip's death two years later. Charles the Bold, however, was not exempt from pressures from certain courtiers. He too had made a crusading vow at Lille. It is also probable that as long as his mother lived (d. 1472) he did not entirely give up the idea of a crusade. One suspects her influence in the translations offered to Charles by Vasco de Lucena, another Portuguese member of her entourage. He translated Quintus Curtius's life of Alexander the Great, pointing out in the Prologue that Alexander's exploits had been achieved with a relatively small army guided by their leader's extraordinary military talents. Therefore, he argued, the duke should not fear a comparable undertaking. Vasco de Lucena thus urged Charles to lead an army to the East "pour reduire l'orient a la foy de Jhesucrist" (to reduce the Orient to belief in Jesus Christ). A similar suggestion is to be found in Lucena's French adaptation of Poggio Bracciolini's Latin translation of Xenophon's *Cyropedia*, likewise dedicated to Charles.[13]

Although Charles never went on a crusade it has been suggested[14] that he took a greater interest in the matter than was previously thought, that he sometimes spoke of a crusade as the ultimate goal, the climax of his life's work—an ambition that he was, of course, not spared to fulfill.

Although undoubtedly disappointed in her failure to influence her husband or her son "constructively," Isabel was not easily deflected from her objectives. She was a worthy sister of Henry the Navigator, and if the direction of the crusade could have been left more directly to her supervision it might indeed have been more successful. Even so, the idea did not die completely, for in 1501 Philip of Cleves, lord of Ravestein and Isabel's grand-nephew through another Portuguese princess, Beatriz of Coimbra, was to be found fighting a Turkish fleet in the Mediterranean for his cousin Louis XII of France.

NOTES

[1]*The Crusade in the Later Middle Ages*, 2nd ed. (New York, 1965), p. 463.

[2]W. J. Entwistle and P. E. Russell, "A Rainha D. Felipa e a sua Côrte," *Congresso do Mundo Português: Publicaçoes*, vol. 2 (Lisbon, 1940), pp. 317-46.

[3]Guillebert de Lannoy, *Oeuvres*, ed. C. Poitvin (Louvain, 1878); *Le Voyage d'Outremer de Bertrandon de la Broquière*, ed. C. Schéfer (Paris, 1892).

[4]M.-R. Thieleman, "Les Croy, conseillers des ducs de Bourgogne," *Bulletin de la Commission Royale d'Histoire* 124 (1959): 1-145.

[5]A. Grunzweig, "Un plan d'acquisition de Gênes par Philippe le Bon, 1445," *Moyen Age* 42 (1932): 81-110.

[6]*The Waning of the Middle Ages* (London, 1924; rept. New York, 1965), p. 463.

[7]"Le Discours du voyage d'Outremer au très victorieux roi Charles VII, prononcé en 1452 par Jean Germain, évêque de Chalon-sur-Saône," *Revue de l'Orient Latin* 3 (1895): 303-42.

[8]Y. Lacaze, "Politique Mediterranéenne et projets de croisade chez Philippe le Bon," *Annales de Bourgogne* 41 (1969): 32-33.

[9]C. Marinesco, "Philippe le Bon, duc de Bourgogne, et la croisade. Part I (1419-1453)," *Actes de VIe Congrès des études byzantines* (Paris, 1950), p. 157.

[10]R. Vaughan, *Philip the Good* (London, 1970), p. 370; Pius II, *Commentaries*, trans. F. A. Gragg and L. C. Gabel, Smith College Studies in History, 42 (1957), pp. 852-57.

[11]Ed. Georges Doutrepont, in *Analectes pour servir à l'histoire ecclésiastique de la Belgique*, Tome 32, 3rd ser. (Brussels, 1906), pp. 5-56.

[12]Barcelona, Archivos de la Corona de Aragon, R. 31 Intrusos, fol. 16v°; R. 21, Intr. fol. 148v° and 132v°.

[13]D. Gallet-Guerne, *Vasque de Lucène et la Cyropédie à la cour de Bourgogne* (Geneva, 1974), Introduction, esp. p. 13.

[14]R. J. Walsh, "Charles the Bold and the Crusade: Politics and Propaganda," *Journal of Medieval History* 3 (1977): 53-87.

NOTES ON CONTRIBUTORS

Jeanette M. A. BEER is Professor of French and Comparative Literature at Purdue University. A native New Zealander and a graduate of the Universities of New Zealand, Oxford, and Columbia, she is the recipient of twenty-three honors and awards in New Zealand, Oxford, and the United States. She is the author of eight books and numerous articles on medieval language and literature, the most recent being *Early Prose in France*, and the editor of *Medieval Translators and Their Craft*. Professor Beer is a member of the Editorial Board of Purdue University Press and an Associate Editor of the Purdue University Monographs in Romance Languages. She has been a Fellow of St. Anne's College, Oxford, and has taught in universities in New Zealand, France, and the USA.

Robert Francis COOK is Professor of French at the University of Virginia and Secretary-Treasurer of the Société Rencesvals, American-Canadian branch. His studies on the Old French Crusade Cycle include *Chanson d'Antioche, chanson de geste: Le cycle de la croisade est-il épique?*, *Le Bâtard de Bouillon, Chanson de geste: édition critique*, and (with Larry S. Crist) *Le Deuxième Cycle de la croisade: Deux études sur son développement*. His most recent book is *The Sense of the Song of Roland* (1987).

John Gordon DAVIES is Emeritus Edward Cadbury Professor of Theology, University of Birmingham (England). He is the author of two dozen books, which cover Church history, liturgy and architecture, and theology in general. His most recent work is *Pilgrimage Yesterday and Today. Why? Where? How?*

[Editor's note: This brief notice was mailed by Professor Davies on 12 December 1990; we learned with regret that he died on the thirteenth. He had been Head of the Department of Theology at the University of Birmingham from 1960 until his retirement in 1986, and was founder and Director of the Institute for the Study of Worship and Religious Architecture at that university. A priest of the Church of England, in 1965 he was made an honorary canon of Birmingham Cathedral.]

Gary DICKSON is Senior Lecturer in History at the University of Edinburgh (Scotland) and a Fellow of the Royal Historical Society. He formerly directed The Antiquary Visiting Scholars Programme. He has written about the cult of saints, and medieval and Renaissance Perugia, and is actively working in this area. The first series of his Studies in Medieval Revivalism (Christian revivalism from Luke's Pentecost to the Florence of Savonarola) is devoted to popular movements during the crusading era and will be completed soon.

Robert Worth FRANK, Jr., is Professor Emeritus of English at the Pennsylvania State University and former head of the department. He is co-founder and editor of *The Chaucer Review* and author of *"Piers Plowman" and the Scheme of Salvation* and *Chaucer and "The Legend of Good Women."* He has held ACLS and Guggenheim fellowships and is a Visiting Fellow of Clare Hall, Cambridge. He is a past president of the New Chaucer Society. His recent work is in miracle literature, Chaucerian pathos, and *Piers Plowman*.

Dorothea R. FRENCH teaches ancient and medieval history at Santa Clara University. Her research on pilgrimage has led her to examine topics such as the motif of death and rebirth in the pilgrimage tradition to St. Patrick's Purgatory, Ireland; pilgrimage rituals; and mapping the sacred center. She is currently completing an anthology of readings on pilgrimage and a video on St. Patrick's Purgatory.

Mary HAMEL is Professor of English at Mount St. Mary's College in Maryland. As MLA-ACLS Fellow in Literature in 1981-82, she completed work on an edition of the fourteenth-century Middle English alliterative poem *Morte Arthure*, which was published in 1984, and she has also published a number of articles and reviews on Middle English literature; she is currently finishing a new edition of the fifteenth-century prose *Life of Alexander* in the Lincoln Thornton MS.

Horst RICHTER is Associate Professor, German Department, McGill University (Canada). His areas of interest are Early Middle High German religious literature, medieval allegory and typology, religious concepts in the reports of the early crusades. Research publications include: *Kommentar zum Rolandslied des Pfaffen Konrad. Teil I.* (1972) and articles on "Das Hoflager Kaiser Karls. Zur Karlsdarstellung im deutschen Rolandslied" and "'Allegoria' und die Metaphorik der frühmittelhochdeutschen Literatur."

Donna M. ROGERS is Assistant Professor of Spanish at The Pennsylvania State University. Her research interests include medieval Catalan and Castilian language and literature, and she is the author of several articles in these fields as well as in computer software for the study of Old Spanish. She has edited two texts by Francesc Eiximenis and is currently translating one of them, the *Regiment de la cosa pública*, into English (*The Rule of the State*). She is at work on a study of late-fourteenth-century Catalan language, as reflected in the works of Eiximenis.

Barbara N. SARGENT-BAUR is Professor of French and Director of the Medieval and Renaissance Studies Program at the University of Pittsburgh. In her published work she has concentrated on medieval and Anglo-French literature in its cultural context. Her articles have in the main discussed Chrétien de Troyes, Béroul, and François Villon. Her latest book is *Brothers of Dragons: Job dolens and François Villon* (1990). She is finishing an edition with translation and commentary of the complete works of Villon, and a long study of Chrétien's *Conte del Graal*.

Susan STAKEL is Associate Professor of French at the University of Denver. She is the author of *False Roses: Structures of Duality and Deceit in Jean de Meun's Roman de la Rose*, a translation with introduction of *The Montpellier Codex*, and articles on the allegory of Jean de Meun, Christine de Pizan, and Charles d'Orléans.

Charity Cannon WILLARD is Professor Emerita of French and Spanish Literature at the former Ladycliff College. Since retirement she has devoted herself to research and writing about late-medieval French literature, especially the works of Christine de Pizan, on which she is a recognized authority, and the court of Burgundy. Among her publications are *Christine de Pizan: Her Life and Works* and a critical edition of the same author's *Livre des trois vertus* (with Eric Hicks, 1989). She has in progress a biography of Isabel of Portugal, duchess of Burgundy.

INDEX

Abel, 71
Abelard, Peter, 62
Abilant, 162
Abraham, 56, 64, 71
Acre, 5, 30 n. 102, 148, 150, 182, 185, 192 n. 22, 193 n. 31
Acts of the Apostles, known world as described in, 60
Adam, 11, 52, 56, 59, 66, 71
Adam-Christ typology, 56, 57, 59, 66, 67, 68
Adam, William, 20; *De modo Saracenos extirpandi*, 20
Adoman (pilgrim), 55, 60
Agremore, 184
Aids to Devotion, 3, 5-6, 14-15, 18-19, 23. See also Itineraries
Aigues-Mortes, 141, 146
Albert of Aix/Aachen, 15, 159, 164
Albigensian crusade, 91
Alexander the Great, life of, 212-13
Alexandria, 144, 160
Alexius I Comnenus, 17
Alfonso V of Aragon, 209
Aljighidai (Mongol general), 141-42, 147
Alpais of Cudot, 84
Alphandéry, P., 17, 89
Alps, crossing, 4

Amalric of Bène, 85
Amalricians, 84-85, 94
Ambrose, Saint, 71
Ambrose (Ambroise) the Minstrel, 14-15, 21, 30 n. 102; *L'Estoire de la guerre sainte*, 21
Amiens, 84-85
Ampullae, as souvenirs, 56, 58
Ancona, 211
Andrew, Brother (order of St. Jacques), 141, 142
Andrew of Longjumeau (Dominican friar), 147
Anthony of Burgundy (son of Philip the Good), 210, 211-12
Antioch, 14, 18, 19, 159, 161, 163, 170, 175 n. 7, 182-83. See also Crusade Cycles
Anti-Semitism, 83, 169, 170, 174, 178-79, 180, 182, 183-84, 186, 189, 190 n. 3
Apulia, 168
Arnold of Nijmegen, 166, 173
Arnold von Harff, 9, 10
Arras, Congress of, 207
Asensio, Eugenio, 129
Athanasius, Saint, 71
Athens, 73
Atiya, Aziz, 167, 189, 205

Aucassin and Nicolette, 95-96
Auctores, 73, 75, 109, 110, 149-50, 202
Augustine, Saint, 11
Auvergne, 168
Avignon, 99 n. 12, 160
¡Ay Jherusalem!, 127-34
Ayub (sultan), 147

Babylon, 144; sultan of, 141, 144, 145, 189, 192 n. 22
Baghdad, caliph of, 141
Baldwin I (Latin emperor), 93, 160
Baldwin of Beauvais, 162
Baldwin of Bourgueuil, 20-21
Balkans, 188
Barbery expedition, 188
Barcelona, 212
Barletta, 168
"Barnwell" chronicle, 88
Baudas, caliph of, 141
Baudouin de Sebourc. See Crusade Cycles
Baudry of Dol (bishop), 3, 16; *History*, 3, 16
Bayezid I (sultan of the Turks), 188
Beatriz of Coimbra, 213
Beatus of Liebana, Saint, 60-61; *Commentary on the Apocalypse*, 60. See also Maps
Beaufort, Henry (cardinal), 207
Bede, on the Holy Places, 9
Bedouins (Saracen), sultan of, 145
Belard of Ascoli, 3
Benedict of Nursia, Saint, 116
Bénézet, Saint, 85, 99 n. 12
Berlière, U., 91
Bernard of Clairvaux, Saint, 96, 123
Bernarde (pilgrim), 36-37
Bernhard von Breydenbach, 12
Berry, 168
Bertrand(on) de la Brocquière, 20, 206, 208

Bethlehem, 50
Blanche of Lancaster, 206
Blanche (queen of France), 86
Bohemond, 19, 162
Boniface VIII (pope), 5
Bonneval, 92
Booty, 15, 113-14, 129, 152, 183, 186
Bordeaux pilgrim, 3, 47
Bounty, 144-45, 152
Bouvines, 94
Bowman, Leonard, 196, 200
Braet, Herman, 197
Bréhier, Louis, 159
Brittania, 62
Bromholm, 6
Bruges, 211, 212
Burchard of Mount Sion, 11, 66-67
Burgos, 13
Burgundian crusade, 205-14

Caesaria, 193 n. 35
Caesarius of Heisterbach, 13
Caiaphas, 186
Cain, 71
Cairo, 5, 144, 145
Calabria, 168
Calaf, 212
Calixtus II (pope), 7
Calvary, Mount, as center of the earth (allegorical, literal), 45-81
Cannibalism, 179-80, 181, 184, 185, 186, 191 n. 12
Canons, conciliar, 2, 12-13, 22
Cartography, 12, 21-22, 45, 46, 48-49, 51, 52, 60-61, 64, 67, 69-70, 73, 75. See also Maps; Matthew Paris
Catalonia, 212
Cathars, crusade against, 90
Cathedral, as microcosm of world, 64-65
Ceuta, 206, 208, 211

Châlons, Council of, 12-13
Chambéry, 14
Chanson de geste, 21. See also
  Ambrose the Minstrel; Crusade
  Cycles; Epic
Chanson de Jérusalem. See Cru-
  sade Cycles
Chanson de Roland, 108, 118, 119,
  162, 166
Chapel of the Place of the Nailing
  of the Cross, 71-72
Charlemagne, 93, 177, 178,
  192 n. 22; cycle, 177; romance,
  188
Charles VI of France, 160, 188, 189
Charles VII of France, 205, 207,
  208-09
Charles the Bold (duke of Bur-
  gundy), 206, 207, 208, 210, 212,
  213
Chartres, 38, 43 n. 13, 64, 85, 89,
  90-92, 94, 95
Chastellain (chronicler), 207
Châteaudun, 85, 92, 99 n. 13
Chaucer, Geoffrey, 12, 35
Chédéville, André, 92, 95
Chétifs, 165
Chevalier au cygne, 165
Children's Crusade, 83-105
Chrétienté Corbaran, 165
Christians, sects in Middle East,
  10; at Holy Sepulchre, 10, 66,
  70, 71-72, 80 n. 62
Christine de Pizan, 195-203, 205;
  L'Avision-Christine, 195,
  198-99, 201, 202; *La Cité des
  dames*, 201; *La Mutacion de
  fortune*, 201; *Le Livre des faits
  et bonnes moeurs du sage roy
  Charles V*, 201; *Le Livre du
  chemin du long estude*, 195,
  197-98, 199-200, 201-02; *Livre
  des trois vertus*, 201

Church of Mount Calvary, 55-56,
  66, 71
Church of the Holy Sepulchre, 53,
  54, 55-56, 66, 70-71, 72
Civetot, 175 n. 7
Clement V (pope), 160
Clermont, Council of, 13, 22, 110,
  121
Climacus, John, 134 n. 7
Cloyes. See Stephen of Cloyes
Codex Calixtinus. See *Liber Sancti
  Jacobi*
Codex Ottobonianus latinus, 3
Col, Gontier, 196
Col, Pierre, 196
Compostela, 3, 7, 14, 19. See also
  James the Apostle, Saint
Constantina of Auxerre, 37
Constantine the Great, 53
Constantinople, 4, 14, 93, 163,
  188, 199, 205, 207, 208
Continents, assigned to sons of
  Noah, 51
Conversion, 113, 116, 117, 141,
  162, 163, 164-65, 170, 178, 184,
  210, 213
Corona vitae, 111-12
Cosmic zones, physical openings
  in, 51-52, 55-56, 67
Crossbow, 143
Crusade as pilgrimage, 13-23, 87,
  157, 161, 168
Crusade Cycles, 157-75
"Cult of carts" at Chartres (1144),
  91
Curiositas, 11
Cyprian, Saint, 115
Cyprus, 136, 141, 142, 146, 147,
  148

Damietta, 135, 141, 142-45, 146,
  148, 150-53
Daniel (Russian abbot), 10-11

Dante Alighieri, 130, 134 n. 7
de Croy, Antoine, 207, 209-10, 211, 212
de Croy, Jean, 207, 209-10, 211
Delaporte, Y., 91
del Carmen Pescador del Hoyo, María, 127
Denis, Saint, 92-93. See also Saint-Denis
Devotio, 84
de Vries, Henk, 129
Deyermond, Alan, 129, 130
Diaries, 3-4, 17, 22. See also Itineraries
Dionysius, 73; *Antiquities*, 73
Dream-vision, 195-203
Dress and insignia, 5, 13, 14, 15, 38, 39, 108, 118, 144, 198
Duby, Georges, 95
Dunois, the. See Stephen of Cloyes
Dupront, Alphonse, 33

Ebedy, 184
Eden, Garden of, 49, 60-61, 64, 199
Egeria (Galician nun), 4, 9, 47
Egypt, 141, 143, 144, 145, 148, 150
Eighth Crusade, 23, 167
Ekkehard, 118
Eliade, Mircea, 60, 64
Emmaus, 13
Enfances Godefroi, 165
Enguerrand of Saint-Pol, 162
Enslavement, 32, 42 n. 10, 144, 145, 152, 181, 183, 184, 185, 187, 189, 192 n. 23, 193 nn. 31 and 35, 212
Ephesus, 4
Epic, 21, 197. See also Crusade Cycles
Epiphanius (monk), 59
Epître à la Maison de Bourgogne, 211
Equitatus Christi, 116-17

Erhard Reuwich of Utrecht, 12
Etienne, Raymond, 20; *Directorium passagium faciendum*, 20
Eton, 8
Eusebius of Caesarea, Saint, 12, 48, 49, 51, 53; *Vita Constantini*, 53
Eustace de Flay, 87
Eutropius, Saint, 7
Evervin of Creil, 162
Ex voto, 32, 40, 41

Famine, 128, 162, 166, 179, 180, 185-86, 187
Fasting, 14, 18, 84, 114, 168
Feast (Banquet) of the Pheasant, 207, 208. See also Lille
Felix Fabri (Dominican, of Ulm), 5-6, 45, 46, 70-75; *The Wanderings*, 5, 45
First Crusade, 13, 14, 17, 18, 22, 62, 91, 93, 110, 115, 117, 121, 122-23, 157, 159, 163, 167, 175 n. 7, 180, 184, 190 n. 3
Flagellants, 97
Fleets, Burgundian, (1444) 207-08, (ca. 1453) 209, (1464) 211-12; of Louis IX. See Jean Sarrasin; *Monjoie*
Florie (queen of Outremer), 163-64
Foulet, Alfred, 147
Fourth Crusade, 154 n. 5
Frescobaldi, 5
Fulcher of Chartres, 13, 15, 17, 28 n. 77, 110, 117-18, 122, 180, 181, 182-83, 184, 193 n. 35; *Historia Hierosolymitana*, 13
Fulk of Neuilly, 154 n. 5

Gabriele Capodilista, 12
Galicia, 4
Gardiner, F. C., 196
Gaul, 86
Gaza, 143

Genoa, 208, 209
Geoffrey de Villehardouin (marshal), 14, 146, 152, 154 n. 5; *La Conquête de Constantinople*, 146
Geoffroy de Thoisy, 208
Geoffroy of Sargines, 142
Gerbert of Sens, 142
Germain, Jean (bishop), 208; *Discours du voyage d'Outremer*, 208-09
Gesta Francorum et aliorum Hierosolymitanorum, 3, 14, 16, 20-21, 21-22; *Descriptio sanctorum locorum*, 16; *Situs Hierusalem*, 21-22
Gesta Francorum Jherusalem expugnantium, 16, 28 n. 77, 159, 182, 183
Giacomo de Verona, 5; *Peregrinationes et indulgentiae Terre Sancte*, 5
Gilbert de Lannoy, Sir, 20
Goderich, Master John, 142
Godfrey of Bouillon (*advocatus sancti sepulchri*), 160, 162-63, 166
Godfrey of Boulogne, 15
Godin, Master (Amalrician leader), 84-85
Golden Legend, 178
Golgotha, 50, 54, 56, 66, 72, 73
Graphia aureae urbis Romae. See *Mirabilia*
Gray, George Z., 87
Great Khan (Gaiouk, Mongol), 141-42, 146, 148
Great St. Bernard, the, 4
Great Schism, 188
Gregory of Nyssa, Saint, 49-51
Gregory the Great, 5, 196; *Moralia*, 5
Grieve, Patricia, 129, 133

Guibert de Nogent, 20-21, 121
Guidebooks, 2, 3, 4, 6-9, 10, 19, 22-23, 45, 47, 75. See also Aids to Devotion; Diaries; Indulgences; Itineraries; Letters
Guides, crusader, 17, 19; pilgrim, 198, 199-200, 202. See also Guidebooks
Guillaume de Lorris, 197, 198
Guillaume de Tyr. See William of Tyre
Guillaume le Breton, 94
Guillebert de Lannoy, 207
Guylforde, Sir Richard. See *Pilgrimage of . . .*

Hadrian (emperor), 53
Hagenmeyer, Heinrich, 18
Handbook, cartographer's, 69
Hathvide (of Valenciennes), 38-39
Helena, Saint, 53, 54
Henry (king of Cyprus), 148
Henry of Derby, 188
Henry II of England, 37
Henry V of England, 20, 205
Henry the Navigator (of Portugal), 206, 213
Heraclius (patriarch of Jerusalem), 163
Herbert le Sommelier, 142
Hermet, 36
Hibernia, 62
Higden, Ralph, 178; *Polychronicon*, 178
Hilarius, Saint, 75
Hilton, Rodney, 96
Historia belli sacri, 117
Hodoeporicon, of Saint Willibald, 11, 20, 26 n. 37
Holy Lance, 161
Holy Land, as center of world, 22. See also Cartography; Jerusalem; Maps

Holy Sepulchre, 10, 15, 53, 66, 71, 74, 75, 80 n. 62, 129, 131, 132, 163, 164, 168, 170, 171. See also Christians, sects; Church of the Holy Sepulchre
Honorius of Autun, 115-16
Hospitallers, 148, 208
Hue de Lannoy, 207
Huizinga, Johan, 208
Hundred Years' War, 160
Hunyadi, John (Hungarian patriot), 207

Ibelin, 148
Iberian crisis (1212), 88-89, 90, 91, 92. See also *Chanson de Roland*; Konrad, *Rolandslied*; *Reconquista*
Iconography, 45, 55, 56, 57, 58, 59, 67, 68, 87, 93
Ile-de-France, 83
Imitatio Christi, 111, 118
Imitatio Dei, 118
Indulgences, 4-5, 8-9, 10, 15, 18; *Libri indulgentiarum*, 4-5, 8-9, 18, 22-23
Information for Pilgrims unto the Holy Land, 8-9, 10
Innocent III (pope) 90, 91, 93, 97
Irish monks, 196
Isaac, 56, 71
Isabel of Portugal, 205-14
Isidore of Seville, Saint, 51, 116; *Etymologiae*, 51
Itineraries, 2-3, 4, 5, 8, 9, 11, 12, 16-17, 19, 20, 22, 47, 66, 94; *Itinerarium Perigrinorum et Gesta Regis Ricardi*, 182, 190 n. 3. See also Guidebooks

Jacob, fountain of, 52, 55; ladder, 130, 131; stone, 131
Jacotin de Ramecourt, 212
Jacques de Vitry, 96

Jaffa, 8, 10
James the Apostle, Saint, 7, 13, 14, 111
James the Less, Saint, 178
Jean de Joinville, 14, 18-19, 20, 147, 148, 150, 151, 152
Jean de Meun, 195, 196
Jean de Montreuil, 196
Jean de Wavrin, 207-08, 212; *Anciennes Chroniques d'Angleterre*, 207-08, 212
Jean le Long (Jean d'Ypres) (abbot), 88-90, 92; *Chronica monasterii sancti Bertini*, 88-89; *Vita Erkembodonis*, 89
Jean le Marchant, 91; *Miracles de Notre-Dame de Chartres*, 91
Jean Sarrasin (chamberlain to Louis IX), letter of, 135-55
Jericho, 15
Jerome, Saint, 4, 12, 47, 48-49, 51, 71, 111, 196
Jerusalem, 3, 6, 8, 10, 13, 14, 15, 17, 18, 20, 23, 35, 45-81, 93, 114, 127-34, 159, 163, 164, 168, 170, 177-94, 200. See also Holy Land
Joan of Arc, 205
Joannes Phocas, 66
Johanna of Constantinople, 206
John, Saint (apostle), 111
John Chrysostom, Saint, 71, 134 n. 7
John of Beaumont, Sir, 142
John of Canterbury, Brother, 4
John of Gaunt, 206
John of Würzburg, 66, 67
John (II) the Good of France, 160
Joseph (of Arimathea), 70
Josephus, 177, 179, 180, 181, 182, 183, 185, 192 n. 26, 193 n. 35; *The Jewish War* (*Bellum Judaicum*), 177, 179, 182
Jordan River, 15

Joshua, 113
Jotapata, 182
Juan II of Aragon, 212

Kerbogha, 162, 163
Khludov Psalter, 59
Knights Templars, 123, 148
Konrad (cleric, of Regensburg),
107-09, 114, 118-23; *Rolands-
lied*, 107-09, 114, 115, 118-23.
See also *Militia Dei*

Labyrinth, 66; in cathedrals,
64-65
La Chanson d'Antioche. See
Crusade Cycles
Lambert of St.-Omer, 50; *Liber
Floridus*, 50
Lamentations, Book of, as related
to fall of Jerusalem, 129-30, 133
Languedoc, 21
Laon Anonymous (chronicler), 84,
85-87, 88, 90, 94, 95, 96, 97
Las Navas da Tolosa, 88-89
Le Bâtard de Bouillon. See
Crusade Cycles
LeBon, Gustave, 90
Legend, 53, 54-55, 56, 57, 59, 67,
71, 72, 149, 178
Lendit (fair), 92, 93, 94
Letters, 1-2, 4, 7, 17-18, 22, 49-51,
86-88, 91, 92, 128, 130-31,
135-55, 187-88, 196, 210, 211,
212
Liber Sancti Jacobi, 7; *Codex
Calixtinus*, 7
Libri indulgentiarum. See Indul-
gences
Lille, 208, 210, 212
Limassol, 141, 142, 147, 148
Limousin, 37
Lisbon, 208
Literature, the (crusader, pilgrim),
1-30; comparison, esp. 22-23

Livre d'Eracle, Rothelin continua-
tion, 135-36, 149-50, 153
Llull (Lull), Raymond, 130,
134 n. 7, 167
Lohengrin 160, 163
Lotharingia (Lorraine), 160
Louis VII of France, 87, 93
Louis IX of France, Saint, 14, 20,
23, 86, 135, 141, 142, 143-44,
145, 146, 147, 148, 150, 151-52,
153, 207. See also Jean de
Joinville; Jean Sarrasin;
Saint-Denis
Louis XI of France, 207, 209, 210,
212
Louis XII of France, 213
Ludolph von Suchem, 62
Luther, Martin, 7-8
Lyons, Council of, 22, 128

Macarius (bishop of Jerusalem), 53
Madrid, 127-28
Magi, 72
Mahomet, 170, 171
Mainz, 12
Mal d'ardents (ergot poisoning), 38
Maps, Plans, and Illustrations, 2,
11-12, 17, 21-22, 47, 48, 49, 60,
62, 69, 70; Beatus map, 60-61;
Ebstorf map, 64, 65; *Mappae
mundi*, 46, 60, 61, 62, 64, 65,
74; T-O maps, 22, 30 n. 105, 50,
51, 52, 60, 62, 63, 64, 69-70.
See also Cartography; Matthew
Paris; Ptolemy, Claudius; *Situs
Hierusalem*
Marco Polo, 69
Margaret of Constantinople, 206
Margaret of Flanders, 206
Margery Kempe, 14
Marguerite d'Anjou (queen of Eng-
land), 212
Marino Sanuti/Sanudo, 12, 167

Markion, 113
Marra, 180, 192 n. 22
Marseilles, 211, 212
Martin Afonso de Oliveira, 208
Matilda (holy woman), 84, 85
Martyrdom, 108, 115-16, 118, 119, 120, 121-23, 131, 152, 166, 173-74
Matthew of Marly, 142
Matthew Paris, 12, 22
Matthias Corvinus (king of Hungary), 210
Maundeville, John, 11, 14
Mecca, 171
Medici Bank, 212
Melchizedek, 56, 71
Mensonge, 197, 202
Midrash, 52
Mileto of Sardis, 47
Militia Dei, 107-26
Militia spiritualis, 109, 112-13, 115, 116, 119-20
Minnis, Cola, 159
Mirabilia, 7-8
Miracle, 31, 32, 34-43, 54-55, 80 n. 62, 84, 86, 87, 91, 92, 104 n. 55, 141, 146
Mohammed, floating tomb of, 166; floating statue of, 171
Mohammed II, 210
Monjoie (ship), 141, 142, 151
Monte Cassino, 9
Morte Arthure, 189
Mosaic (at Daphni), 67, 68
Motive, crusader, 13, 15, 16, 18, 66, 107, 108, 109, 110, 115-16, 117, 118-19, 121-23, 128, 168, 169, 170-71, 172, 173, 177, 178, 186-87, 189, 190 n. 3, 205-06; pilgrim, 4, 11, 12-13, 15, 16, 31-32, 39, 45, 47, 48, 64-66, 196, 200. See also Crusade as pilgrimage

Mountjoy, 14
Mount of Olives, 20, 50
Mount Sion, Franciscan monastery on, 6, 8
Mulberton (Norfolk), 10

Naples, 208
Navigators, Mediterranean, 69, 208, 209
Nazareth, 9
Nero, 178
New Jerusalem, 133, 200
Nibelungenlied, 109
Nicaea, 183
Niccolò of Poggibonsi, 9, 10; *A Voyage beyond the Seas (1346-50)*, 10
Nice, 209
Nicholas V (pope), 208
Nicholas Arrode, 35, 141, 145
Nicholas de Martoni (notary), 9-10
Nicholas of Cologne, 87, 101 n. 26
Nicholaus Germanus (Benedictine, in Florence), 70
Nicodemus, 70
Nicopolis (1396), 160, 179, 188, 189, 205
Nicosia, 141
Nile River, 73, 144, 145, 150, 153
Notre Dame de Rocamadour. See Rocamadour

Odoric, Friar, 69
Olivier de la Marche, 208
Origen, 113-15
Orosius, 51; *Historia*, 51
Otto of Freising (bishop), 87
Outremer, 93, 163-64
Overpopulation, rural, 92

Palestine, 9, 10, 11, 19, 45-81, 166
Palmer, J. J. N., 179, 188
Paris, 14, 84-85, 88, 92, 101 n. 27, 135, 145-46, 148, 150, 152, 153, 199; masters, 86, 94

Parts of a church, symbolism of, 9
Pastores, crusade of (1251), 83, 86, 95, 98 n. 5
Paten (Siberian), 56, 57
Patrides, C. A., 130
Paul, Saint, 109, 110-16, 117, 196
Paula (Roman matron), 4, 47
Paulinus of Nola, 15
Pauperes, crusade of. See Peter the Hermit
Pedro of Portugal, 212
Peregrinatio puerorum, 83. See also Children's Crusade
Peregrinus, 13, 87
Persia, 142
Peter de Abano (of Padua), 73
Peter, Saint, 113-14, 122, 173
Peter the Deacon (librarian), 9
Peter the Hermit, 83-84, 87, 157, 164
Piers Plowman, 187
Philip of Cleves, 213
Philip (II) Augustus of France, 83, 86-88, 91, 93-94, 185
Philip (IV) the Fair of France, 160
Philip VI of France, 160
Philip the Bold, 206
Philip the Good (duke of Burgundy), 205-14
Philippe de Mézières, 160, 167, 187-88, 189; *Letter to King Richard II*, 187
Piacenza pilgrim, 3
Pilgerbuch, 9
Pilgrim plays, 196
Pilgrimage of Sir Richard Guylforde to the Holy Land, A.D. 1506, The, 10
Pius II (pope), 210-11; *Commentaries*, 211
Planck, Stephen (printer), 9
Poggio Bracciolini, 213
Poirion, Daniel, 202
Poissy, 142

Portinari, Giovanni, 212
Processional for Pilgrims to the Holy Land (Franciscan), 5, 23
Propaganda, 20, 21, 93, 148, 157-75, 188-89
Ptolemy, Claudius, 46, 47, 48, 69-70, 73; *Geographia (Atlas)*, 48, 69-70, 73
Pueri, meaning of, 95-96
Pynson (printer), 5

Quarrel of the Rose, 195
Quintus Curtius, 212-13

Rabbi ben Gurion, 52
Raedts, Peter, 85, 88, 95, 96
Raimbaut Creton, 162
Rallying cries, 14
Rates of exchange, 8
Raymond of Aguilers, 17
Reconquista, 127, 133
Relics, 7, 14, 42 nn. 2 and 11, 54, 90-91, 93, 142, 143, 210
Renaud de Mouçon (bishop of Chartres), 91
Renaud Porchet, 162
René d'Anjou, 212
Return of Cornumarant, 163
Rhodes, 208
Riant, P., 17
Richard Coer de Lyon, 177, 178, 180-81, 182, 184-85, 186, 187, 189, 192 n. 22
Richard Coeur de Lion (king of England), 14-15, 182, 189, 192 n. 22, 193 n. 31
Richard, Jean, 22
Richard of Chaumont, 162
Richard II of England, 160, 188, 189
Richard of Poitou (count), 190 n. 3
Richard the Pilgrim, 161
Riley-Smith, Jonathan, 83-84
Robert de Clari, 14, 154 n. 7; *Conquête de Constantinople*, 14

Robert de Torigny, 37
Robert (patriarch of Jerusalem), 128
Robert the Monk, 20-21, 190 n. 3
Roberto de Sanseverino, 14
Rocamadour, 31, 34-43; narratives, 33-43; Notre Dame de, 34; Virgin of, 31, 34, 35, 36, 38, 39
Roland. See *Chanson de Roland*; Konrad, *Rolandslied*
Rolandslied. See Konrad; *Militia Dei*
Roger d'Argenteuil, 190 n. 5; *Bible en françois*, 190 n. 5
Rolin, Nicolas (chancellor of Burgundy), 207, 210
Roman de la rose, 195, 197, 198, 202
Rome, 3, 7, 12, 19, 36, 90, 171, 173, 177, 187, 210; St. Peter's, 177, 188, 211; Stations at, 9
Rothelin continuation. See *Livre d'Eracle*
Rousset, Paul, 159
Rye (England), 10

Sacral power and pilgrimage, 31-43, 45-81. See also Saint-Denis
Saewulf (Anglo-Saxon merchant), 3
Saint-Denis, 84-88, 90, 92-94; gonfalon, 142-43, 144; oriflamme, 93
Saladin, 80 n. 62, 157, 162, 164-65, 193 n. 31
San Domingo de Silos, 13
Santiago. See Compostela
Scourging, 14. See also Flagellants
Second Crusade, 87, 93, 167
Sege off Melayne, 178, 189
Seventh Crusade, 153, 167. See also Jean Sarrasin
Shepherds. See Stephen of Cloyes
Siege engines, 182-83, 192 n. 22
Siege of Jerusalem, The, 177-94

Sigal, Pierre-André, 33
Sigeric, 3
Sigurd of Norway, 15
Simon Semeonis (Irish Franciscan), 11
Sinai, 5
Sir Ferumbras, 177, 192 n. 22
Sirventes, 21
Situs Hierusalem, 21-22
Sluys, 212
Songe, 197
Song of Roland. See *Chanson de Roland*
Sowdone of Babylone, The, 177, 184, 192 n. 22
Spearing, A. C., 179
St. Gilles, 14
St. Guilhelm-le-Desert, 38
Stacyons of Rome, The. See Vernon manuscript
Stephana of Rouergue, 34-35, 42 n. 8
Stephen of Blois, 162, 175 n. 7
Stephen of Cloyes, 83-105
Struss, Lothar, 159
Swan Knight. See Lohengrin
Syrene, 73
Syria, 21, 67, 148

"Taking the cross" (literal), 14, 118, 144. See also Dress and insignia
Tancred, 162, 164
Taticius (guide), 17
Templar of Tyr, the, 148
Templars. See Knights Templars
Temple (Jerusalem), 12, 52, 54, 55, 56, 178
Tertullian, 115
Tervagan, 170; Tervogant, 173
Theoderich, 66
Third Crusade, 15, 93, 157, 159, 177
Thomas Aquinas, Saint, 11

Thomas of Marle, 162
Thomas Paleologus, 210
Thule, 62
Titus and Vespasian, 186-87
Titus (emperor), 178, 180, 183,
   185, 187, 192 n. 26, 193 n. 35
Toghtekin of Damascus, 162
Torkington, Sir Richard (rector),
   10, 14
Torture, 129, 131, 132, 181, 186-87
Tosez, Geraud, 35-36
Tower of Babel, 64
Travel Accounts, 2, 4, 9-11, 14-15,
   19-21, 22, 23. See also Diaries;
   Guidebooks
Travel by ship, 8, 128, 142, 143,
   149, 150
Tripoli, 17
Troubadours, 21
True Cross, 6, 54-55, 56, 80 n. 62,
   142, 143, 193 n. 31. See also
   Calvary, Mount
Turner, Victor and Edith, 33
Turpin, 108-09, 122

Urban II (pope), 13, 110, 121, 184,
   190 n. 3

van der Essen, Léon, 89
Varna, 207
Vasco de Lucena, 212-13
Vendôme, 86, 88, 101 n. 27; Vin-
   docinum, 99 n. 13
Venice, 8, 10, 19, 208, 209, 210
Vernacular texts, 1, 7-8, 8-9, 13-14,

91, 136-40, 145, 149-50, 168-74,
   178, 179, 180, 181, 182, 183,
   184, 185, 186-87, 192 n. 22,
   212-13
Vernon manuscript, 5; *Stacyons of
   Rome, The*, 5
Veronica, Saint, 178
Vespasian, 178, 183, 187,
   192 n. 26
Villefranche, 208
Vindicta Salvatoris, 178
Virgil, 198
Virgin of Rocamadour. See Roca-
   madour
Vocabularies, 9, 10

Walerand de Wavrin, 207-08
Wilkinson, J. D., 3
William cycle, 166
William of Andres, 89
William of Julich (duke), 10
William of Tyre, 13, 14, 16-17, 20,
   135-36; *Historia Hierosolymi-
   tana*, 136. See also *Livre
   d'Eracle*
William Wey, 8, 12; *The Itiner-
   aries*, 8
Willibald, Saint. See *Hodoepori-
   con*
Wills, 142
Wilton Diptych, 188
Wynkyn de Worde, 8

Xenophon, 213; *Cyropedia,* 213
Xerigordon, 175 n. 7